Uncle John's

THIRD BATHROOM READER

by

The Bathroom Readers' Institute

St. Martin's Griffin
New York

Marlene Dietrich was an expert
at playing the musical saw.

 For information, address St. Martin's Press, 175 Fifth Avenue, New York, N.Y. 10010

Produced and Packaged by Javnarama
Design by Javnarama
Cover directed by Michael Brunsfeld, *executed by* Richard Kizu-Blair

Library of Congress Cataloging-in-Publication Data

Uncle John's third bathroom reader / Bathroom Reader's Institute.
p. cm.
ISBN 0-312-04586-7
1. American wit and humor. I. Bathroom Reader's Institute (Berkeley, Calif.)
PN6153.U454 1990
818'.5407—dc20 90-37309
CIP

If you're reading this page, you must have finished the rest of the book—or you haven't started yet. Listen, you won't be able to make head or tails of this "Library of Congress" stuff. We've been writing books since the early '80s, and we still can't figure it out. Skip it—get to the good stuff.

Oh, by the way—thanks for your support. And go with the flow!

"Blowin' in the Wind," "The Archies," "Black & White," "The Australian Beatles," "Monkee Business," "Blue Suede Shoes," "Ain't That a Shame," and "Real People" originally appeared in *Behind the Hits*, Copyright © 1985, by Bob Shannon and John Javna. Reprinted by permission of the authors.

"Moore to Come," "The Best of Groucho," "Saturday Night Live," "Bewitched," "Say Goodnight, Gracie," and "Alfred Hitchcock Presents" originally appeared in *Cult TV*. Copyright © 1985, by John Javna. Reprinted by permission of the author.

"Landslide Lyndon" Copyright © 1990 by Michael Dorman. Reprinted by permission of the author.

Disney Stories Copyright © 1990 by Jim Morton. Reprinted by permission.

Excerpts from *UNAUTHORIZED AMERICA* ("Elvis-O-Rama," "Elvis: Still Dead?") by Vince Staten. Copyright © 1990 by Vince Staten. Reprinted by permission of Harper Collins Publishers.

"The Paper Chase" Copyright © 1989 by Ron Barlow, originally appeared in *The Vanishing American Outhouse*, published by Windmill Publishing House. Reprinted by permission of the author.

"Tissue Talk" by Harry L. Rinker, originally appeared in *Antiques and Collecting* magazine. Reprinted by permission of the publisher.

THANK YOU

The Bathroom Readers' Institute sincerely thanks the people whose advice and assistance made this book possible.

Eric Lefcowitz
Larry Kelp
John Javna
Derek Goldberg
Michael Goldberger
John Dollison
Jim Morton
Michael Brunsfeld
Richard Kizu-Blair
Gordon Van Gelder
Stuart Moore
Fifth Street Computers
Jay Nitschke
Penelope Houston
Bob Shannon
Jack Mingo
Patty Glikbarg
Robin Kipke Alkire
Lyn Speakman

The city of Domme
"Weird Brain"
Antiques and Collecting magazine
Harry L. Rinker
Ron Barlow
Michael Dorman
Vince Staten
Anita Sethi
Dan Simon
Bill Batson
David Davis
Duane Dimock
Sandra Konte
The EarthWorks Group
Reddy Kilowatt
Rocky
Bob Migdal
Lenna Lebovich
The Sharp Fax Machine

This page is for Emergency Use Only.

CONTENTS

NOTE

Because the B.R.I. understands your reading needs, we've divided the contents into length as well as subject.

Short—a quick read

Medium—1 to 3 pages

Long—for those extended visits when something a little more involved is required.

BATHROOM LORE
Short
Uncle John's Mailbag.............8
Bathroom News....................67
Loose Ends..........................140
Medium
The Paper Chase..................10
Tissue Talk.........................189

THE NAME GAME
Short
Name & Place......................76
College Names...................163
Name & Place....................183
Medium
Edible Names.......................15
Familiar Names....................26
Rock Names.......................103
The Name is Familiar........124

LAW 'N' ORDER
Short
Reel Gangsters.....................39
It's the Law........................150
Medium
Pardon Me...........................73
Strange Lawsuits................112
Public Enemy #1................196

MEDIA-FILE
Short
Bonehead Ads...................... 19
Viewer's Choice.................. 29
Radio Stunts........................ 96
Medium
Mars Attacks........................ 41
Real Ads.............................. 55
Great Newspaper Leads....... 70

YOU BE THE JUDGE
Medium
A Small Step...................... 159
Long
Blowin' In the Wind........... 87

MOUTHING OFF
Short
Quayle Quips....................... 31
Fit for a King....................... 40
Honestly, Abe...................... 86
Fuller Ideas........................ 126
Stengel-ese........................ 156
Edison Enlightens.............. 161
Goldwynisms..................... 188
Allenisms.......................... 194

AMUSEMENTS
Short
Travels with Ray I 18
Travels with Ray II 66
Travels with Ray III 131
Military Double-Talk 158
Travels with Ray IV 218

MYTH AMERICA
Short
The Boston Tea Party, Ford and Other Myths 37
The Alamo, Thoreau, and Washington 105
Medium
The Columbus Myth 157

WORDPLAY
Short
Common Phrases 14
Assorted Maniacs 28
Definitions 52
Common Phrases 184
Film Terms 136
Famous Last Words 147
Medium
Wordplay 62
Don't Quote Me on That 175

GOOD SPORTS
Short
All-American Sports 195
Medium
Just Say No-Hit! 48
The Old Ballgame 139
Long
Who's On First? 107
The Baseball Myth 204

SPACE CADETS
Short
Space Junk 47
Pigs in Space 102
Asteroids 148
Long
Space Nazis 164

SCIENCE
Short
Dumb Science 85
Body Parts 99
Frog Facts 123
Recycling Facts 162
Body Language 179
Shark!! 180

THE PERSONAL COLUMNS
Short
Oh, Zsa Zsa! 17
Elvis-O-Rama 92
Groucho Gossip 172
Situation Tragedy 181
Medium
Celebrity Hypochondriacs 20
Lucy the Red 100
Elvis: Still Dead? 185

TV QUOTES
Short
Primetime Proverbs 25
Groucho & Guests 79
Primetime Proverbs 93
Late Night 114
Kung Fooey 152
Good E-e-evening 202

TV FACTS
Short
Bombs Away! 23
Medium
Moore To Come 57
The Best of Groucho 77
Saturday Night Live 121
Bewitched 145
Say Goodnight, Gracie 192
Alfred Hitchcock Presents . 200

POLITICS
Short
Jocks in Politics 59
Lincoln & Kennedy: Weird Coincidences 120
Long
Dick Nixon, the Coach 43
Close Calls 127
Landslide Lyndon 208

MUSIC: BEHIND THE HITS
Medium
Black & White 53
The Australian Beatles 83
Monkee Business 115
Blue Suede Shoes 142
Ain't That a Shame 177
Real People 221

CARTOON CORNER
Medium
Cartoon Origins 35
Cartoon Origins 137
The Archies 170

POP-POURRI
Short
Just Your Type 34
Secret Recipes 60
Simpul Spelling Moovment 69
Flake-Out 72
Oh Say Can You See? 94
Custom-Made 95
Give Us a Hand 117
Medium
Fabulous Fakes 49
Invasion! Part I 61
Amazing Coincidences 64
The Great Titanic 118
Invasion! Part II 132
Invasion! Part III 203

DISNEY STORIES
Medium
Snow White 32
Sleeping Beauty 81
Cinderella 134
Pinocchio 168
The Little Mermaid 198

BANNED IN THE USA
Short
Banned in the USA 80
Banned Books 173
Medium
The Hayes Office 97
Don't Look Now 153

UNCLE JOHN'S MAILBAG

Our first two Bathroom Readers brought in lots of mail with interesting stories and comments...Here's a random sample:

Gentlemen:
If you recall, several weeks ago, astronomers discovered rings around Uranus. Well, after spending several hours engrossed in your book, so did I!

—*John M., Fort Mill, South Carolina*

Fellow Bathroom Readers:
Whenever I have a relative or guest at my house, they always come out of the bathroom and ask me why there is a stack of magazines on the back of the toilet. When I answer them, they just chuckle and call me "silly."

I'm glad to see there's finally an offical bathroom reader's publication that I can leave on the toilet so people can answer the question for themselves. Keep up the good work!

—*Duane J., Palm Bay, Florida*

Dear Uncle John:
I was beginning to think that Excremeditation was a dying cultural phenomenon, a lost art. Uncle John's Second Bathroom Reader is the simmering potpourri in the Great Outhouse of Life.

—*F. Lee S., Charlottesville, Virginia*

Dear B.R.I.:
We would like to sit down and be counted. We read the first book in the bathroom, but since we're traveling for a year, we read the second book out loud to each other while driving. We enjoyed driving on Route 66...which we didn't even know existed until we read your book...And, hey, whatever happened to Burger Chef, Burger Queen, and Jack-in-the-Box? Any chance you'll write about them in a future edition?...FYI: Your books make great housewarming gifts! We are waiting with our pants around our ankles for book #3!

—*Amy & Rex Y., Athens, Michigan*

Before 1859, baseball umpires didn't crouch behind the catcher—they sat in rocking chairs.

Dear Uncle John:
I was reading the Bathroom Reader when I noticed I was out of toilet paper. Unfortunately, I had to make the most out of what I had. Will you please send me a copy of pages 38-39? Thanks.

Arnie P., Seattle, Washington

Dear B.R.I.:
I'd like to admit that one day I read the Bathroom Reader in 20° weather in an outhouse. Thanks, you guys helped me keep my mind off the cold.

—Robert W., Old Tappan, New Jersey

Dear Uncle John:
Thanks a ton. Now my husband *lives* in the john.

—Renee G., Los Angeles, California

Dear Uncle John:
Info on Kelsey—

1. My nickname is Kelley.
2. I'm 14 years old.
3. I love to read (especially on the pot).

—Kelsey B., Cedar Rapids, Iowa

Dear Sirs:
After reading your book, I had to take time out from the "business at hand" to write this letter. Having been a bathroom reader for many years, I found your book to be very "moving." There's a lot of very good information to "pass" on to others.

—Jim B., Canyon Country, California

Dear Uncle John:
Who is that guy on the back cover of both your books? Is it you? And what's he doing with the clipboard? I've just got to know—I read both your books cover-to-cover, and have spent hours staring at that picture, "passing" the time.

—Glenn W., Montpelier, Vermont

Glad you asked, Glenn. He's not Uncle John; he's Larry Kelp, a music critic at an urban newspaper. Of course, he's busy recording data about America's bathroom reading habits. Keep up the great work, Lar!

Julius Caesar's autograph is worth $2 million dollars.

THE PAPER CHASE

At the B.R.I., we get a lot of questions about toilet paper. Heck, we even get them written on toilet paper. Recently, one of our "field representatives" discovered a couple of selections that should satisfy even the most finicky T.P. afficianado. The first is this piece adapted from a self-published book called The Vanishing American Outhouse, *by Ronald Barlow It should unroll a few mysteries.*

YESTERDAY'S PAPER

"Toilet paper is a fairly modern invention. Today's thoughtfully perforated product was patented by an Englishman named Walter J. Alcock, in the early 1880s. At first there was little demand for toilet paper by the roll. British pharmacy owners stocked this item under their counters and out of sight; T. P. was an affront to Victorian sensibilities.

"But Mr. Alcock was undaunted by the public's reserve and promoted his product religiously. His singleminded missionary zeal eventually paid off. By 1888 toilet paper fixtures (roll-holders) were stocked in most hardware stores, and today Alcock's original factory exports two-ply tissue to a world-wide market."

★ ★ ★

BEFORE PAPER

"What did folks use before paper was in wide circulation? Affluent Romans used sponges, wool, and rosewater. The rest of the world grabbed whatever was at hand, including shells, sticks, stones, leaves, hay, or dry bones. Royalty in the Middle Ages was fond of silk or goose feathers (still attached to a pliable neck) for this delicate clean-up task."

★ ★ ★

NO CORNY JOKE

"Rural Americans traditionally relied on corncobs instead of T.P. James Whitcomb Riley wrote a poem commemorating the experience:

The torture of that icy seat could make a Spartan sob,
For needs must scrape the gooseflesh with a lacerating cob.

Riley's family privy must have had an outdated supply of corncobs because old timers tell me that fresh ones are not all that uncomfortable. The term: 'rough as a cob' could perhaps apply to produce left out in the sun and rain for a year or so, but not to the supply of month-old corncobs used in privy confines. Guests often had a choice of colors, even before the invention of toilet paper. According to privy folklore, red cobs outnumbered white ones by a two to one ratio. The modus operandi was to use a red cob first and then follow up with a white one to see if another of the red variety was necessary."

★ ★ ★

T.P. BY MAIL

"Mail order catalogs came into general outhouse use in the late 1880s. Prior to that time they consisted of less than a dozen pages and could not compete with newspapers, dress patterns and other *uncoated* paper stock. Concerned mothers routinely removed the 'female undergarment' and 'personal hygiene' sections of these catalogs before consigning them to the outhouse. By the early 1930s most magazines and mail-order catalogs had converted to slick clay-coated pages and fell into general disuse as a T.P. substitute.

"The following letters, adapted from Bob Sherwood's 1929 book, *Hold Everything*, illustrate how important the thick semi-annual Sears catalogs were to many country households:

The Letter

Dear Sears & Roebuck:

Please find enclosed money order for one dollar ($1.00) for which please send me ten packages of your Peerless Toilet Paper.

Yours sincerely, Abner Bewley, Sr.

The Reply

Dear Sir:

We acknowledge receipt of your order with enclosure of $1.00 in payment for ten packages of Peerless Toilet paper. We assume you have taken this price from one of our old catalogs. On account of the recent increase in the cost of manufacturing this article, the price is now listed at $1.50 for ten packages. On receipt of an

Americans eat about 22 pounds of tomatoes every year—mostly in ketchup and tomato sauce.

additional fifty cents, we will forward at once.

Very respectfully, SEARS & CO.

The Back-Fire

Gentlemen:

I am in receipt of your reply to my letter ordering ten packages of Peerless Toilet Paper.

If I had had one of your old catalogs, I would not have needed any toilet paper.

Please send me your latest catalog, and return my money.

Yours Sincerely, Abner Bewley, Sr.

P.S. After thinking the matter over you had better send two catalogs, as we have a very large family."

★ ★ ★

FOREIGN PAPER

"There are enough different varieties of toilet paper to inspire a major collection. (Smithsonian...are you listening?)

• One can write very easily in pen and ink on modern day Czechoslovakian toilet issue, which is of the consistency of writing paper. My son's college roommate just sent him a long letter on some of this 'poor man's stationery.'

• German-made bathroom tissue is light gray in color and rather coarse textured. The brand used on railway trains is imprinted 'Deutsche Bundesbahn' on every single sheet.

• In England, museum-going tourists are quick to notice that each square of paper is plainly marked 'Official Government Property.'

• In some Scandinavian restrooms the extra heavy roll is simply too large to carry away.

• Mexico solved her paper pilfering problem in airport and bus station 'baños' by not supplying any at all. Be prepared and bring your own, or you'll be forced to borrow from an adjacent stall-holder.

• Upscale European consumers are switching to a new luxury brand of paper; the pre-moistened, perfumed squares, sealed separately in foil envelopes, are not unlike the 'wet wipes' mothers buy in American supermarkets.

★ ★ ★

AUTOMATIC WIPE

According to a 1988 article in *The San Diego Union*, fully 11.5% of all Japanese homes are now equipped with deluxe flush toilets which have built-in hot-water cleansing and hot-air drying mechanisms; these features preclude the need for any sort of tissue at all.

What are the chances of a Japanese-owned electronic-potty-maker locating its manufacturing facilities in San Diego, or some other U.S. city? 'Almost nil,' stated a spokesman. 'Only the quality control standards in Japan are strict enough to produce these devices without fear of public-liability lawsuits.' "

★ ★ ★

RECOMMENDED READING

The Vanishing American Outhouse is an oversized paperback full of color photos of outhouses, and goes where no man has gone before in its detailed study of American outhouse history. To order a copy, send $15.95 plus $1.50 for postage and handling to: Windmill Publishing Co., 2147 Windmill View Rd., El Cajon, CA 92020.

✍ ✍ ✍

TWINKIE POWER

• It's been estimated that the cake in a Twinkie will outlast the wrapper—which is made of plastic, and probably takes about 200 years to decompose. But according to William Poundstone in *Bigger Secrets*, that's just a rumor. He says that the Continental Baking Company, makers of America's favorite cremed cake, pulls unsold boxes of Twinkies off grocery store shelves every four days. Believe it or not.

• When James A. Deware invented the Twinkie in 1930, he called it, "The best darn-tootin' idea I ever had." How good was it? A Continental Baking Company executive claims that one man lived for 7 years solely on a diet of Twinkies and Cutty Sark.

COMMON PHRASES

What do these familiar phrases really mean? Entymologists have researched them and come up with these explanations.

SIAMESE TWINS
Meaning: Identical twins who are physically attached.
Background: Eng and Chang Bunker were always close—in fact, the twin brothers from Siam were born joined at the liver. P.T. Barnum hired the Bunkers and exploited them on the carnival and sideshow circuit during the mid-1800s. Though the brothers were really three-quarters Chinese, Barnum thought "Siamese" had a more exotic ring, and coined the term we still use today. (Side note: Eng and Chang lived long lives, married twin sisters and fathered more than twenty children).

LONG IN THE TOOTH
Meaning: Old.
Background: Originally used to describe old horses. As horses age, their gums recede, giving the impression that their teeth are growing. The longer the teeth look, the older the horse.

TO GO BERSERK
Meaning: To go mad, or to act with reckless abandon.
Background: Viking warriors were incredibly wild and ferocious in battle, probably because they ate hallucinogenic mushrooms in pre-battle ceremonies. They charged their enemies recklessly, wearing nothing more than bearskin, which in Old Norse was pronounced "berserkr" or "bear-sark."

TO FACE THE MUSIC
Meaning: To deal with a troubling situation.
Background: All actors have experienced stage fright, but eventually they must stand upon the stage and face the audience and orchestra (the music).

A-OKAY
Meaning: All correct, or all systems working.
Background: NASA engineers added 'A' onto "OKAY" because the 'O' sound sometimes got lost in radio static.

Toto's real name was Terry.

EDIBLE NAMES

Like fast food? Try this list. You still may not know what you're eating, but at least know what's it's named after.

McDONALD'S. Named after two brothers who were scenery movers in Hollywood during the 1920s—Richard and Maurice ("Mac") McDonald. They started the first modern fast food joint in San Bernardino, California after World War II and sold out to Ray Kroc for $2.7 million in 1961.

• Sidelight: They gave up the rights to use their own names, so when they wanted to open another fast food restaurant, they had to call it "Mac's." Kroc was so incensed they were competing with him that he opened a McDonald's across the street from "Mac's" and drove the McDonald brothers out of business.

ARBY'S. Forest and Leroy Raffel wanted to open a fast food restaurant called Big Tex, in Akron, Ohio...but someone else already owned the name. So they settled for Arby's—R.B.'s—after the first initials of *R*affel *b*rothers.

TACO BELL. No, it has nothing to do with mission bells. The chain was founded in 1962 by Glen W. Bell.

JACK IN THE BOX. There was a huge, square metal ventilation unit on the roof of Robert Peterson's restaurant. It was really ugly, but he couldn't remove it...So he covered it up instead, disguising it as a jack-in-the-box. Then he changed the name of his restaurant, making it seem as though the whole thing had been planned.

HARDEE'S. Founded by Wilbur Hardee, who opened the first Hardee's in Greenville, North Carolina in 1960.

BOB'S BIG BOY. In 1937, local orchestra members told 19-year-old Bob Wian they wanted "something different"; so the young owner of the ten-stool Bob's Pantry served up the "Big Boy" double-decker hamburger. It became so popular that Bob changed the name of his eatery to match it.

In Italy, a whole year's salary is the proper amount to pay for an enagement ring.

PIZZA HUT. Frank Carney, a 19-year-old engineering student at the University of Wichita, opened a pizza parlor in 1958 with his older brother Dan. It was in a rented, hut-shaped building with a sign that only had room for eight letters and a single space. Pizza Hut was the perfect name because it described the restaurant *and* fit the sign.

CHURCH'S FRIED CHICKEN. George W. Church, who'd previously sold incubators and run a chicken hatchery, founded the chain after he retired.

DAIRY QUEEN. In 1938, Sherb Noble put together a 10¢ All-You-Can-Eat promotion for his Kankakee, Illinois store. He offered a brand new kind of "semi-frozen" ice cream called "Dairy Queen," and was dumbfounded by the public's response—they bought 16,000 servings of it in two hours. Two years later, Noble opened a food stand that sold nothing but Dairy Queen.

KENTUCKY FRIED CHICKEN. "Colonel" Harlan Sanders had a restaurant in Corbin, Kentucky. His speciality was fried chicken.

WHITE CASTLE. In 1921, Walter Anderson needed money to open his fourth hamburger stand. He borrowed the money—$700—from a local real-estate and insurance salesman named Billy Ingram, who suggested that the restaurant be called the "White Castle," symbolizing cleanliness and strength. Since it was Ingram's money, Anderson humored him.

WENDY'S. Dave Thomas, an executive at Kentucky Fried Chicken, decided to open his own chain of fast food restaurants in 1969. The first one was located in Columbus, Ohio. It was named for Thomas's third daughter, Wendy.

NOW THAT YOU'RE HUNGRY... SOME NUTRITION INFO

• From *Best Worst And Most Unusual*: "If one is really starving, consider licking some postage stamps. The glue is a mixture of cassava (the source of tapioca) and corn...starchy but nutritious."

OH, ZSA ZSA!

Sure, you've read about her in the National Enquirer (only while you're waiting in line at the supermarket, of course). But what do you really know about Zsa Zsa Gabor? You might surprised to learn that a century ago, while she was still a young lady, she was quite beautiful and...yes, we admit it—pretty clever. A few words from, and about, this national institution.

WHAT ABOUT ZSA ZSA?

"She not only worships the golden calf, she barbecues it for lunch."

—*Oscar Levant*

"I feel a little like Zsa Zsa Gabor's fifth husband. I know what I'm supposed to do, but I'm not sure how to make it interesting."

—*Senator Al Gore, the 24th speaker at a political dinner*

"As a graduate of the Zsa Zsa Gabor School of Creative Mathematics, I honestly do not know how old I am."

—*Erma Bombeck*

ZSA ZSA SAYS...

- "I'm a marvelous housekeeper...Every time I leave a man, I keep his house."
- "You never really know a man until you've divorced him."
- "Macho does not prove mucho."
- "A man in love is incomplete until he has married. Then he's finished."
- "I want a man who's kind and understanding. Is that too much to ask of a millionaire?"
- "I never hated a man enough to give him his diamonds back."
- "Husbands are like fires. They go out when unattended."
- "I know nothing about sex because I was always married."

...BUT THEY'RE NOT ALL BIMBOS

"I will do anything to initiate world peace."

—*Jayne Mansfield*

Confederate General Robert E. Lee didn't own slaves. He didn't believe in it.

TRAVELS WITH RAY

Perplexing adventures of the brilliant egghead Ray "Weird Brain" Redel. Answers are on page 223.

Only a few men in modern history have been known specifically for their ability to think. There's Albert Einstein, Buckminster Fuller, and of course the most famous of all, Ray "Weird Brain" Redel. As I'm sure you've heard, "Weird Brain" 's reputation for solving word problems inspired friends to spring practical jokes on him constantly. Everyone wanted to be the one to say he or she had stumped him.

A few years ago, "Weird Brain" and I went to Egypt together for the International Smart Guys Conference. After listening to boring highbrow discussions for two days, we escaped to the local marketplace. It was refreshing to wander through the crowd, listening to people bark prices at each other instead of scientific theories.

Suddenly, a man in a white suit appeared before us, clutching something in his hand. He staggered and groaned and pointed to the object in his hand. I felt as though I was in a Hitchcock movie. The man managed to gasp, "*If you feed it, it will live. If you give it water, it will die.*" Then he swooned.

Alarmed, I looked for the police. But Ray just reached into his pocket, pulled out something, and tossed it to the prostrate man. "Here, Humphrey," he said—for the "dying" man was really "Weird Brain" 's Hollywood drinking buddy, Humphrey Bogart—"Nice try, but I think this is what you want."

What did "Weird Brain" toss Bogart?

The next day, we decided to do a little sightseeing. The cab driver offered to suggest a destination. "Sure," I said, "where should we go?" The driver grinned and said in broken English, "*It has a bed, but never sleeps; and has a mouth, but never eats.*" "Weird Brain" yawned. "Casey," he told the driver, who was New York Yankees manager Casey Stengel, an old pal, in disguise—that one's so old everyone knows it. But if it'll make you happy, take us there.

Where did Casey take us?

BONEHEAD ADS

Businesses spend billions of bucks on ads every year—but some of them backfire. A few amusing examples:

SAY WHAT?

Translating U.S. ad slogans into other languages doesn't always work.

• In China, a Coca-Cola ad used Chinese symbols to sound out "Coca-Cola" phonetically. The soda company withdrew the ad after learning the symbols "Co" "Ca" "Co" " La" meant "Bite the wax tadpole."

• In Brazil, an American airline advertised that its planes had "rendezvous" lounges, not realizing that in Portuguese "rendezvous" means a place to have sex.

• "In Taiwan," according to a book called *The Want Makers*, "Pepsi's 'Come Alive with the Pepsi Generation' was reportedly translated on billboards as 'Pepsi brings your ancestors back from the dead.'"

• "In French Canada, Hunt-Wesson attempted to use its 'Big John' brand name by translating it into French as 'Gros Jos,' a colloquial French phrase that denotes a woman with huge breasts."

• When the gringos at General Motors introduced the Chevrolet *Nova* in Latin America, it was obvious they didn't know their Spanish. Ads all across Latin America heralded the arrival of the new, reliable *Nova*, which in Spanish means "Doesn't go."

SMELL IT LIKE IT IS

Two of the most ludicrous Scratch'n'Sniff ads ever:

• In June, 1977, the Rolls-Royce Motor Car Company introduced a campaign entitled "This, In Essence, Is Rolls Royce." Apparently, the company's executives hired scientists to analyze the smell inside a Rolls. They came up with a scent strip that was supposed to smell like leather upholstery.

• In 1989, BEI Defense Systems ran a Scratch'n'Sniff ad for its Hydra 70 weapons system in *The Armed Forces Journal*. It pictured two battling helicopters; when scratched, it gave off the smell of cordite, the odor left in the air after a rocket explosion.

Dirt Cheap: The United States bought Alaska from the Russia for about 2 cents an acre.

CELEBRITY HYPOCHONDRIACS

Everyone's at least a little afraid of getting sick, but some people take it to extremes. Here are some of history's most famous hypochondriacs:

THE CELEBRITY: Howard Hughes

THE SYMPTOMS: When he was a little boy, the billionaire-to-be's mother fussed over every change in Howard's physical and emotional conditions. One result: Hughes developed a low tolerance to pain.

• After crashing one of his planes in Hollywood in 1946, Hughes began to display an irrational fear of dust and germs. He used Kleenex tissues on everything, and refused to touch doorknobs or let other people use his bathroom. (He once spent 26 straight hours in the bathroom; he also suffered from severe constipation).

• His fastidiousness got out of hand when he wrote out nine-step instructions to his housekeepers on how to open a can of fruit. He became a virtual recluse.

• One of the most bizarre manifestations of his obsession with health was a urine collection, purportedly for medical testing.

• Ironically, towards the end of his life, Hughes lost all pretenses of hygiene. He stopped taking care of himself—letting his hair and fingernails grow outrageously long—and stopped eating; he weighed only 93 pounds when he died.

THE CELEBRITY: Charles Darwin

THE SYMPTOMS: The father of the theory of evolution, staunch believer in the "survival of the fittest," apparently wasn't such a hardy specimen himself. Darwin was a life-long hypochondriac who suffered from stomach aches, chronic insomnia and fatigue.

• In 1849, he began a daily diary which included a running commentary on the state of his health. He kept it up for six straight years.

• In one entry, he wrote gloomily, "It has been a bitter mortification for me to digest the conclusion that the 'race is for the strong' and that I shall probably do little more but be content to admire the strides others made in science." He lived forty-one years after making that statement.

• Some have speculated that Darwin's ailments were brought about by the stress of his "heretical" theories; others have claimed they were an easy solution to meeting social obligations.

THE CELEBRITY: Napoleon Bonaparte

THE SYMPTOMS: Napoleon had a lifelong fear and hatred of medicine. As a student, he studied anatomy but was too squeamish to continue. He reportedly claimed, "I believe in the doctor, not medicine."

• The "Little Emperor" suffered a plethora of maladies, most of them the result of stress, including: skin disorders, ulcers, dysuria (difficulty urinating) and a nervous cough.

• To combat his hypochondria, Napoleon took steaming hot baths, sometimes 1-1/2 hours long. He also developed meticulous grooming habits, including gargling with brandy and water, and showering himself with eau-du-cologne.

• One doctor's report of Napoleon from the battlefields of Russia said, "The constitution of the Emperor was highly nervous. He was very susceptible to emotional influences...divided between the stomach and the bladder."

• Some scholars even doubted the diagnosis of Napoleon's death (stomach cancer) during his exile in St. Helena, claiming he died of hysteria brought on by boredom.

THE CELEBRITY: Alfred Lord Tennyson

THE SYMPTOMS: According to one of Tennyson's friends, the poet laureate of England worried "more about his bowels and nerves than about the Laureate wreath he was born to inherit."

• Throughout his life, Tennyson was beset by seizures, fits and trances, which including seeing animals floating across his field of vision.

• An admitted hypochondriac, Tennyson was obsessed with going bald and blind. Among the treatments he sought was a radical form of water therapy called hydropathy, which included being rolled naked into wet blankets and then plunged into water.

• Three of his major poems, "In Memoriam," "The Princess" and "Maud" alluded to his preoccupation with mental illness.

Home-Sweet-Home: One-fifth of Americans spend their vacations at home.

• In reference to his hypochondria, Tennyson was once quoted as saying, "I'm black-blooded like all Tennysons." He lived past 80.

THE CELEBRITY: H.L. Mencken

THE SYMPTOMS: The irascible essayist, one of the most respected American journalists of the 20th century, rationalized his hypochondria by once stating "the human body is a complex organism in a state of dubious equilibrium. It is almost unthinkable for all parts of it be operating perfectly at any one time."

• Mencken suffered an obsessive-compulsive need to continually wash his hands.

• Among his real-or-imagined maladies was a chronic sore throat (which resulted in three operations), hives, low blood pressure, lumbago, sinus infections, ulcers and hemorrhoids. He also suffered from terrible allergies, which, Mencken wrote, "I accept philosphically as a reasonable punishment for my errors."

• For years, Mencken kept a medical diary of his hay fever, which included log entries of his temperature, the weather conditions and the medicine he was taking. He also subjected himself to many new miracle cures, which lead him to describe himself as a "sort of laboratory animal" for medical experimentation.

THE CELEBRITY: Florence Nightingale

THE SYMPTOMS: The woman who revolutioned modern nursing was also a confirmed hypochondriac; she suffered from migraine headaches, chronic coughs, breathlessness, fainting and nervous distress.

• After her heroic deeds in the Crimean War, Nightingale became convinced that her heart trouble placed her in imminent danger.

• Starting in 1859, she became a virtual recluse, confined to bed and sofa, where she continued to write letters and books about nursing.

• Though she often claimed she was on the edge of death, Nightingale lived a long life. She died in 1910, at the age of 90.

AND DON'T FORGET... Michael Jackson. The thriller of pop and dance music is often seen in public wearing a surgical mask. Once, he tried to buy a germ-free hyperbaric oxygen chamber to sleep in, but the manufacturer refused to sell it to him.

People in the Southern U.S. watch more TV than people in any other region.

BOMBS AWAY

Sitcoms don't have to be dumb...but they usually are. Here are the premises of some of the dumbest and most obscure sitcoms flops ever. Yes, they really aired on national TV.

MY LIVING DOLL (1964-65) An Army psychiatrist who lives with his sister brings home a gorgeous woman one day, explaining that she's got severe mental problems and needs constant care. He neglects to explain that she's not really a person at all—she's a robot who's so lifelike and sexy that men lust after her. She calls the psychiatrist "Master," and she'll do anything (yes, anything) he tells her to. So what does he do? What would you do? Well, all he wants is to teach her good manners. That's more than enough to make this show unbelievable.

MONA McCLUSKEY (1965) A Hollywood star makes 40 times as much money as her husband, an Air Force sergeant (he gets $500 a month, she gets $5000 a week). But the guy won't let her spend any of her dough—they live on his salary or nothing. Well, she's so in love that she agrees: She moves into a two-bedroom apartment and then spends all her time trying to figure out ways to secretly use her own money. The show lasted longer than the marriage would have—seven months.

IT'S ABOUT TIME (1966-67) Two astronauts accidentally break through the time barrier and wind up in a prehistoric era. There they coexist with a bunch of Neanderthals until they fix their space capsule—and then they head for L.A. But whoops! A couple of cavemen hitch a lift into the present. Intelligently, the astronauts hide the Neanderthals in an apartment and try to teach them about modern life. This inanity could only come from the fertile mind that also gave us "Gilligan's Island" and "The Brady Bunch."

RUN BUDDY RUN (1966-67) A couple of goofy assassins try to catch and kill a guy who accidentally overheard their secret plans in a Turkish bath. Some fun.

THE SECOND HUNDRED YEARS (1967-68) The cryogenics sitcom. A 33-year-old prospector is frozen alive in an avalanche in 1900. Sixty-eight years later he thaws out. Surprise! He's still 33 and full of pep. He goes to live with his son, who's now older than ol' dad, and his grandson, who's the same age. In fact, he and his grandson look exactly alike. What a coincidence!

THE GIRL WITH SOMETHING EXTRA (1973-74) Sally Field gave up her nun's habit and stopped flying. Now she's got ESP. And she's married to John Davidson. She says she can read his mind, but how can she be sure there's really something in it? The premise sounds like a *National Enquirer* story.

THE WAVERLY WONDERS (1978) Among television critics, this show is already a legend. Who thought it up? Is he still allowed into Hollywood? Joe Namath was the star, playing a basketball coach/history teacher at a small Wisconsin high school. Joe didn't know anything about history, as you might imagine. And his players didn't know anything about basketball. So what's the joke? The inept teacher? The inept basketball team? The inept TV network?

APPLE PIE (1978) The ultimate absurdity in family sitcoms. It broke all sitcom records for brevity too, lasting exactly two weeks. The plot: In 1933, a hairdresser decided she wanted a family. So she advertised for one in the local paper. The result: a collection of weirdos that rivals *King of Hearts*—a con-man "husband," a "son" who thinks he's a bird, a "grandpa" who's barely still moving, and a "daughter" who likes to tap dance around the house.

TURNABOUT (1978) A husband and wife, in an idle moment, wish they could switch places. They're only kidding around, but they speak in the presence of a magic Buddha statue—and Buddha *doesn't* kid around. Overnight, their spirits switch bodies—the man becomes a cosmetics exec in a woman's body, and the woman becomes a male sports reporter.

MR. MERLIN (1981-82) Merlin the Magician shows up in the 1980's as a garage mechanic. Merlin the Mechanic. Next time you tell a repairman he's a real wizard, think twice. You might be inventing a sitcom.

The U.S. Department of Defense spends about $6,000,000 on recruiting—every day.

PRIMETIME PROVERBS

Here are some more TV quotes from the book Primetime Proverbs, *by Jack Mingo and John Javna.*

ON LOVE

"Ah—love— the walks over soft grass, the smiles over candlelight, the arguments over just about everything else..."

Max Headroom,
Max Headroom

"I'm looking for a serious commitment—someone who'll stay the night."

—Stewardess,
Married...With Children

THE FACTS OF LIFE

"There's an old Moroccan saying—trust in God, but tie your camel tight."

—Annie McGuire
Annie McGuire

"There are three things you don't get over in hurry—losing a woman, eating bad possum, and eating good possum."

—Beau La Barre
Welcome Back, Kotter

"Reservations are the condoms in the birth of new ideas."

—Twiggy Rathbone
Heavy Metal

ON SEX

"If sex were fast food, you'd have an arch over your head."

—Carlotta Winchester,
Filthy Rich

[After his first time] "I'm so excited. It's like discovering America, or a third arm or something. This is the greatest thing that ever happened to me. I should have started this ten years ago. I mean, the hell with television."

—Billy Tate,
Soap

"I haven't had much experience saying 'No' to a woman. The closest I've ever come is, 'Not now, we're landing.' "

—Sam Malone,
Cheers

ON WOMEN

Dwayne Schneider:
"A woman is like a bathtub full of water— once you get it hot, it doesn't cool off too fast."
Barbara Cooper: " And once it does, it has a ring."

—One Day at a Time

FAMILIAR NAMES

Some people achieve immortality because their names become commonly associated with an item or activity. You already know the names—now here are the people.

Giovanni Casanova. A European diplomat. At age 16, his "immoral behavior" got him expelled from a seminary. Later, he was so notorious as a lover that his name became synonymous with seduction.

Count Paul Stroganoff. A 19th-century Russian diplomat. He funded archaeological expeditions, supervised a Russian educational district, and ate huge amounts of the sauce now named after him.

Daniel Elmer Salmon. A veterinary surgeon. He first identified the rod-shaped bacteria, *salmonella*, that causes food poisoning.

Adolphe Sax. A Belgian musical-instrument maker. In the early 1840s, he turned the music world on its ear with his invention, the *saxophone*.

Ambrose Everett Burnside. A Union General in the Civil War. His full side-whiskers (to complement his moustache) were so distinctive that they were called "burnsides." Over time, the word has been transformed into *sideburns*.

James Smithson. An English chemist. It took ten years of debate before Congress accepted his bequest for a Washington, D.C. *Smithsonian Institution*, for "the increase and diffusion of knowledge among men."

Oliver Fisher Winchester. An American men's shirt manufacturer. His special talent was improving on others' inventions, notably the Winchester repeating rifle invented by Benjamin Henry.

Mr. and Mrs. Legrand Benedict. After complaining that there was nothing new being served by New York restaurants, this "high society" couple cooked up the idea of *eggs benedict*.

According to M magazine, 84 percent of bicyclists think about sex while cycling.

Rudolph Boysen. An American horticulturist. After years of experimentation breeding hybrid berries, he finally came up with a *boysenberry*.

John Montague. The 4th Earl of Sandwich. A compulsive gambler who would not leave any game to dine, he had his valet serve him a piece of cold meat placed between two slices of bread.

Captain Bo. A legendary English fighter. His exploits inspired other combatants, who used a variation of his name, *boo*, as a bloodcurdling war cry.

Julius Caesar. The Roman Emperor was allegedly the first person delivered via *caesarian section*, through his mother's abdominal wall.

James Thomas Brudenell. The 7th Earl of Cardigan. The button-up sweater is named after him.

Thomas "Stonewall" Jackson. A Confederate General in the Civil War. He is credited for "standing like a stone wall" against Union troops at the first battle of Bull Run. Today we call similar holding actions *stonewalling*.

John Macadam. An Australian chemist. He discovered the *Macadamia nut*.

Vidkun Quisling. Leader of Norway in 1940. His surname became synonymous with *traitor* after he collaborated when they occupied his country.

Joseph Pulitzer. A newspaper publisher. His will created and funded the Pulitzer Prize for journalism.

Josh Billings. A 19th century humorist. He popularized a bantering comedy style which became known as *joshing*.

Charles Moncke. A British blacksmith. He is credited with inventing the monkey wrench (which the British call a "spanner").

ASSORTED MANIACS

You've heard of pyromaniacs and kleptomaniacs, but chances are you've never heard of these loonies. Do you know a...

Coprolalomaniac: Someone who compulsively uses foul language.

Doromaniac: Someone who compulsively gives presents.

Cresomaniac: Someone suffering from delusions of wealth.

Timromaniacs: Someone obsessed with postage stamps.

Emetomaniac: A person who always feels like throwing up.

Ablutomaniac: Someone obsessed with taking baths.

Hellenomaniac: Someone who compulsively uses Greek or Latin words.

Ailuromaniac: A person obsessed with cats.

Philopatridomaniac: Someone who's always homesick.

Dromomaniac: A compulsive traveler.

Phagomaniac: Someone who constantly craves food.

Xenomaniac: Someone obsessed with foreign customs.

Oniomaniac: A person who compulsively buys things.

Klazomaniac: Someone who always feels like shouting.

Micromaniac: Someone suffering from delusions of a shrinking body.

Titillomaniac: A compulsive scratcher.

Erythromaniac: Someone who's always blushing.

Catapedamaniac: Someone who always feels like jumping from high places.

Chionomaniac: Someone obsessed with snow.

Theomaniac: Someone who's sure he or she is God.

Nudomaniac: A person obsessed with nudity.

Ichthyomaniac: Someone who's just crazy about fish.

Arithomaniac: Someone who compulsively counts objects.

Cynomaniac: Someone obsessed with dogs.

Onychotillomaniac: A person who constantly picks his or her nails.

Bruxomaniac: Someone who grinds his or her teeth all the time.

Lycomaniac: Someone suffering from delusions of being a wolf.

VIEWER'S CHOICE

Hollywood producers often use sneak previews to shape the way their movies end. Here are some examples of the ways preview audiences have influenced the final versions of recent films.

COCKTAIL

Initial tests by the Disney Company revealed that audiences found this Tom Cruise vehicle a snooze. So Disney executives decided to shoot more footage—including bar scenes of Cruise mixing drinks and dancing up a storm in front of bikini-clad bathing beauties and presto!—they had a hit. *Cocktail* went on to gross $160 million.

PRETTY IN PINK

In the original ending of the film, Molly Ringwald ended up with her awkward friend Duckie (Jon Cryer) instead of the slick and wealthy Blaine (Andrew McCarthy). When preview audiences disapproved, director John Hughes re-filmed the ending to conform to their wishes, including a romantic liason between Ringwald and McCarthy.

LITTLE SHOP OF HORRORS

In both the original film and off-Broadway musical production, the "Little Shop Of Horrors" ended with Audrey, the people-eating plant, munching down the lead characters. During preview tests for the 1986 film version of the musical, however, audiences expressed their displeasure that Rick Moranis and Ellen Greene became plant food. The cast and crew flew back to England to film an entirely new—and happy—ending where the plant was killed instead.

FIRST BLOOD

Preview audiences were asked to vote on whether Rambo, played by Sylvester Stallone, should die at the end of movie. Two endings had already been filmed. One showed Rambo shot by his enemy, Richard Crenna (which was how the 1972 novel on which the movie is based, ended). The other showed an emotionally-drained Rambo being led away by Crenna alive. Audiences were split on

Only one carat in every 23 tons of ore mined is a diamond.

the decision, but apparently the producers made the correct choice by letting Rambo live. The sequels, *Rambo: First Blood Part II* and *Rambo III*, were box-office bonanzas.

THE BIG CHILL

Lawrence Kasdan's cult movie about '60s college pals reuniting in the '80s originally had a different ending—a flashback to the group's hippie days at the University of Michigan. Preview audiences, however, refused to accept the actors dressed up as college-age kids and the ending was cut.

An exception to the rule:

STAR WARS

Marketing research for the 1976 mega-hit was conducted by the staff of Twentieth Century Fox. It concluded that "you can't use war in the title," and that "robots could turn off the mass majority of moviegoers." Director George Lucas ignored the advice and obviously the force was with him—*Star Wars* is one of the top-grossing films of all time.

MISCELLANEOUS MOVIE FACTS:

• **Bizarre Movie Titles:** *Betta, Betta in the Wall, Who's the Fattest Fish of All* (United States, 1969), *She Ee Clit Soak* (United States, 1971), *Recharge Grandmothers Exactly!* (Czechoslovakia, 1984), *I Go Oh No* (Taiwan, 1984), *Egg! Egg?* (Sweden, 1975), *Phfft* (United States, 1954), and *Film Without Title* (East Germany, 1947).

• **Sound Stomachs:** To create the language of the mutants in *Island of Lost Souls* (United States 1932), sound-man Loren L. Ryder recorded a mixture of animal sounds and foreign languages, then played them backwards at alternating speeds. The effect: the sound induced nausea—audiences vomited in the theaters.

• **The Amazing van der Zyl:** Sometimes beautiful movie actresses don't have beautiful voices to go with their good looks. Enter Nikki van der Zyl, the voice of the James Bond Girls. In *Doctor No* (1962) Miss van der Zyl is the voice of all but two women in the film. She also dubbed the neanderthal grunts for Racquel Welch in *One Million Years BC (1962)*. Of course, the films don't credit her.

That's the breaks: A major league baseball team can break $150,000 worth of bats in one year.

QUAYLE QUIPS

Vice President Dan Quayle may not be articulate, but he's quotable. Here are some of his more memorable remarks.

"What a waste it is to lose one's mind. Or not to have a mind. Do I mean that?"

"Republicans understand the importance of the bondage between parent and child."

"We're going to have the best-educated American people in the world."

When asked by state GOP *chairman to consider running for Congress:* "I'll have to check with my dad."

"Hawaii has always been a very pivotal role in the Pacific. It is in the Pacific. It is part of the United States that is an island that is right here."

On his decision to join the National Guard in 1969:
"Well, growing up in Huntington, Indiana, the first thing you think about is education."

On which vice president he might model himself after:
"I don't know if there's one that comes to mind."

"It's rural America. It's where I come from. We always refer to ourselves as real America. Rural America, real America, real, real America."

On the ethics of his admission into law school:
"I deserve respect for the things I did not do."

On the Holocaust:
"An obscene period of our nation's history."

"Verbosity leads to unclear, inarticulate things."

On the meaning of Thanksgiving:
"The first would be our family. Your family, my family—which is composed of an immediate family of a wife and three children, a larger family with grandparents and aunts and uncles. We all have our family, whichever that may be."

At the Inauguration:
"I'm not used to going in front of President Reagan, so we went out behind the Bushes."

Dan Quayle's favorite film is "Ferris Bueller's Day Off."

DISNEY STORIES: SNOW WHITE

"Snow White and the Seven Dwarfs" was Walt Disney's first full-length cartoon feature, and it was nearly his last. Hollywood, appalled at the money he was pouring into it, dubbed it "Disney's Folly." It premiered in L.A. on December 21, 1937—and received a standing ovation. It also received a special Academy Award—"a full-size Oscar and seven little ones." Of course, the Disney version and the Grimm fairy tale were substantially different. Here are some examples of how the tale was changed.

THE DISNEY VERSION

Snow White's stepmother, the Wicked Queen, is jealous of Snow White's beauty. So she sends Snow White to the forest with one of her hunters. He's supposed to kill the young Princess and bring her heart to the queen as proof the girl is dead...but he can't do it. He lets Snow White go free, kills a wild boar and brings the boar's heart to the Queen instead.

• This trick almost works. But the queen consults her magic mirror and learns that Snow White is still alive.

• Meanwhile, Snow takes up residence with the seven dwarfs.

• One day, the wicked queen shows up looking like a hag and offers Snow White a poison apple. The dwarfs catch the queen in the act, but they're too late; Snow White dies. The dwarfs chase the queen to a rocky cliff where she falls to her death.

• A handsome Prince shows up and kisses the dead princess. Snow White is revived; she and the Prince live happily ever after.

THE ORIGINAL VERSION

• To small children, Disney's version is nightmarish enough. We can only wonder what children would think of the gruesome goings-on in the original fairy tale.

• The Queen doesn't ask for Snow White's heart—she wants the princess's lungs and liver. When the hunter brings her the boar's innards, the Queen—thinking they're Snow White's—has them boiled in salt and eats them.

• In the original story, the Queen tries to kill Snow White three times. The first two attempts fail. Since the Queen uses the same disguise all three times, we have to assume Snow White, although pretty, is a little short in the brains department.

• The dwarfs—who don't have cute names like Sneezy and Grumpy—do put Snow White in a glass coffin. But the Prince doesn't wake her with a kiss. In fact, kissing her never enters his mind. He just thinks she's pretty (albeit dead), and wants to keep her around his castle.

• On the way back to the castle, servants carrying the casket trip and drop it. This dislodges the poison apple from Snow White's throat and she's revived.

• In this tale, the Queen makes it back to her castle after apparently killing Snow White. A little later, she's invited to a wedding. The wedding, it turns out, is Snow White's. When the Queen arrives, Snow and the Prince have a pair of red-hot iron shoes waiting in the fireplace. The Queen is forced to wear the shoes and dance until she drops dead.

SAMPLE PASSAGES (FROM THE ORIGINAL)

"The Queen summoned a huntsman and said, 'Take the child out into the forest. I never want to lay eyes on her again. You are to kill her and bring me back her lungs and liver as proof of your deed'...The cook was ordered to boil [the boar's organs] in salt, and the wicked woman ate them and thought that she had eaten Snow White's lungs and liver."

The Queen receives an invitation to Snow White's wedding. She's stunned, because she was sure Snow White was dead.

"The evil woman uttered a loud curse and became so terribly afraid that she did not know what to do. At first she didn't want to go to the wedding celebration. But she couldn't calm herself until she saw the young queen. When she entered the hall, she recognized Snow White...and she was so petrified with fright that she couldn't move. Iron slippers had already been heated over a fire, and they were brought over to her with tongs. Finally, she had to put on the red-hot slippers and dance until she fell down dead."

It was illegal in Nazi Germany to name your horse "Adolph."

JUST YOUR TYPE

Have you ever wondered why the letters on a typewriter are arranged so strangely? Here's the answer:

BUILT FOR SPEED

In 1872, Charles Latham Sholes and two partners developed a bizarre-looking machine they called the "Type-Writer." It wasn't the original typewriting machine, but it was the first to go beyond the experimental stage.

However, shortly after Sholes and his partners started selling it, they ran into a problem: The machine couldn't keep up with quick-fingered typists; the keys would jam if they were struck too closely in succession. Sholes spent long hours in his workshop, but still couldn't find a way to quicken the machine's keystrokes.

NOT SO FAST

One day in his lab, the desperate inventor had a brainstorm—a clever idea which still affects typists today. Since he couldn't speed up the machine to accomodate typists, he decided to slow down typists to accommodate the machine. He set out to design the most inconvenient, awkward, and confusing arrangement of typewriter keys possible.

After weeks of research, Sholes settled on what is now called the QWERTY keyboard (after the first six letters of the typewriter's third row). With this new keyboard, Sholes was confident everyone would have to "hunt and peck"—and even an expert typist would be slowed enough to use his machine. He marketed a model with the altered keyboard as a "groundbreaking advancement," boasting that a typist could now type the word "typewriter" without having to leave the third row.

Today we type on high-speed machines that Sholes couldn't have imagined in his wildest dreams. But we still use the keyboard he devised to save his primitive machine.

SWEET DREAMS... Where did the term *lollipop* come from? According to *How Did They Do That*: "George Smith, who invented the candy on a stick in the early 1900s, had other money-making interests: Lolly Pop was one of the finest racehorses of the time."

CARTOON CORNER

A few facts about the origins of your favorite cartoon characters.

THE FLINTSTONES. This half-hour cartoon, introduced in 1960, was TV's first animated sitcom...and the first prime-time cartoon show ever. Hanna-Barbera Studios originally planned to take a standard sitcom—"a young couple with a kid and a dog"—and transpose it to prehistoric times. But that wound up too much like "Blondie." So Joseph Hanna turned it into a prehistoric "Honeymooners" instead, complete with an Art Carney-type next-door neighbor.

The original stars were Fred and Wilma Flagstone; the program was going to be called "Rally 'Round the Flagstones." But Mort Walker, creator of the comic strip "Hi and Lois," objected. Pointing out that Hi and Lois's last name is Flagston, he insisted that "Flagstone" was too similar to his creation, and asked Hanna-Barbera to change the name.

Receiving this news, one furious Hanna-Barbera producer suddenly had a vision of a Stone Age man rubbing two stones together to make fire—two flint stones. And that became the new name. Footnote: "The Flintstones" was the first cartoon ever to rank among the Top 20 shows of a year, ranking at #18 in 1960.

MIGHTY MOUSE. In 1939, DC comics introduced Superman; by the early 1940s, Superman was so popular that the comics had been joined by a Superman radio show and a series of animated cartoons. Paul Terry, a veteran cartoon-maker (Terrytoons), decided to capitalize on the Superman craze. So in 1942, he introduced an invulnerable flying rodent (dressed in a Superman-style costume, complete with a red cape) named Super Mouse. The public loved it. A year later, anxious to avoid a lawsuit, Terry changed Our Hero's name to Mighty Mouse.

ROCKY AND BULLWINKLE. In 1948 Jay Ward and his partner, Alex Anderson, decided to create a cartoon series especially for TV—which had never been done. For their stars, they had in mind an animal duo—a smart little creature (the hero) and a big dumb one (the sidekick). They proposed two shows:

• "Crusader Rabbit," featuring a rabbit and his towering, dimwitted tiger buddy.

• "Frostbite Follies," featuring a flying squirrel and a big, dumb moose.

The first one they developed, "Crusader Rabbit," was immediately successful...so they didn't bother working out the second one. Then, in the mid-1950s, Ward sold his rights to "Crusader" and started work on a new cartoon show that adults would appreciate, too. He went back to the squirrel and moose concept.

He'd already picked the name Bullwinkle for the moose. It was inspired by a car salesman in Berkeley, California, where Ward lived. "Every day I'd drive by this sign, Bullwinkle Chevrolet or something," he recalled several decades later, "and I'd think to myself, 'If I ever do another cartoon character, I'm gonna name it Bullwinkle.'" The name Rocky for the little squirrel was a takeoff on tough-guy, macho names. Ward worked on the show for several years. It finally debuted as "Rocky and His Friends" in 1959.

GOOFY. Mickey Mouse's pal made his screen debut in the 1932 cartoon Mickey's Review, as Dippy Dawg. (At the time, "dippy" was popular slang for "someone foolish or slightly mad.") The inspiration: country folks whom Pinto Colvig, Goofy's voice, had known in Oregon. Over the next 6 years Dippy Dawg became a regular character, but his name was changed to Dippy, then Dippy the Goof, and finally Goofy (although for a while in the '40s, his name changed again, to Mr. Geef). His first-ever appearance as Goofy was in the 1939 short, *Goofy and Wilbur*.

TWEETY BIRD. Created by Bob Clampett, a Warner Brothers animator. The inspiration for Tweety's wide-eyed stare and little body was a nude baby photograph of Clampett himself. The canary's famous phrase, "I tawt I taw a puddy-tat," originated in a letter Clampett wrote to a friend on MGM stationery. He drew a surprised baby bird pointing at Leo the Lion, saying "I tink I taw a titty-tat!" Clampett's friend wrote back that he got "quite a kick" out of the "titty-tat" gag. (It was a little off-color for the times). "Titty-tat" was turned into "Puddy-tat" for the big screen.

MEL BLANC. Believe it or not, the man who provided Bugs Bunny's voice was allergic to carrots.

The New York League for the Hard of Hearing says 50% of D.J.s suffer hearing damage.

MYTH AMERICA

You may have believed these myths all your life; after all, they were taught to us as sacred truths. But here's another look...

REMEMBER THE ALAMO

The Myth: The defenders of the Alamo fought for justice, political freedom, and independence.

The Truth: It was as much an issue of slavery as it was independence. In the 1820s Texas was a part of Mexico, and much of its land was being settled by slave-owning farmers and ranchers from the southern U.S. But in 1830, the Mexican government passed a law outlawing slavery. Soon after, American settlers revolted, and the Alamo was defended—at least in part because American settlers wanted to keep their slaves.

BAR-B-COW

The Myth: Mrs. O'Leary's cow kicked over a lantern while being milked and started the Great Chicago Fire of October 8, 1871.

Background: The cow was merely a scapegoat . . .or scapecow. Michael Aherns, a reporter whose newspaper account first broke the legendary cow story, later admitted he made the whole thing up to boost his paper's circulation.

The Truth: The fire did start somewhere near the O'Leary house, but the Chicago Fire Department never found the real cause of the blaze.

THE FATHER OF OUR COUNTRY

The Myth: George Washington was the first president of the United States.

The Truth: Washington was the first to serve as America's president under the Constitution of 1789, but the United States was a sovereign nation 13 years before the Constitution was written. In 1777, the Congress adopted the Articles of Confederation, which were ratified by the states in 1781. Later in 1781, this new legislative body convened and elected John Hanson as "President of the U.S. in Congress assembled." Hanson had been a member of the Maryland assembly and the Continental Congress, where he played a key role in convincing Maryland, the only state against

37% of Americans say they are excellent drivers. 2% think others drivers are equally skilled.

the Articles of Confederation, to ratify them. Washington himself sent Hanson a letter of congratulations on his "appointment to fill the most important seat in the United States." However, Hanson and the *seven* other presidents who served before George Washington have been forgotten.

THOREAU-LY SURPRISING

The Myth: Henry David Thoreau was a recluse who spent his Walden years in solitude, far from civilization.

The Truth: During his two years at Walden, Thoreau kept a pretty busy social schedule. He made frequent trips to the nearby town of Concord to spend time with friends and enjoy some of his mother's home cooking. In addition, he often played host to whole groups of visitors in his "secluded" cabin. Ralph Waldo Emerson was a frequent visitor, as was Bronson Alcott, who dropped by weekly. One day, April 1, 1846, Thoreau had about 30 people over for a meeting. According to Walter Harding's *The Days of Henry Thoreau*, "hardly a day went by that Thoreau did not visit the village or was not visited at the pond."

The Myth: Thoreau spent an extended period of time in prison for refusing to pay poll taxes which would support the Mexican War of 1846 and slavery.

The Truth: Thoreau did do jail time for his act of civil disobedience—one night of it. He was bailed out the following morning by an unidentified woman rumored to be his Aunt Maria, or Ralph Waldo Emerson in disguise. Legend has it Thoreau begged to stay in jail, but the jailer would have none of it.

CHARGE!

The Myth: Teddy Roosevelt commanded his hardy band of Rough Riders on their charge up Cuba's San Juan Hill in the Spanish-American War.

The Truth: Contrary to the popular image of the courageous cavalry charge on horseback, the cavalry unit was on foot; their horses had accidentally been left in Florida. And Roosevelt wasn't even on San Juan Hill. He did take part in the charge on nearby Kettle Hill, but only watched from there as Colonel C. Wood led the Rough Riders up San Juan Hill.

REEL GANGSTERS

If you're an old movie buff, you've probably seen classic gangster films like Scarface, Little Caesar, *and* Public Enemy. *Here's some behind-the-scenes trivia about how the films were made.*

BIG AL IS WATCHING YOU

Scarface (1932) was the best known of all early gangster films. Director Howard Hughes and screenwriter Ben Hecht modeled the main character, Tony Camonte (played by Paul Muni), after Chicago mobster Al Capone. Capone heard about it. And just to make sure *Scarface* was to his liking, he sent some of his own men to monitor the filming, as "advisors."

How do you spell relief? Capone enjoyed the film so much he bought a print of it and threw a huge party for Hawks in Chicago.

THE UN-NATURAL LOOK

Edward G. Robinson's portrayal of vicious killer Caesar Enrico Bandello in *Litte Caesar* (1930) made him a star. But he actually hated firing guns; in fact, every time he shot one in the film, he shut his eyes. Director Mervin LeRoy wanted a "cold and unblinking" killer, so he taped Robinson's eyelids open.

RIGHT GUY, WRONG PART

James Cagney was brought to Hollywood by Darryl Zanuck, and was immediately miscast as a smooth character in *The Millionaire*. One day Zanuck was watching unedited cuts of the film, wondering why Cagney wasn't working out. A scene ended; Cagney turned to the camera, sneered, and said, "For God's sake, who wrote this crap?" Zanuck realized the tough-talking Cagney was perfect for the gangster roles he was having such a hard time casting. It made Cagney's career.

In the most famous 1930s gangster scene, Cagney (*Public Enemy*, 1931), smashed half a grapefruit in Mae Clark's face. It wasn't in the script. Cagney and Clark staged it as a practical joke to shock the film crew, but director William Wellman liked it and left it in. Later in life, Cagney wasn't able to finish a meal in a restaurant without being offered a free half-grapefruit.

At the wedding of Ronald Reagan's daughter Patti: 134 guests and 180 security personnel.

FIT FOR A KING

A few thoughts from Maring Luther King, Jr., winner of the Nobel Peace Prize and one of the greatest leaders of the 20th Century.

"Human salvation lies in the hands of the creatively maladjusted."

"I live each day under a threat of death. I know I can meet a violent end."

"Philanthropy is commendable, but it must not cause the philanthropists to overlook the circumstances of economic injustice which make philanthropy necessary."

"He who passively accepts evil is as much involved in it as he who helps to perpetrate it."

"Freeedom is never voluntarily given by the oppressor; it must be demanded by the oppressed."

"War is a poor chisel to carve out tomorrows."

"All progress is precarious, and the solution of one problem brings us face to face with another problem."

"Nothing pains some people more than having to think."

"We will have to repent in this generation not merely for the vitriolic words and actions of the bad people, but for the appalling silence of the good people."

"Injustice anywhere is a threat to justice everywhere."

"The means by which we live have outdistanced the ends for which we live."

"Our scientific power has outrun our spiritual power. We have guided missiles and misguided men."

"A man has no right to live until he has found something to die for."

"Shallow understanding from people of goodwill is more frustrating than absolute misunderstanding from people of ill-will."

MARS ATTACKS

On October 30, 1938, over a million-and-a-half listeners tuned in to the most famous radio broadcast of all-time—War Of The Worlds, *a dramatization of* H.G. *Wells' classic science fiction novel about a Martian invasion. Here's what happened.*

HERE THEY COME

The radio version of *War of the Worlds* was just an elaborate Halloween joke played by actor Orson Welles and the regulars of "Mercury Theatre on the Air." But it caused a nationwide panic. Some terrified families fled from their homes; others prepared for a full-scale Martian war.

ON THE SPOT

Welles insisted on making the broadcast of *War of the Worlds* as realistic-sounding as possible. At first, the announcements that Martians had landed came in the form of news bulletins interspersed between live big-band remotes. Gradually the tone of the broadcast became more hysterical. Some of the bulletins ("We take you now to Washington for a special broadcast on the national emergency...") sounded particularly unnerving to a nation on the verge of World War II.

I CAN'T LOOK

Since the show had no sponsors, there were only a few interruptions to announce that the show was a dramatic presentation. Listeners tuning in mid-broadcast heard frightening "on the scene" descriptions of the attacking Martians. "Good heavens, something's wriggling out of the shadow like a grey snake. Now it's another one, and another. They look like tentacles to me. There, I can see the thing's body. It's large as bear and it glistens like wet leather. But that face...it's indescribable. I can hardly force myself to look at it. The eyes are black and gleam like a serpent. The mouth is V-shaped with saliva dripping from its rimless lips that seem to quiver and pulsate."

Although he was oblivious to the hysteria his program was stirring up, Welles was still clever enough to give the show a happy ending—the Martians are conquered and calm is restored. Welles concluded the broadcast by saying, "And if your doorbell rings and nobody's 'there,' that was no Martian...it's Halloween."

THE PANIC

By the time the broadcast was completed, millions of Americans were convinced that a Martian invasion had occurred. Police switchboards were flooded from coast to coast by calls from terrified listeners. Among the reactions:

• One New Jersey resident mistook a water tower for the Martians and blasted it with a shotgun.

• Twenty families from one apartment building evacuated their homes with wet towels on their faces to avoid deadly Martian rays.

• Pennsylvania's governor offered troop support to New Jersey, where the invasion was supposedly taking place.

• A woman paged her husband at a Broadway play to warn him of the attack—and many audience members fled with him.

• A husband in Pittsburgh came home to find his wife with a bottle of poison in her hand, saying "I'd rather die this way than that."

Despite the hysteria, no deaths resulting from the broadcast have ever been documented.

FALL OUT

• Police stormed CBS studios after the broadcast and held the cast and crew for questioning (Mercury employees hid the tape of the show, fearing that it would be confiscated). After a few hours of intense grilling, the police let everybody go.

• Welles became an instant nationwide celebrity. The day after the broadcast, he seemed as incredulous as anybody about all the hoopla: "I'm extremely surprised to learn that a story, which has become familiar to children through the medium of comic strips and many succeeding novels and adventure stories, should have had such an immediate and profound effect upon radio listeners."

• In 1947, the citizens of Ecuador had a similar hysterical reaction to Radio Quito's dramatization of the Mercury script. Once again, panic-stricken residents fled into the streets. Later, when a mob of terrified listeners found out the broadcast wasn't real, they burned down the radio station (Ecuador's oldest) in anger. One radio station employee died in the blaze.

DICK NIXON, FOOTBALL COACH

Judging from Watergate, you might say strategy wasn't Richard Nixon's strongest suit. But that didn't keep Nixon from trying to "coach" two football teams—the Washington Redskins and the Miami Dolphins—while he was serving as president.

BACKGROUND
• Nixon was an acknowledged football freak, an armchair quarterback who often peppered his speeches with allusions to the game.
• He once referred to Congress as "a fourth-quarter team," adding, "in the last quarter, we have to score a lot of points."
• The White House used the code name "Operation Linebacker," for a secret Pentagon strategy in Vietnam during Nixon's presidency. Nixon's personal code name was "Quarterback."

COLLEGE DAYS
• Nixon was never much of a football player. He made the freshman squad at Whittier College in California, but later in his college career was only allowed to practice with the team and sit on the bench.
• He later recalled: "I played on the C team...and I didn't even make that."
• In 1969, a few days before being inaugurated, he finally received a varsity letter from Whittier.

THE COACH AND THE PREZ
• George Allen, who coached the Redskins during Nixon's tenure at the White House, had previously been Whittier's football coach.
• The two met at a college sports banquet in 1952 and became very close. Allen, who spoke often to the president, publicly praised him, saying, "The president thinks football is a way of life. He is a competitor."
• Allen, like Nixon, wasn't known for his scruples. Once, while he was coach of the Redskins, Allen traded away a draft choice he didn't have. Football officials fined him $5,000.

PEP TALK

• In November, 1971, President Nixon visited the Redskins at their practice camp in Virginia. He gave them a pep talk: "I've always said that in life, as well as in sports, politics, and business, what really makes a team or a country is when it has lost one, it doesn't lose its spirit. I think this team has the spirit it takes. I think government has it. You're going to go on and win."
• The president was wrong. Washington lost the National Football Conference championship game that season to the San Francisco 49ers, partly due to Nixon's playmaking.
• Late in the second quarter of the game, with the Redskins on the verge of a touchdown, Coach Allen ran a play that Nixon had especially requested—a flanker reverse with Roy Jefferson. The play resulted in a 13-yard loss, throwing the Redskins from the 49ers' 8-yard line to the 21-yard line. The Skins had to settle for a field goal.
• When the 49ers won the game, 24-20, many sportwriters claimed Nixon's play had been the turning point of the game.

SWITCHING SIDES

• Following the Redskins' loss to the 49ers, Nixon quickly switched allegiances to the Miami Dolphins, claiming he had followed the team from his vacation home in Key Biscayne, Florida.
• The Dolphins defeated the Baltimore Colts, 21-0, for the American Football Conference title. That night, their coach, Don Shula, received a 1:30 am phone call from the president. "I thought it might be some nut calling," Shula later recounted. "But his aide said, 'Is this Mr. Shula?' Then he said, 'The president is calling.' I thought it might be a hoax. I was listening to make sure it was his voice."

SINKING THE DOLPHINS

• Shula would soon regret Nixon's interest.
• Somehow it became public knowledge that the President had suggested the Dolphins run a specific play for their star wide-receiver, Paul Warfield, against the Dallas Cowboys in the upcoming Super Bowl. "I think you can hit Warfield on that down-and-in pattern," Nixon told Shula.
• The Dolphins failed to complete the play three times in the 1972 Super Bowl, which the Cowboys won handily, 24- 3.

Say What?: In Albania, nodding the head means "no" and shaking the head means "yes."

• After the game, Warfield complained that the Cowboys had keyed on him thanks to Nixon. "They had two weeks to prepare and they made sure that under any circumstances we wouldn't be able to catch that pass," he said.

NO BONES ABOUT IT

• More than a few Cowboys fans took umbrage at Nixon's support of the Dolphins. The Bonehead Club of Dallas, a group of Dallas businessmen, awarded their annual "Bonehead of the Year Award" to Nixon two days prior to the Super Bowl.

• Nixon accepted the award "in the spirit in which it is given . . . in good humor."

CSONKA'S COMPAINT

• Larry Csonka, the Dolphins' star running back, wasn't all that pleased with Nixon's playmaking either. He later complained, "President Nixon may identify with football players, but I don't identify with him, and I haven't met a player yet who does. The man upset me with his role as superjock. Here he is, the one man in the world who has, at his fingertips, all the information and influence to make a lot of people's lives better. But what's he doing calling football players on the telephone and giving pep talks to teams? It just brainwashes people more, makes people think football is a lot more important to them than it really is. He's either hung up on the violence or else he's pulling off a master con job on a lot of sports fans. He's implying that he's one of them and he's hoping to get their votes in return."

KILMER'S COMPAINT

• Despite his coaching ineptitude, Nixon kept meddling with the Redskins the following season.

• Billy Kilmer, the Redskins' quarterback, became so frustrated that he told the *Washington Post*, "He's really hurting us. He calls all the time. He told some guy from Cleveland he met in New York that Cleveland had a good team but they had quarterback problems. Then Cleveland got all psyched up and they were much harder to beat. I think I'm going to ask George Allen to tell the president not to talk about the game until after we've played it."

Flies can get athlete's foot.

POSTSCRIPT

• By 1978, both Nixon and Coach Allen had lost their jobs. But unlike the ex-President, Allen had landed a new one as the head coach of the Rams.

• Surfacing to express confidence in his old pal, Nixon fearlessly predicted that Allen would coach the Rams to the Super Bowl.

• "I'm not saying they will win the Super Bowl," he told the *Los Angeles Herald Examiner* in 1978, "but I think he'll get them there at least."

• Not exactly. Allen was fired early in the season; the Rams lost in the playoffs. Nixon was later spotted in Yankee Stadium, rooting for the New York Yankees. Apparently, he'd become a baseball fan.

☛ ☛ ☛

AD-VERSARIES: WOULD YOU BUY A USED CAR FROM THESE GUYS?

• **Mr. Clean versus Mr. Bush:** In 1985, Procter & Gamble took a poll to see how many people could identify Mr. Clean, the genie character used as a trademark for one of their cleaning products. 93% of consumers could identify him. That year, *People* magazine also took a poll and found that only 56% of the same shoppers could identify then-Vice President George Bush.

• **TV Time:** The average American teenager will see some 350,000 TV commercials by the time he or she graduates from high school.

Obsolescent Ads

• **Planned:** During the 1984 Super Bowl, Apple Computer showed a commercial that depicted a procession of robot-like people marching off a cliff. The idea: Most computer buyers pick the same old thing, but choosing an Apple is daring to be different. The widely-praised ad, which cost over $500,000 to produce, was intentionally never shown again.

• **Un-Planned:** In 1989, Pepsi paid Madonna a whopping $5 million for one two-minute commercial featuring her new hit "Like A Prayer." Ironically, the ad was abruptly cancelled by Pepsi after a month when consumers confused the commercial with Madonna's video of the same song, which featured "sacreligious" images like burning crosses.

A horse has 10 more bones than a man.

SPACE JUNK

Since Sputnik I was launched in 1957, nearly four thousand satellites have been put into orbit. Many just exploded; others have been deliberately blown up. As a result, there are literally billions of pieces of man-made debris now circling the earth...a veritable junkyard in space. So here's some "space junk" trivia.

Seven U.S. Delta rockets and a French observation satellite have exploded in space.

In 1961, Cuban premier Fidel Castro charged that a chunk of a U.S. spacecraft had fallen on Cuba and killed a cow.

In 1962, a 21-lb. fragment of Soviet Sputnik IV landed at the intersection of Park and North 8th Streets in Manitowoc, Wisconsin.

In 1978, a Soviet satellite came crashing back to Earth, contaminating hundreds of square miles of Canadian territory with radiation. What caused the crash? Scientists' best guess: the satellite collided with space junk, which caused it to go off its orbit.

Lost and never found: Astronaut Ed White lost a white glove during the Gemini 4 flight in 1965; George "Pinky" Nelson lost two minature screws while attempting to repair a satellite on a space shuttle mission in 1984.

In 1981, a Soviet navigation satellite exploded into 135 pieces after colliding with space debris.

Over 7,000 objects floating in space are being tracked from earth; only five percent are satellites.

Dodging space junk is a dangerous occupation. A 0.5 millimeter metal chip could puncture a space suit and kill an astronaut walking in space. A particle as small as ten millimeters could damage and possibly even destroy an orbiting space vehicle.

Before it blew up in 1986, the space shuttle Challenger was hit by a flake of paint measuring 0.2 millimeters, which damaged a window during one of its missions.

Americans make $500 million worth of illegal long distance phone calls annually.

JUST SAY NO-HIT!

Although quite a few public figures dabbled in pyschedelics during the late '60s and early '70s, few played major league baseball. Dock Ellis did...and pitched a no-hitter on LSD.

BACKGROUND

Dock Ellis was a premier pitcher from 1968 through 1979, winning 138 games while playing for the Pittsburgh Pirates, New York Yankees, Oakland Athletics, Texas Rangers and New York Mets. Of all his achievements, which include pitching in two World Series, his biggest was the no-hitter he pitched as a Pittsburgh Pirate against the San Diego Padres on June 12, 1970.

Fourteen years later, Ellis revealed he had accomplished this feat while under the influence of LSD.

A LONG STRANGE TRIP

Apparently, Ellis took the dose at noon and then realized he had to pitch at 6:05 p.m. that night. "I was in Los Angeles and the team was playing in San Diego, but I didn't know it," Ellis told the *Pittsburgh Press* in 1984. "I had taken LSD. I thought it was an off-day."

THE ACID TEST

The game was the first in a twi-night doubleheader between the Pirates and the Padres. Despite the powerful effects of the LSD, Ellis pitched brilliantly for nine innings, allowing no hits (he walked eight and hit a batter). "I can only remember bits of pieces of the game," Ellis later recounted. "I was psyched. I had a feeling of euphoria." According to one source, Ellis believed the ball was talking to him, telling him what pitches to throw.

THE AFTERMATH

Ellis didn't dare admit what he'd done. In fact, he never pitched on psychedelics again. Years later, Ellis was treated for drug dependency and became the coordinator of an anti-drug program in Los Angeles.

In 1985, hailstones weighing over 2.25 pounds each fell in Bangladesh.

FABULOUS FAKES

There are plenty of little lies and hoaxes in the newspapers every day—from President Reagan pretending to light the White House Christmas tree, to votes of confidence for baseball managers about to be fired. But some hoaxes capture the public's imagination, and fool the experts at the same time. Here are some classics.

THE PILTDOWN MAN

THE DISCOVERY: In 1912, the remains of the fabled "missing link" between man and ape were found at an English excavation site. The exciting discovery included nine pieces of a skull and a jawbone.

THE HOAX: Charles Dawson was a British lawyer and amateur archeologist when he "discovered" the remains of the half-ape/half-man in a pit at Piltdown Common near Sussex, England. Dawson claimed the fossils were proof that human life had origins in England—a notion that appealed to British sensibilities.

In 1915, Dawson made a similar discovery two miles away from the first, proving the "Piltdown Man" was part of a race of people. The problem was, no one could get close enough to the bones to either prove or disprove Dawson's theory—he kept them locked up and only provided plaster cast models of the fossils.

THE UNMASKING: Dawson died in 1916, but it wasn't until 1953 that scientists finally got a chance to test the authenticity of the bones. They quickly proved the "Piltdown Man" was a fraud and concluded that Dawson probably bought the bones in an auction and tried to pass them off as "the missing link" as a practical joke.

THE CARDIFF GIANT

THE DISCOVERY: In 1869, workers digging near a well in Cardiff, New York discovered the petrified remains of a ten-foot tall man. Newspapers dubbed him "the Cardiff Giant" and hailed the discovery as the paleontogical "find of the century." "Cardiff Giant fever" swept the country.

THE SCHEME: The Cardiff Giant was the brainchild of a cigar manufacturer named George Hull, from Binghamton, New York.

Young Guns: The average age of U.S. Military personnel is 25.

Hull bought a 5-ton block of gypsum in Iowa and had it shipped to Chicago, where two marble cutters, with him as their model, spent three months carving out a likeness of a naked man.

According to Stephen Jay Gould in *Natural History* magazine: "Hull made some crude and minimal attempts to give his statue an aged appearance. He chipped off the carved hair and beard because experts told him that such items would not petrify. He drove darning needles into a wooden block and hammered the statue, hoping to simulate skin pores. Finally, he dumped a gallon of sulfuric acid all over his creation to simulate extended erosion." Hull then had the statue buried in Cardiff (in the backyard of a friend who was in on the hoax), where it was not-so-accidentally "discovered" by two unsuspecting workmen hired to dig a well there.

THE UNMASKING: A Yale paleontologist named O.C. Marsh exposed the fraud a few weeks later. After giving the Cardiff Giant the once-over, he declared that the Giant "was of very recent origin and a decided humbug." Shortly thereafter, under intense pressure, Hull confessed to his fraud.

AFTERMATH: Hull had managed to sell the rights to the Cardiff Giant—for $30,000 to a consortium of businessmen—before revealing the hoax. Although the Cardiff Giant was no longer the acknowledged "Eighth Wonder of the World," people still paid 50¢ apiece to see it. P.T. Barnum later made a copy of the fake and also put it on exhibition in New York City. Reportedly, his model outdrew the original when both were on display at the same time. The original Cardiff Giant is still on display at the Farmer's Museum in Cooperstown, New York.

THE ORANGE MOONMEN

THE DISCOVERY: In 1835, a New York *Sun* writer named Richard Adams Locke broke the stunning news that a British astronomer had seen furry, orange creatures living on the moon. The public was fascinated.

THE HOAX: Locke claimed that British astronomer Sir John Herschel had been trying out a new telescope when he noticed bison grazing on the moon. Supposedly, Herschel also saw blue goats, tropical forests and white beaches. Locke made the moon sound like a vacation spot. And the most amazing revelation was...there were apparently orange humanoid creatures, sporting leather wings, living on the lunar surface.

THE UNMASKING: Locke's chicanery was quickly exposed. Herschel disavowed the story and Locke owned up. He made up the entire thing to satirize an astronomer from Scotland who'd been claiming that he had discovered plant life on the moon.

BATS IN THE BELLE-FRY

THE DISCOVERY: During the Civil War, Ida Mayfield, a beautiful belle from Louisiana, became the toast of New York society. She was among the most beautiful, well-bred women in the city, and married Ben Wood, a newspaper magnate and congressman. She wore the finest gowns and jewels, danced with the Prince of Wales, was presented to Empress Eugenie of Austria, and entertained President Cleveland. Then, during the financial panic of 1907, she disappeared without a trace.

THE HOAX: Ida Mayfield was really Ellen Walsh, the penniless daughter of an immigrant textile worker, using a borrowed dress, the name of respected Louisiana family, and her innate charm. Wood never knew her real identity.

THE UNMASKING: In 1931, Ida Mayfield was found blind, deaf and shrunken. She was 94 years old, and living in a dingy New York hotel room, wearing a "dress" made only of two hotel towels pinned together. Her room was a mess of yellowed newspapers, letters and boxes, all scattered in disarray. She was judged incompetent and was made a ward of the court.

However, when they opened the boxes, they found securities worth hundreds of thousands of dollars. A diamond and emerald necklace was hidden in a box of crackers. And to top it off, fifty $10,000 dollar bills were contained inside a pouch tied around her waist. When collectors took this from her, she died.

FABULOUS FAKES ADDENDUM:

In 1708, English writer Jonathan Swift was so sick and tired of an astrologer that he wrote and published a fake obituary about the man, whose career subsequently took a dive.

DEFINITIONS

How's your vocabulary? In the first two Bathroom Readers we included some obscure words and their meanings, so you could impress your friends and neighbors. Here's another batch.

Labrose: Thick-lipped

Xenoepist: Someone with a foreign accent

Nosocomephrenia: Depression resulting from prolonged stay in the hospital

Hebetate: To become stupid or boring

Palpebrate: To wink

Quakebuttock: A coward

Glock: To swallow in large gulps

Brumous: Foggy or misty

Noyade: Mass execution by drowning

Ergophile: A workaholic

Weener: A trustworthy or believable person

Phrontistery: A place to study

Crurophilous: Liking legs

Dactylgram: Fingerprint

Valgus: Knock-kneed or bow-legged

Fample: To feed a child

Thuften: Having webbed toes

Errhine: Causing sneezing

Sphragistics: The study of engraved seals

Subrahend: The amount subtracted

Cygnet: A young swan

Misocapnist: Someone who dislikes tobacco smoke

Culch: Meat scraps

Recrement: A bodily secretion that is re-absorbed

Dentiscalp: A toothpick

Sorbile: Drinkable

Glabella: The space on your forehead between your eyebrows

Vespertilonize: To turn into a bat

Misodoctakleidist: Someone who dislikes practicing the piano

Deglutible: Capable of being swallowed

Spasmatomancy: Fortune-telling based upon body twitches

Bonnyclabber: Sour, coagulated milk

Peen: The end of a hammer opposite the striking end

Opsigamy: Marriage late in life

Hesternal: Having to do with yesterday

Shoding: The part in a person's hair

The chairman of Hyundai is called "The Chairman," even by his wife and kids.

BLACK AND WHITE

In 1972, Three Dog Night hit #1 on the pop charts with a tune called "Black and White" ("The ink is black, the page is white..."). Here's the amazing true story behind it.

LEGAL HISTORY

In 1896, in a decision called *Plessy v. Ferguson*, the United States Supreme Court ruled that racial segregation was constitutional—as long as blacks were given facilities which were "separate but equal" to those provided to whites. This ruling was the basis for institutionalized segregation in America.

Fifty-eight years later, the NAACP and a group of black families, with the support of Attorney General Herbert Brownell, sued the Topeka, Kansas school system, claiming that segregation was discriminatory and violated their constitutional rights. In an historic decision known as *Brown v. the Board of Education*, the court ruled in their favor, unanimously overturning the *Plessy* verdict. "In the field of public education, the doctrine of 'separate but equal' has no place," the court ruled.

During the months following the decision, more than 150 school districts integrated. Others fought the decision, and eventually lost. But the decision's impact was not merely on schools. It was one of the turning points of the Civil Rights movement, and marked an awakening of black activism that changed the face of American culture forever.

A SONG IS BORN

To jubilant Americans like Earl Robinson, an activist-songwriter who composed "Joe Hill," the *Brown v. Board of Education* ruling was a triumph. He and David Arkin, actor Alan Arkin's father, wrote "Black and White" to commemorate the event. It was a modern folk song.

"It was done in the '50s to celebrate a Supreme Court decision on segregation in the schools," Robinson says. "It was a famous decision, and this was kind of a celebration song, written actually, with children in mind, and no ideas whatsoever about it going popular."

On average, the French take twice as long on their business lunches as we do.

Robinson was a performer himself, and sang the song whenever he gave concerts ("The first place it was performed was in Elizabeth Irwin High School in the New York area, by the junior high school class there"). Thus it was passed around among New York folksingers , until it landed in...Guyana?

Robinson says: "In the late '50s, I got a call from CBS, which wanted to use my song, 'The Ink Is Black'—which isn't the title—for a documentary film they were making. It seems there was some kind of a Peace Corps that was working in French Guyana, and CBS wanted to clear the song because it was being used by them there, to teach the French Guyanese how to speak English! In the film, they showed a blackboard with a pointer, so you would hear [sings] 'The Ink Is Black...' and they'd point to the words as it went along. That became a theme song for this whole film, which was about how the American group was helping them build a recreation hall."

BACK TO AMERICA

"So then Sammy Davis Jr. got ahold of it through a publisher of mine, and he sang it and pressed 5,000 copies for the Anti-Defamation League of B'nai B'rith, which he was strongly connected with—and this was kind of like a flash in the pan. Pete Seeger also recorded it. He did it with a bunch of kids, and I wasn't too impressed, although I was happy that Pete did it.

"Anyway, it kept on being sung around, spreading slowly, by word of mouth until I got called on the phone in the early '70s. Someone told me, 'Three Dog Night is singing your song, did you know that?' I didn't even know who the Three Dogs were, to tell you the truth. I had no concept of it. You know, they told me later, when I went to attend a concert where they were singing, that they had heard the song in Holland, over a radio, where it was being sung by a Jamaican group. Now, I remembered this Jamaican group, but we paid very little attention to them because very little royalties were coming in from them. But the guys in Three Dog Night told me that they knew immediately it was going to be a hit when they heard it." And it was. Six weeks after it was released, it reached #1 in the nation. But virtually none of the millions of fans who bought it had any idea of what it was really about.

REAL ADS

Some ad characters—Charmin's Mr. Whipple, for instance—are so believable that we forget they're simply actors playing parts. Just to remind us, here's some inside info on a few of them.

THE STAR: Clara Peller in "Where's the Beef?"
BACKGROUND: Joe Sedelmaier, a producer of commercials, was filming a scene in a Chicago barbershop when he discovered that nobody had hired a manicurist. He sent an assistant to a local beauty shop to find one and she returned with Clara Peller, an octogenarian manicurist who had worked in a nearby salon for 35 years. She looked at Sedelmaier and said gruffly: "How ya doin', honey?" Sedelmaier realized he had found a "natural." "She's a counterpart to all those sweet little old ladies," he explained.
THE AD: In 1984, Sedelmaier convinced Wendy's Old Fashioned Hamburgers to design an ad campaign around Peller, who growled the catchy phrase, "Where's the beef?" Almost immediately, Wendy's sales jumped 15%. The slogan "Where's the beef?" entered the popular lexicon when Presidential candidate Walter Mondale used the phrase against his Democratic rival, Gary Hart, in the primary campaigns.

Meanwhile, the 82-year-old Peller became an instant cult star with a national fan club. She ended up making $500,000 for the Wendy's ad, plus merchandising. Before she passed away in 1987, Peller said "I made some money, which is nice for an older person, but Wendy's made millions because of me."

THE STAR: Jim Varney in "Hey, Vern!"
BACKGROUND: John R. Cherry III, a Nashville ad executive, was searching for an innovative ad campaign to publicize an amusement park that, in his words, was "so bad we couldn't show it on television." His solution: a fictional character named Ernest P. Worrell, a nosy country bumpkin with a penchant for injuring himself, who continually harasses an off-screen character named Vern.

To fill Ernest's silly shoes, Cherry picked Jim Varney, who'd appeared on the TV show "Fernwood 2-Night," as a "mobile home daredevil." Ironically, Varney was a trained Shakespearean actor.

Every year, Americans buy 5 million copies of *Cliffs Notes* for *The Scarlet Letter*.

THE AD: Although the amusement park closed after three months, Ernest was an immediate success. Sensing Ernest's potential, Cherry and Varney cleverly decided to license the character to any company that wanted him—rather than identifying Ernest with one particular product. Eventually, the duo collaborated on over 3,000 Ernest commercials (sometimes filming as many as 20 a day) plugging everything from Toyota cars to Snickers bars. In 1987, Ernest made it to the movies in "Ernest Goes To Camp," a $4 million feature that outdrew its competition, the $45 million "Ishtar." Since then, two other features, "Ernest's Christmas" and "Ernest Goes To Jail"—both huge box-office successes—have been released. No doubt more are on the way.

THE STAR: David Leisure in "You Have My Word On It."
BACKGROUND: David Leisure was an unemployed actor when an ad agency chose him to star in a series of Isuzu TV ads that were based on the character of "The Liar," popularized by Jon Luvitz on "Saturday Night Live." After auditioning several candidates, the agency hired Leisure "because he could lie like a pro." Leisure's previous biggest screen role had been as a Hare Krishna in the film "Airplane!"
THE AD: The ads featured Leisure playing Joe Isuzu, a car salesman who made outlandish claims about Isuzu cars while the words "he's lying" appeared under him. The campaign caught the public's imagination and Isuzu car sales jumped 18%. Meanwhile, the character became a household name. In the 1988 Presidential race, Michael Dukakis compared George Bush's tax promises to Joe Isuzu.

THE STAR: Dick Wilson in "Don't Squeeze The Charmin."
BACKGROUND: In 1964, Proctor and Gamble was looking for an actor to portray Mr. Whipple, an uptight supermarket manager who (for some strange reason never fully explained) begged his shoppers to stop squeezing Charmin toilet paper. Dick Wilson, an ex-vaudevillian, won the role over 80 potential Mr. Whipples. The first ads were filmed in Flushing, New York.
THE AD: Mr. Whipple caught on; Charmin became the bestselling toilet paper in the country. One 1970s survey found that more people recognized Mr. Whipple than Jimmy Carter. Unfortunately, Wilson became typecast. "When I go through the toilet paper section," he told People magazine, "I get some very strange looks."

Poetry in Ocean: According to experts, whale songs rhyme.

MOORE TO COME

In a recent poll, TV critics called "The Mary Tyler Moore Show" one of the 5 best sitcoms ever. As the first program to feature a single career woman competing on equal terms with men, it was certainly among the most influential. Here are some interesting facts about the show:

HOW IT STARTED

From 1961 to 1965, Mary Tyler Moore co-starred in the popular TV program "The Dick Van Dyke Show." But after she left the show, her career didn't fare too well. She tried movies, and wound up in films like *Change of Habit*, with Elvis Presley (she played a nun). She gave Broadway a shot (a musical version of *Breakfast At Tiffany's*), and the play closed before opening night. People began to notice that she'd never made it on her own, and suspected that she'd just been lucky on TV. She needed to do something to prove herself.

Then in 1969 she was invited to co-star with Dick Van Dyke in a TV special called "Dick Van Dyke and the Other Woman." Van Dyke's previous TV special, which co-starred singer Leslie Uggams, hadn't done well. But the Moore-Van Dyke show got high ratings, and Mary got the credit. The result: she received an offer from CBS that was too good to pass up; if she'd star in a new sitcom for them, they'd give her total creative freedom in developing it—plus part-ownership of the series. If it succeeded, she'd be rich. She accepted the offer.

Moore chose her new character carefully. She didn't want to be a housewife because she'd been "married" in "The Dick Van Dyke Show" (and wanted to avoid typecasting). She didn't want to be another sitcom "widow." So she decided to become a divorcee. Her writers created a pilot in which a recently-divorced woman (Mary) struggled with a career as an associate TV producer, and CBS loved it—except for the divorce. America wasn't quite that liberated yet. The network requested a change, saying they were afraid viewers would assume she had "divorced" Van Dyke. So the part was re-written to make Mary a refugee from a love affair. That was fine with CBS. The series debuted in Sept. 1970, and was a hit from the start. For three years in a row, it was among the Top 10 TV shows in America.

According to a Yale study, you think better in the winter than in summer.

SCOREBOARD

• The *Mary Tyler Moore Show* was the most honored show in Emmy history. It received 27 awards, including three for best comedy show, one for directing, and five for writing. Moore, Ed Asner (Lou Grant), and Valerie Harper (Rhoda Morgenstern) received three Emmys each; Ted Knight (Ted Baxter) and Betty White (Sue Ann Nivens) received two apiece; and Cloris Leachman (Phyllis, the land-lady) was presented with one.

• Even more impressive, the show spawned more successful spinoffs than any other sitcoms: *Rhoda*, *Phyllis*, and *Lou Grant*. In the 1975 season, two of the spinoffs placed in the Top Ten of the Year (*Phyllis* was #6, *Rhoda* was #8), outstripping even *Mary*, which ranked at #19.

REVENGE

Ironically, the only major cast-member who never received an Emmy for his work on the *MTM Show*—Gavin Macleod (Murray)—went on to the biggest TV success of all of them. He wound up as captain of the *Love Boat*, which ranked in the Top 5 several years in a row—higher than Mary or any of its spinoffs ever got. Amazing, but true.

HOME SWEET HOME

Remember that quaint house at 119 North Weatherly, where Mary supposedly had her apartment? It was owned by a University of Minnesota humanities professor. She was initially delighted to let MTM Productions shoot its exterior for use on the show (the interior scenes were done in the studio).

But when the program became popular, doorbell ringers began showing up regularly, asking for Mary, Rhoda, and Phyllis. The professor's life was so disrupted that she refused to let MTM film the outside of her house anymore. When MTM ignored her wishes and showed up to film the outside of her house anyway, the professor hung banners reading "Impeach Nixon" out of the windows that were supposed to be Mary's. That stopped the film crew.

Soon after, Mary "moved" to a high rise.

ANGLERS TAKE NOTE: In Tennessee and Washington, it's illegal to fish with a lasso.

That's relief: Scientists say that sex can relieve arthritis pain for up to 6 hours.

JOCKS IN POLITICS

Are all jocks dumb? Not necessarily. Some wind up making laws, starting revolutions, even running countries. A few examples:

George Bush. Right after World War II, Yale had the best baseball team in the East; it won the Eastern Division NCAA championships twice. Bush was the team's starting first baseman, and was even named captain in his senior year (1948). Five members of the Yale team signed pro contracts after graduation. Bush supposedly thought about going pro, too.

Mario Cuomo (governor of New York). Tried professional baseball for a single season, then quit. In 1952, he played with a minor league team in the lowly Class D Georgia-Florida League. His record: A .244 batting average, with one homer in 254 at bats. His strength, according to a scouting report was that he would "run right over you."

Fidel Castro. A star pitcher at the University of Havana in the 1940s. Cuba once had a minor league team (the Havana Sugar Kings) and when Castro took over the country, he enthusiastically supported it. In fact, Premier Castro once pitched an inning in the minors, striking out 2 batters—on called strikes (after which he left the mound and shook the umpire's hand). In another game, his team was losing in the 9th inning—so he declared that the game would go into extra innings. They played until Castro's team won.

Jack Kemp (former New York congressman, secretary of HUD). Spent 13 years as a pro quarterback, leading the AFL's Buffalo Bills to championships in 1964 and 1965. He used his standing as a local Buffalo hero to run for Congress—and won.

Bill Bradley (U.S. senator from New Jersey). Star of the Princeton University "Cinderella" basketball team in 1965, Rhodes Scholar who returned to the U.S. and signed with the New York Knicks. He was a starting guard on their world championship 1970 and 1973 teams. In 1978, he was elected senator; and in the '80s, he was the architect of major tax reform legislation.

An ice cream sundae will warm you more than hot chocolate. The reason: more calories.

SECRET RECIPES

Here's some fascinating data we found in a wonderful book called Big Secrets *by William Poundstone.*

TWINKIES

In 1976, the *Snack Food Yearbook* reported "[Twinkies inventor James] Deware says [the Twinkies] formula is a secret...He always refers to [the filling] as a creamed filling, emphasizing the need to add the 'ed.' " So what's really in the filling? Among other things:

- Sugar and corn syrup. (40%)
- Shortening content (25%). Here's what's written on the label: "partially hydrogenated vegetable and/or animal shortening (contains one or more of the following: soybean oil, cottonseed oil, palm oil, beef fat, lard)." Hydrogenated vegetable shortening is oil turned into a wax-like solid. Beef fat is...well...the fat from beef.
- Skim milk (7%). The "nutritional" part.
- Butter flavoring (1%).

KENTUCKY FRIED CHICKEN

The Colonel's "secret recipe" is a special combination of eleven herbs and spices, right? Not even close. In a laboratory analysis, the "eleven herbs and spices" were revealed to be a sum total of zero herbs and only four spices, namely salt, pepper, flour, and Monosodium Glutamate (MSG).

OREOS

What's the creme filling in America's favorite sandwich cookie? Mostly sugar and shortening, with hydrogenated coconut oil the favored shortening. Lard is also used occasionally, but not beef fat.

COCA-COLA

Does Coca-Cola, which is made with coca leaves, have any cocaine in it? Trace amounts, almost certainly. Even if 99.99999999 percent of the cocaine from the coca leaves was removed, millions of cocaine molecules would remain floating in each can of Coke. Regardless, Coca-Cola is still 99.5% sugar water.

In a single year, over 200,000 pounds of barnacles collect on the bottom of a steamship.

INVASION! PART I

European history is full of invasions. But since it became a nation in 1776, the U.S. has rarely been the target of foreign attacks. In fact, we could only think of five of them. Here's one.

THE INVADERS: The British.

THE DATE: August 24, 1814.

BACKGROUND: During the early 1800s, relations between Britain and America were strained. One reason: the English had broken their promise to leave Canada after the Revolutionary War. Another: the British fleet had begun seizing American ships that were headed for France (which was at war with England).

Ultimately, the dispute over free trade led to open conflict—on June 18, 1812 President James Monroe declared war. (Historians call it the War of 1812). Two years of fighting ensued. In 1814, the U.S. mounted a particularly destructive attack on the British stronghold in York, Canada, burning down several government buildings. The British decided to retaliate.

THE INVASION: Under the command of British General Robert Ross, 4,000 British troops sailed through Chesapeake Bay, headed for Washington. There was virtually no resistance. British soldiers marched into America's capital and burned down government buildings—including the Capitol, the Library of Congress, and the White House.

President James Madison and his wife, Dolly, were warned of the attack and managed to escape, taking only the White House drapes, Gilbert Stuart's famous portrait of George Washington, and some fine china with them. Ravenous British soldiers raided the White House and polished off all the food they could find. Then, using rockets and gunpowder, they incinerated the place. That night, a drenching thunderstorm put out the fire, but not in time to save the young nation's symbol of power.

AFTERMATH: Later that year, the Treaty of Ghent was signed between the two nations, ending the War of 1812. Conquered territories were returned and hostilities ceased. Four years later, on January 1, 1818, the Madisons moved into the newly restored White House. No foreign power ever occupied it again.

Marco Polo introduced fireworks to the Western World.

WORD PLAY

Here are some more origins of common phrases.

SON OF A GUN
Meaning: An epithet.
Background: In the 1800s, British sailors took their wives along on extended voyages. When babies were born at sea, the mothers delivered them in a partitioned section of the gundeck. Because no one could be sure who the *true* fathers were, each of these "gunnery" babies was called a "son of a gun."

PUT UP YOUR DUKES
Meaning: Raise your fists and get ready to fight.
Background: In the early 1800s, the Duke of York, Frederick Augustus, shocked English society by taking up boxing. He gained such admiration from boxers that many started referrring to their fists as the "Dukes of York," and later, "dukes."

HAVING AN AXE TO GRIND
Meaning: Having a hidden agenda.
Background: The expression comes from a story told by Benjamin Franklin. A man once praised Franklin's father's grindstone and asked young Benjamin to demonstrate how the grindstone worked. As Franklin complied, the stranger placed his own axe upon the grindstone, praising the young boy for his cleverness and vigor. When the axe was sharpened, the man laughed at Franklin and walked away, giving the boy a valuable lesson about people with "an axe to grind."

NO BONES ABOUT IT
Meaning: Without a doubt.
Background: The *Oxford English Dictionary* traces this phrase to a 1459 reference to eating stew. Stew-eaters had to be careful not to swallow bones. If a bowl of stew had no bones in it, one could eat it without hesitation. Bone appetit.

People in the Soviet Union don't chew gum.

UPPER CRUST

Meaning: Elite.

Backround: In the Middle Ages, nobility and royalty were served the choice part of a loaf of bread, the upper crust, before it was offered to other diners.

HIS NAME IS MUD

Meaning: Fallen into ill-repute or disrespect.

Backround: John Wilkes Booth, the man who assassinated President Lincoln, broke his leg as he escaped the scene of the crime. Samuel Mudd, a country doctor who hadn't heard of the assassination yet, treated Booth's injury. When he received news of the assassination the following day, Mudd notified the authorties that his patient might have been the assassin. But the doctor had a second surprise coming—he was arrested as a conspirator and sentenced to life in prison.

President Andrew Johnson, Lincoln's successor, commuted Mudd's sentence after the doctor helped stop a yellow fever outbreak at the jail. However, Mudd's family was still trying to clear his name as recently as the 1980s.

MEET A DEADLINE

Meaning: Finish a project by an appointed time.

Backround: The phrase originated in prisoner-of-war camps during the Civil War. Because resources were scarce, the prison camps were sometimes nothing more than a plot of land surrounded by a marked line. If a prisoner tried to cross the line, he would be shot. So it became known as the "deadline."

TOE THE LINE

Meaning: To behave or act in accordance with the rules.

Backround: In the early days of the British Parliament, members of Parliament wore swords in the House of Commons. To keep the Members from fighting during heated debates, the Speaker of the House of Commons forced the Government and Opposition party to sit on opposite sides of the chamber. Lines, two sword-lengths plus one foot apart, were drawn in the carpet. Members were required to stand behind the lines when the House was in session. To this day, when a member steps over the line during a debate, the speaker yells: "Toe the Line."

UPS ships 12 million packages daily. 20 million a day around Christmastime.

AMAZING COINCIDENCES

How many bizarre coincidences have you experienced in your life? We'll bet that none of them were as weird as these.

PSYCHIC LINC

Abraham Lincoln's eldest son, Robert Todd Lincoln, was on the scene of *three* separate presidential assassinations.

• First, he was summoned to his father's side after his father was mortally wounded at Ford's Theatre in 1865.

• The second occurred in 1881, when Lincoln was Secretary of War under President Garfield. Lincoln went to Union Station in Washington to inform the president he could not travel with him due to work overload. By the time Lincoln arrived, Garfield had been shot by Charles Guiteau.

• The third assassination occurred 20 years later in 1901, when Lincoln accepted an invitation from Presdent William McKinley to meet him at the Pan-American Exposition in Buffalo, New York. When Lincoln entered the festival he noticed a crowd had gathered—William McKinley had just been mortally wounded by Leon Czolgosz.

WHAT ABOUT HYMN?

In 1950, *Life* magazine reported that 15 people barely missed disaster by an intricate stroke of luck. The 15, members of a church choir in Beatrice, Nebraska, were supposed to meet at 7:15 pm for practice. Each one got delayed...each for a different reason! For example, one had car trouble, another was finishing house chores, another was catching a radio show, etc. Whatever the reason, they were all lucky to be late: The church was destroyed in an explosion at 7:25.

BASIC TRAINING

A distraught architect threw himself in front of a train in the London Underground in a suicide attempt. Luckily, the train stopped inches from his body; in fact, it had to be jacked off its tracks to allow his removal. When questioned, however, the driver informed officials he hadn't stopped the train. An investigation revealed that one of the passengers, unaware of the suicide attempt, had independently pulled the emergency brake. Postscript: London Transport officials considered prosecuting the passenger for illegal use of the emergency brake but ultimately decided against it.

GEORGE, BY GEORGE

George D. Bryson, a businessman from Connecticut, decided to change his travel plans and stop in Louisville, Kentucky, a place he'd never visited before. He went into a local hotel and made preparations to check into Room 307. Before he could do so, a hotel employee handed him a letter addressed to his exact name. It turned out the previous occupant of Room 307 was another George D. Bryson.

NUMBER, PLEASE

In 1983, a woman told British Rail authorities about a disturbing vision she had of a fatal train crash involving an engine with the numbers 47 216. Two years later, a train had a fatal accident, similar to one the woman had described. The engine number, however, was 47 299. Later, someone noticed that the number had previously been changed by nervous British Rail officials. The original number: 47 216.

WHAT'S THE GOOD WORD?

Several secret code words were devised by Allied military commanders during their preparations to invade Normandy in World War II. Among them: "Utah," "Neptune," "Mulberry," "Omaha," and "Overlord." Before the invasion could begin, however, all of these words appeared in a crossword puzzle in the *London Daily Telegraph.* After interrogating the puzzle's author, an English school teacher, authorities became convinced that it was sheer, inexplicable coincidence.

THE MOST AMAZING

On three separate occasions—in the years 1664, 1785, and 1860—there was a shipwreck in which only one person survived the accident. Each time that one person was named Hugh Williams.

The Mona Lisa has no eyebrows.

TRAVELS WITH RAY

Perplexing adventures of the brilliant egghead Ray "Weird Brain" Redel. Answers are on page 223.

One weekend Ray "Weird Brain" Redel, the man who inspired Rodin's statue "The Thinker," decided to go backpacking at Yosemite National Park. "I've been pushing this old brain too hard," he told me as we set off for the mountains.

"I don't see how you can tell," I muttered.

At that, "Weird Brain" slapped his forehead. "Here's proof," he groaned. "I just realized I've forgotten something terribly important."

"Did you forget to turn off the stove at home?" I grumbled.

"No, no, nothing like that. I just forgot to bring something."

I was getting exasperated. "What? What did you forget to bring?"

He glared at me. "Don't use that tone of voice. You want to know what I forgot? Figure this out: *It has cities, but no houses; it has forests but no trees; it has rivers but no fish.*"

I smiled. "Well, why didn't you say so. Let's just get another one."

What did "Weird Brain" forget?

When we finally got to Yosemite, "Weird Brain" ran into an old friend—a photographer named Ansel Adams.

"Anse, m'boy, what are you doing around here?" he asked the shutterbug.

"Well, Weirdo, I think Yosemite's the best place to enjoy my favorite thing in nature."

"Which is..."

Adams smiled, and I could tell he was testing "Weird Brain"'s fabled ability to solve riddles. "*What can pass before the sun without making a shadow?*" he asked. "That's what I love best.

What was Adams saying he loved?

BATHROOM NEWS

Here are a few of the stories we flushed out during the past year.

JUST WHAT WE NEEDED

October, 1989: A North Carolina company has introduced "Talking Tissue," a novelty gadget which fits the standard toilet paper dispenser. Each time you pull the tissue, you hear one of four recordings: "Yuk-yuk," "Stinky-stinky," "Nice one-nice one," or alarm bells. Batteries not included.

DOWN IN THE DUMPS

January, 1990: A man in Lawrence, Kansas, spent a night underneath an outhouse after he fell through the seat trying to retrieve his wallet. He was rescued by Sheriff Loren Anderson, who said the man wasn't injured, "but in a pretty ugly mood."

UNCLE SAM SAT HERE

November 6, 1989: Archaeologists recently discovered Uncle Sam's toilet six feet under Ferry Street in Troy, New York. The site is where 19th century meatpacker Sam Wilson used to live (see *Uncle John's Second Bathroom Reader* for more info). During the War of 1812, Sam labelled his meat-crates "U.S.," which led American soldiers to joke that they were being fed by Uncle Sam. A developer is building a supermarket and a park on the site, but Uncle Sam's bathroom floor and house foundation will be preserved for visitors to view.

RIGHT BACK AT YA

January, 1990: Over 20 toilets and urinals in the King County, Washington, Court House erupted after being flushed. Apparently, a plumber who was making repairs mistakenly switched an air compressor with a water line.

SINGAPORE STAKE OUT

June, 1989: Undercover agents arrested six men for not flushing urinals in Singapore public restrooms.

In a separate investigation, Singapore courts fined a man $75 for urinating in an elevator. Police nabbed him in the elevator after the *urine detector* locked the elevator doors. A hidden video camera recorded the whole event and the footage was later used as evidence.

THE JOHN POLICE

December 19, 1989: Police employees in Concord, California, filed a $30 million lawsuit against the Concord Police Department after they found a hidden camera installed above a urinal in the men's room. Police Chief George Straka explained that the surveillance was necessary to catch the culprit who had clogged the urinal a few times, causing it to flood the chief's office downstairs.

HIGH-TECH TOILETS

October 29, 1989: "New high-tech toilets from Japan can do it all, including check your health. Here are a few features of some of the latest models:"

• No paper is needed. The push of a button sends a jet of cleansing water upward. A control panel allows the user to adjust the angle, pressure and temperature of the stream. Drying blasts of hot air and mists of perfume follow seconds after. As the commercial for the Toto Ltd. *Toto Queen* says, "Even your bottom wants to be washed."

• The "intelligent bowl" automatically drops a strip of litmus paper into the bowl. Optical sensors analyze urine levels of protein, sugar and other substances. Blood pressure and pulse data are measured if the user inserts his finger in the blood pressure device on the side of the toilet. All test results are revealed on a display screen beside the toilet.

POTTY-PARITY

Setpember, 1989: The American Society of Interior Designers honored Sandra Rawls, an assistant Professor at the University of Missouri, Columbia, for her research which revealed that women's restrooms need more toilets, because women need more time than men. The states of California, New York and Virginia have listened to Rawls's advice and have intoduced so-called "potty-parity" laws.

THE SIMPUL SPELLING MOOVMENT

At the turn of the century, Andrew Carnegie spent over $200,000 in an attempt to simplify spelling. Here are a few of the details of that forgotten episode in American history.

E-Z DUZ IT: In 1906, millionaire industrialist Andrew Carnegie was approached by Melvin Dewey, the head of the New York libraries, and Brander Matthews, a Columbia University professor, with a revolutionary plan to simplify spelling. Carnegie was enthusiastic. He believed that easier spelling could lead to world peace. Together, the threesome formed the Simplified Spelling Board; their expressed goal was to convince authorities to begin changing the spelling of 300 words.

Among the words targeted were though (tho), confessed (confest), dropped (dropt), through (thru), kissed (kist), fixed (fixt), enough (enuf), prologue (prolog), thoroughfare (thorofare) and depressed (deprest).

ENUF ALREDDEE: Theodore Roosevelt was an instant convert to the simplified spelling plan. On August 29, 1906, he ordered the U.S. Printer to use the new spelling on all executive branch publications. For an instant, it looked as if simplified spelling would be instituted nationwide.

Roosevelt's plan met instant oppostion. It even made front-page news—both here *and* abroad. In England, the *London Times* ridiculed the American president with a headline reading "Roosevelt Spelling Makes Britons Laugh."

Congress was equally outraged by Roosevelt's decree. In late 1906, they debated the idea on the floor of the House. Sensing an embarrassing political defeat, Roosevelt quickly withdrew his support for the plan.

WEL, THATZ THAT: Carnegie was deeply disappointed. Eventually he dropped his financial support for the Simplified Spelling Board, writing, "I think I hav been patient long enuf...I have a much better use of $25,000 a year."

GREAT NEWSPAPER LEADS

The first paragraph in a newspaper story is called the "lead." Technically, it's supposed to answer five questions: Who? What? Where? When? and Why? Here are some of the greatest leads in newspaper history.

"John Dillinger, ace bad man of the world, got his last night—two slugs through his heart and one through his head. He was tough and he was shrewd, but he wasn't as tough and shrewd as the Federals, who never close a case until the end. It took 27 of them to end Dillinger's career, and their strength came out of his weakness—a woman."

—Jack Lait for the *International News Service*, July 23, 1934

"Death and destruction have been the fate of San Francisco. Shaken by a trembler at 5:13 o'clock yesterday morning, the shock lasting 48 seconds, and scourged by flames that raged diametrically in all directions, the city is a mass of smouldering ruins."

— *The San Francisco Call, Chronicle and Examiner*, April 19, 1906

"In the darkness of night and in water two miles deep the *Titanic*, newest of the White Star fleet and greatest of all ocean steamships, sank to the bottom of the sea at twenty minutes past two o'clock yesterday morning. The loss of the *Titanic*—costliest, most powerful, greatest of all the ocean fleet—while speeding westward on her maiden voyage will take rank in maritime history as the most terrible of all recorded disasters at sea."

—*New York Herald*, April 15, 1912

"Steel-nerved Alan B. Shepard Jr., rode a rocket into space today, exclaimed 'What a beautiful sight' as he looked down on the earth, and then dropped to a safe landing in the Atlantic ocean. To the wiry, 37-year-old navy commander, the historic adventure obviously was no more frightening than many earlier flights he had made

In 1936, a cabin on the Hindenburg airship cost $750 for a trans-Atlantic flight.

in experimental aircraft. 'It's a beautiful day,' he told marines on the helicopter that plucked his space capsule out of the water after a soaring flight 115 miles above the earth and 302 miles southeast from the Cape Canaveral launching pad. Then his nonchalance gave way to excitement as he declared: 'Boy, what a ride!' "

—Ralph Dighton for the *Associated Press*, May 5, 1961

"War broke with lightning suddeness in the Pacific today when waves of Japanese bombers attacked Hawaii this morning and the United States Fleet struck back with a thunder of big naval rifles. Japanese bombers, including four-engine dive bombers and torpedo-carrying planes, blasted at Pearl Harbor, the great United States naval base, the city of Honolulu and several outlying American military bases on the Island of Oahu. There were causalities of unstated numbers."

—*The New York Times*, December 8, 1941

OTHER NEWS:

Here are some items from a great "bathroom reader" called *News Of the Weird.*

• An Alaskan assemblyman authored legislation to punish "public flatulence, crepitation, gaseous emission, and miasmic effluence," with a $100 penalty.

• Firefighters in Thurston, Washington slept through a fire in their own station. A passing police officer noticed the blaze and called in the alarm.

• In 1986, firefighters used wire cutters and pliers to free a San Jose, California woman from a tight pair of designer jeans.

• In the 1988 Massachusetts Democratic primary, Herbert Connolly dashed from a late campaign appearance to the polling place to cast his ballot. He got there fifteen minutes late, and lost his seat on the Governor's council. The final tally: 14,716 to 14,715.

• The Internal Revenue Service fined George Wittmeier $159.78 for not paying all of his taxes. He was a penny short on his return.

FLAKE-OUT

When financial analysts say baseball cards are a better investment than the stock market, you know collecting has become a way of life. But cereal boxes? It's strange but true. Here are some examples.

CORN FLAKES. One of the most collectible cereal boxes is the 1984 Kelloggs' Miss America commerative Corn Flakes Box. The box features Vanessa Williams, the first black Miss America, with a congratulatory endorsement on the back panel that claims the limited edition box is "a lasting reminder that America remains the land of opportunity...and we must continue to promote the American dream and encourage all Americans to freely pursue life, liberty and happiness." Ironically, the box was recalled immediately after *Penthouse* magazine published pictures of Williams in the buff.

WHEATIES. In the 1950s Wheaties stopped using athletes on their boxes and started using Walt Disney figures. Within a year, sales went down 15%. General Mills had a huddle, kicked Disney out, and recalled their sports stars. But the Disney boxes are valuable today.

SWISS MIX. The psychedelic generation of the late 1960s didn't miss out on cereal boxes—pop-artist Peter Max designed a surreal cereal box for an imported Swiss Mix cereal called LOVE. It's now collectible.

WHEAT AND RICE HONEYS. A pair of 1969 Wheat and Rice Honeys boxes featuring the Beatles in "Yellow Submarine" recently sold for $7000.

COUNT CHOCULA. In 1981, General Mills released a cereal called Count Chocula. The box featured a cartoon Count Dracula in front with a Bela Lugosi Dracula in the background. The "Bela" Dracula was wearing a six-point star pendant. A religious group objected to what they felt was a "Star of David" and the box was recalled. Today collectors pursue it religiously.

Moose are very nearsighted. Some try to mate with cars.

PARDON ME

The Constitution gives our president the power to grant pardons. This doesn't mean he can overturn guilty verdicts—it only gives him the authority to remove the legal penalties. You hardly ever hear about presidential pardons, but they're granted all the time. Here are a few of the more interesting ones.

RICHARD NIXON

The most famous pardon in U.S. history occurred on September 8, 1974, when Gerald Ford granted Richard Nixon "a full, free, and absolute pardon" for any crimes connected with the Watergate scandal. The decision was extremely controversial. A Gallup Poll conducted after the pardon found that 56% of the American public thought Nixon should have been brought to trial for Watergate.

An August, 1983 article in *Atlantic* magazine by journalist Seymour Hersh alleged that Ford and Nixon had cut a deal for a pardon before the latter's resignation on August 9, 1974. According to the article, Nixon made a threatening phone call to Ford on September 7—one day before the pardon—to make sure the deal was still on. Ford "really resented it," an unnamed Ford aide told Hersh.

ARMAND HAMMER

Armand Hammer, multi-millionaire head of Occidental Petroleum, was pardoned by George Bush in August, 1989, for making an illegal $54,000 contribution to Nixon's 1972 re-election campaign. Hammer was found guilty and placed on a year's probation for the offense—making a political contribution in the name of another person—in March, 1976. He was fined $3,000.

GEORGE STEINBRENNER

In January, 1989, George Steinbrenner, shipbuilder and ex-owner of the New York Yankees, was pardoned by Ronald Reagan. Steinbrenner had been convicted of making an illegal $100,000 contribution to Richard Nixon's re-election campaign in 1972.

Every year, Mexico City sinks about 10 inches.

Steinbrenner was fined $15,000 in 1974 and later suspended for two years by Baseball Commissioner Bowie Kuhn after pleading not guilty to the charges. Kuhn lifted the suspension in March 1976 after 16 months had been served.

✍ ✍ ✍

TOKYO ROSE

In one of his last official acts as president in 1977, Ford pardoned Iva Toguri D'Aquino (aka, Tokyo Rose), who had served six years in jail for making pro-Japanese propaganda broadcasts during World War II. D'Aquino, an American citizen of Japanese descent, had gone to Japan to visit a sick aunt in July, 1941, just before war broke out between the two countries. Unable to return to the U.S., she was recruited by Japanese authorities to try to demoralize American troops. According to the *New York Times*, "For the G.I.s in the South Pacific, the broadcasts were as much a part of the routine as Spam. In between familiar selections of American music there was the voice of a woman telling American servicemen that their wives and girlfriends were being taken over by the civilians who remained behind and that there was really no point in fighting on any further because the Japanese were going to win anyway. The G.I.s began calling her Tokyo Rose. To most soldiers and sailors the broadcasts were a pleasant joke."

D'Aquino was indicted for treason and was sentenced to 10 years in prison beginning in 1949 (she was released in 1956 for good behavior). She also paid a $10,000 fine.

✍ ✍ ✍

DRAFT RESISTERS

On January 21, 1977, in his first act as president, Jimmy Carter issued an unconditional presidential pardon to Vietnam draft resisters. Prior to Carter's proclamation, Gerald Ford had granted a limited amnesty to Vietnam draft resisters in 1974 if they swore allegiance to the U.S. and agreed to perform two years of public service. 21,700 people took advantage of Ford's program. Carter's unconditional pardon—which excluded deserters and veterans with less-than-honorable discharges—affected between 100,000 and 500,000 people.

Holy cow!: 2.2 pounds of steak costs $1.50 in Buenos Aires, and $51 in Tokyo.

...AND TWO PARDONS REFUSED

• Samuel A. Mudd, a physician who aided assassin John Wilkes Booth, (he set his broken leg after the assassination) pleaded for a pardon for his inadvertant role in the death of Abraham Lincoln. Mudd was paroled in 1869 from a life sentence, but was never pardoned. In 1988, his grandson, Dr. Richard Mudd, gave up a 61-year campaign to clear his name after the Reagan White House refused to grant one.

• In 1914, journalist George Burdick, a writer for the *New York Tribune*, broke a story about prominent officials who were going to be indicted for smuggling. A Federal grand jury demanded to know his sources, but Burdick refused to reveal them. President Wilson stepped in and offered a full pardon, but Burdick refused. This set a precedent—no one had ever refused a pardon before. Eventually, the Supreme Court upheld Burdick's right to refuse Wilson's pardon, arguing it preserved the privilege against self-incrimination. The case was widely regarded as a major victory for freedom of the press. Burdick never revealed his source.

ODDS & ENDS

• In 1795, George Washington issued the first presidential pardon to two instigators of the Whiskey Rebellion. They'd led a mob that attacked and burned a tax collector's home on July 17, 1794.

• During the War of 1812, President James Madison announced amnesty for pirates and smugglers "in the vicinity of New Orleans who helped fight the British."

• Abraham Lincoln pardoned over 10,000 Confederate soldiers for their role in the Civil War. His successor, Andrew Johnson, issued a full pardon in 1865 to all Confederates, except leaders, as long as they took an oath of allegiance to the United States. Then in 1868, Johnson granted an unconditional amnesty to "all persons engaged in the late rebellion."

• During his two terms as president, Ronald Reagan granted 380 pardons. Among the offenses for which people were pardoned were tax evasion, possession of untaxed whiskey, possession with intent to distribute cocaine, illegal transfer of machine guns, and copyright infringement.

NAME & PLACE

Would you want to live in Hell Station, Accident, or Dildo? You can. Here are the strange names of some real places.

Frozen Run, West Virginia: A man saved his own life by wrapping himself in the skin of a recently killed buffalo. His friends had to thaw it to get him out.

Preacher's Head, New Mexico: A rock resembling the face of a serious-looking man overlooks the town.

Dildo, Newfoundland: Coincidentally, it's the birthplace of Shannon Tweed, *Playboy* magazine's 1982 Playmate of the Year.

Anxiety Point, Alaska: Sir John Franklin, a British explorer, was afraid that bad weather would prevent his team from reaching a point on the Alaskan coast. They made it, and left this permanent reminder of his nervousness.

Nipple Mountain, Colorado: One formation on the mountain is named "Clara's Bird's Nipple."

Chilly Buttes, Idaho: A cold place in the winter.

Chicago, Illinois: From the Algonquin word meaning "onion-place."

Hell Station, Michigan: Locals say it freezes over every winter.

Art, Texas: As one resident explained, "Well, it's not for Arthur or Artesian, and far as I know people here weren't ever especially arty. We've heard they picked it just because they wanted a real short name."

Sacul, Texas: A reverse spelling of (John) Lucas, an early settler in the area.

Lake Italy, California: The lake is shaped like a boot.

Accident, Maryland: In 1774, surveyors marked off a parcel of land by mistake. They decided to immortalize the error.

YOU BET YOUR LIFE

To a generation of viewers who only know the Marx Brothers from their films, it may come as a surprise that Groucho was also a radio and TV star...as the host of a quiz show called "You Bet Your Life," which aired from 1950 to 1961.

HOW IT STARTED

In 1947, radio was the most popular entertainment medium in America. Groucho Marx was no longer a movie star, but he did a guest spot on *The Bob Hope Show* that turned into a hilarious ad-lib free-for-all. The act impressed a successful radio producer named John Guedel, who happened to be in the audience that night. When it was over, Guedel approached Groucho and asked him if he could ad-lib like that all the time. Groucho replied that he'd done it all his life.

Guedel was excited. He thought Groucho's talent was wasted with scripts—he ought to do a show in which he was allowed to interact with "real people," ad-libbing. Groucho, who'd hosted four different radio shows and had bombed every time, was open to anything. But when Guedel suggested a quiz show, Groucho balked. He said he had to think about it.

Groucho wondered if he could live with himself as a game-show host...and decided he could. ("What the hell, nothing else had worked.") So he made an audition tape. But no network was interested. So Guedel, convinced that America would love tuning in to the real Groucho, took the tape directly to a sponsor and got it on the air that way. Within a few years Guedel looked like a genius and Groucho's career was revived—"You Bet Your Life" was one of America's top 10 radio shows.

At that time, TV networks were snapping up popular radio programs and adapting them to television. Everything from "Burns and Allen" and "The Jack Benny Show," to "Gangbusters" and "The Lone Ranger" wound up on the tube. Naturally, Groucho was approached about bringing his show to TV. CBS and NBC both wanted it—but in the ensuing battle for Marx's talents, CBS head William Paley offended Groucho by referring to the fact that they were both Jewish and that Jews should stick together. NBC head Robert Sarnoff was also Jewish. Groucho chose NBC.

All continents have deserts—except for Europe.

INSIDE INFO

Stiff Upper Lip.

Without his mustache, Groucho was unrecognizable to the public; he could walk the streets without being stopped by fans. For radio and TV he refused to use the phony mustache he wore in his movie days ("That character is dead," he said). But he did agree to grow a real mustache.

TV or Not TV?

When Groucho's show moved to TV, NBC wanted to add all kinds of visual gimmicks "to make it more interesting." They also wanted to resurrect his movie persona. But Groucho insisted on keeping things simple, as they had been in the radio format. No funny walks, no costumes. Just Groucho in a business suit, sitting in front of a curtain with his guestrs. It turned out to be a good idea: From the time the show debuted in 1950 to the time it was cancelled 11 years later, "You Bet Your Life" was the most consistently popular game show on TV.

Nobody Loses.

Groucho wasn't comfortable with some aspects of being a game show host. He complained, for example, that he felt bad when people had to leave the show broke. He said, "Can't we ask them a simple question, like who's the President of the U. S., or who's buried in Grant's Tomb?" So that became part of the show. Whenever someone lost, Groucho asked the easiest question possible, and the contestant got a few bucks as a consolation.

Close Encounters.

In 1973, NBC started burning original negatives of the 250 reels of *You Bet Your Life* to make space in their warehouse. Fortunately, someone thought to call the show's producer, John Guedel, and ask if he wanted a few negatives as souvenirs; they'd already burned 15 of them. A shocked Guedel stopped the destruction and made a deal with NBC to take over syndication of *The Best of Groucho*. In 1973, a Los Angeles TV station aired reruns at 11:00 p.m. as a favor to Groucho. The ratings were so good that stations all over the country picked it up, and the show was revived.

Video Mania: On average, Americans rent over 6 million videos a day.

GROUCHO & GUESTS

No one could ad-lib like Groucho. Here are a few spontaneous remarks from "You Bet Your Life."

Groucho: "What's it like in South Carolina?"
Woman: "Oh, it's wonderful, Goucho, Southern hospitality and wonderful folks."
Groucho: "Well, we want you to feel at home here, Marie, so we'll pay you in Confederate money."

Groucho: "How did you meet your wife?"
Man: "A friend of mine."
Groucho: "Do you still regard him as a friend?"

Groucho (to husband & wife with arms around each other)**:** "How long have you been married?"
Wife: "Two and a half years, Groucho."
Groucho: "Why are you holding on to each other? Are you afraid if you let go, you'll kill each other?"

Groucho: "What are you gonna do with your money?"
Man: "I'm gonna make my wife happy, Groucho."
Groucho: "What are you gonna do—get a divorce?"

Groucho: "You don't mind if I ask you a few questions, do you?"
Woman: "If they're not too embarrassing."
Groucho: "Don't give it a second thought. I've asked thousands of questions on this show, and I've yet to be embarrassed."

Woman (explaining herself)**:** "I'm afraid you don't follow me."
Groucho: "Even if I did, you'd have nothing to be afraid of."

Groucho (to the father of triplets)**:** "Do you have a job?
Man: "Yeah."
Groucho: "What is it?"
Man: "I work for the California Power Company."
Groucho: "My boy, you don't work for the California Power Company. You *are* the California Power Company."

Groucho: "What's your husband's name?"
Woman: "Milton August."
Groucho: "What's his name in September?"

BANNED IN THE U.S.A.

Censorship is a big issue for bathroom readers. After all, we don't want anyone telling us what we can read in here...or if we can read in here at all! So we've included a few tidbits on censorship in this edition, to remind us all to sit down and be counted.

AND STAY OUT!

Bring us your tired, your wretched...etc.? Not in the early '50s. In 1952, at the height of our Cold War hysteria, a provision was added to the Immigration and Nationality Act of 1952 to keep certain "undesirable" people from entering the U.S. The law, known as the McCarran-Walter Immigration Act, was vetoed by then-President Harry S Truman, but overriden by Congress. Usually, "undesirable" meant "suspected Commies," although the 33 provisions included categories for people who engaged in espionage, polygamy and "deviant sexual behavior."

But the bill was actually a political tool, designed to keep people with controversial views (like John Lennon) out of the country. In 1984 alone—32 years after the act was passed—8,000 people from 98 different countries were banned from the U.S.A. under the auspices of the bill, because of their political beliefs.

WHO'S WHO?

Among the people banned from the U.S.A. since 1952 were actors, singers, writers, and politicians. Two examples:

• *Gabriel García Márquez*, Colombian author and winner of the Nobel Prize. Márquez, a critic of U.S. foreign policy, was denied a visa in 1963. Eight years later, he was allowed in temporarily to accept an honorary degree from Columbia University. The terms of Márquez's restricted visa included the stipulation that an FBI agent would accompany him everywhere he went.

• *Pierre Trudeau*, future Prime Minister of Canada. He was denied entry because he had participated in an economic conference in Moscow in 1952 and was labeled a "Communist sympathizer." Trudeau was eventually allowed to travel in the U.S. after immigration officials interviewed him in Montreal and gave him "clearance."

Postscript: Congress finally repealed the law in January, 1990.

91% of Americans surveyed have bought their pets holiday gifts.

DISNEY STORIES: SLEEPING BEAUTY

In 1959, Walt Disney released Sleeping Beauty, an adaptation of the classic fairy tale. It took 6 years and $6 million (an incredible sum at the time) to finish. But it was a disappointment at the box office, taking in just $5.3 million that year. Since then, it has grossed almost 5 times that much. Of course, the Disney version and the original story were substantially different. Here are some examples of how the tale was changed.

THE DISNEY VERSION

A King and a Queen in a faraway kingdom throw a party for their newborn daughter. They invite everyone from miles around...except a Wicked Witch, who's really upset about it. She shows up anyway, and casts this spell on the baby: On her 15th birthday, the young Princess will prick her finger on a spinning wheel spindle and die.

• A Good Fairy attending the party softens the curse, changing it to 100 years of sleep instead of death.

• The King tries to avoid the curse by burning every spinning wheel in the kingdom. No luck; on her 15th birthday, the Princess discovers a tower chamber where an old woman is working a spinning wheel. The Princess tries her hand at it, pricks her finger, and falls asleep. So does everyone else in the kingdom.

• Thick, impenetrable brambles grow around the castle. 100 years later, a young Prince shows up.

• The Witch throws the Prince into her dungeon. When he escapes, the Witch turns herself into a dragon and attacks him. The Prince slays her, enters the castle, and kisses the Princess, who wakes up (along with the rest of the people in the castle). The Prince and Princess live happily ever after.

THE ORIGINAL VERSION

• Disney's version of Sleeping Beauty is based loosely on Charles Perrault's telling of this ancient fairy tale. But Disney only tells half the story.

• In the original, the Wicked Witch disappears from the story after casting her spell. No brambles grow up around the castle.

• The Prince just happens to arrive at exactly the moment Sleeping Beauty is supposed to wake up. The Prince secretly marries her, and they have two children—a daughter (Aurora) and son (Day). It isn't until his father dies and he becomes king that the Prince invites Sleeping Beauty to his castle.

• The Prince's mother, it turns out, is an Ogress. While he's away at war, the Queen Mother orders the chef to slaughter and cook the daughter, then the son, and eventually Sleeping Beauty herself. The chef can't bring himself to do it—he hides the trio and serves other animals instead.

• Eventually the Queen Mother discovers the truth. She orders Sleeping Beauty and her children to be thrown into a cauldron of carnivorous reptiles. In the nick of time, the new King arrives home and the Queen Mother leaps into the cauldron herself.

SAMPLE PASSAGE (FROM THE ORIGINAL)

"The Prince—now the King—had no sooner left than the Queen Mother sent her daughter-in-law and the children to a country house in the wood so that she might more easily gratify her horrible longing. She followed them there a few days later, and one evening she said to her head cook, 'I will eat little Aurora for dinner tomorrow.'

"'Oh no, Madam,' the cook exlaimed.

"'Yes, I will.' said the Queen Mother, and she said it in a voice of an Ogress longing to eat fresh meat. 'And I want her served with my favorite sauce.'

"The cook, seeing that an Ogress isn't someone to trifle with, took his knife and went up to Aurora's room. She was about four years old, and she came jumping and laughing toward him, threw her arms around his neck, and asked him if he had any candy for her. He burst into tears, dropping the knife; then he went into the farmyard and killed a little lamb, which he served up with such a delicious sauce that the Ogress assured him she'd never eaten anything so tasty. Meanwhile, he carried Aurora to his own home and gave her to his wife to hide, so the Queen Mother wouldn't find her."

Mr. Green Jeans's nickname in real life was "Lumpy."

THE AUSTRALIAN BEATLES

When Beatlemania and the British Invasion hit the U.S. in the mid-sixties, many musicians suddenly found themselves out of work. Here's the story of a creative solution that turned into one of the all-time great rock'n'roll hoaxes.

It was rock 'n' roll news in 1965. A new band had arrived in America. Direct from the outbacks of Australia—Armstrong, Australia, aborigine country—came the "Down Under" continent's answer to the Beatles! The Strange brothers, Miles, Niles and Giles, known professionally as the Strangeloves. They were strange, indeed. They dressed in loud striped outfits and wore native hats. And the three didn't look at all alike. But that, they explained, was because they had the same mother and different fathers.

The boys had rhythm, too. Playing jungle drums, they brought back the old Bo Diddley beat with a great song called "I Want Candy," which took off like a frightened kangaroo, hopping up the American charts into the Top 10. The Strangeloves toured three times with the Beach Boys, who thought the brothers were the most insane people they'd ever met. They appeared on Radio Caroline in England. And they had the time of their lives on NBC-TV's "Hullabaloo." An unbelievable feat for a group that didn't exist. They were real people, of course, but they weren't named Strange. And they weren't from Australia. The Strangeloves came straight from the Brill Building in New York City.

The Brill Building was rock'n'roll's Tin Pan Alley in the early '60s. It was the home of songwriters like Ellie Greenwich and Jeff Barry, Carole King and Gerry Goffin, and Neil Sedaka and Howie Greenfield, who had been the source of hundreds of hit songs in the early sixties. But in 1965, no one wanted to hear American groups. So songwriters/producers Bob Feldman, Jerry Goldstein, and Richard Gotterher got the idea to put together a fake "British Invasion" act. They donned bizarre costumes, learned their accents

Six out of seven gynecologists are men.

from a Britisher named Doug Moody, and the Strangeloves were born. After writing "I Want Candy" and recording it for their record label, Bang Records, the act went on tour. First stop, the dome at Virginia Beach, where Feldman recalls, "There were 3,000 kids with banners saying, 'Welcome to the U.S., Strangeloves.' And the mayor gave us the key to the city and there we were. We had to go through with it!"

The Beach Boys knew the truth; nobody else did, except the Strangeloves' immediate families. In fact, the group turned down a $10,000 offer to appear on "The Ed Sullivan Show" because Richard didn't want his elderly Jewish grandmother to see him on TV in a wild leopard-skin outfit. The Strangeloves' "Australian" accents, filtered through their native Brooklynese, must have sounded pretty authentic. They eventually appeared with almost every major British act and they never got caught. But the ruse did lead to some unexpected close calls. One time on a local Pittsburgh dance show, host Clark Race unexpectedly brought out a boomerang and handed it to Miles (Feldman), who was supposedly a champion thrower. As Bob was about to throw it, Clark stopped him and said, "Miles, that's not the way to hold a boomerang." Bob looked right into the camera and said, "Clark, that's why I'm the champion and you're not." "Miles" then proceeded to throw it. He hit the cameraman on the shoulder, barely missing his head, and knocked him to the floor. As the cameraman fell, his camera went with him.

At nearby Kennywood Park, the Strangeloves were hired without a backup band. They had their jungle drums with them and wowed the crowd with a 45-minute version of "Shout." Bob then went for some fun on an amusement park ride called "The Magic Carpet Ride," forgot to hug his knees as instructed, and fell over the top. He was carried to the infirmary where they tended to his injured shoulder...but he found out that he couldn't even drop his pose there! The head nurse was from Sydney, Australia, and she recognized him. As Bob tells it, "She said, 'You're one of those Strange boys, aren't you?'...Now I had to cry out in pain with an accent, too!"

Mercifully, the Strangeloves' pose only lasted until 1966.

The song sung most often in America is "Happy Birthday to You."

DUMB SCIENCE

Ever wonder what scientists do in their laboratories all day? Here are a few real-life examples.

THE EXPERIMENT: James McConnell, head of the University of Michigan's Planaria Research group, wanted to see if memory "can be eaten and reused." So he trained a batch of worms, ground them up, and fed them to a second group of untrained worms.

THE CONCLUSION: According to McConnell, it worked. The untrained worms demonstrated behavior he'd taught the ground up worms. Minor problem: He never got the same results again.

THE EXPERIMENT: A scientist named Spalding brilliantly theorized that a baby chick's instinct to follow a mother hen originates in its brain. In an 1873 experiment, he removed the brains of baby chicks and placed the chicks a few yards from a mother hen.

THE CONCLUSION: Spalding's groundbreaking paper, "Instinct," tells us: "Decerebrated chicks will not move towards a clucking or retreating object."

THE EXPERIMENT: To test the rumor that Coca-Cola is an effective spermicide, Harvard University researchers added sperm samples to test tubes, each containing a different type of Coke.

THE CONCLUSION: A minor success. Diet Coke was the most effective, followed by Classic Coke, New Caffeine-Free, and in last place, New Coke. Researchers suggest that levels of acidic pH and perhaps some secret formula components were the determining factors. In any event, a Coca-Cola official was quoted to say: "We do not promote Coca-Cola for medical purposes. It is a soft drink."

THE EXPERIMENT: Are rats psychic? In 1974, two parapsychologists named Craig and Treuriniet decided to find out. They put rats in a lab maze with only two exits—one leading to freedom, the other to death. (They would kill the rats).

THE CONCLUSION: Half chose the correct path; half didn't. Unsatisfied with the results, Craig and Treuriniet theorized a correlation between the rat's psychic powers and phases of the moon.

According to a recent study, housewives feel more stressed than working women.

HONESTLY, ABE

Abraham Lincoln, our 16th president, was surprisingly quotable. Here are a few of his better-known sayings.

"The best way to destroy your enemy is to make him your friend."

"God must love the common man, he made so many of them."

"No man is good enough to govern another man without that other's consent."

"It's been my experience that people who have no vices have very few virtues."

"No matter how much cats fight, there always seems to be plenty of kittens."

"People who like this sort of thing will find this the sort of thing they like."

"Public opinion in this country is everything."

"Human action can be modified to some extent, but human nature cannot be changed."

"A man's legs must be long enough to reach the ground."

"Those who deny freedom for others deserve it not for themselves."

"My father taught me to work, but not to love it. I never did like to work, and I don't deny it. I'd rather read, tell stories, crack jokes, talk, laugh—anything but work."

"Tact is the ability to describe others as they see themselves."

"The things I want to know are in books; my best friend is the man who'll get me a book I ain't read."

"The man who is incapable of making a mistake is incapable of anything."

"The ballot is stronger than the bullet."

"As I would not be a slave, so I would not be a master. This expresses my idea of democracy."

"The best thing about the future is that it comes only one day at a time."

Americans report about 10 U.F.O. sightings every day.

YOU BE THE JUDGE

Blowin' in the wind is one of the best-known folk songs in American history. It was written by Bob Dylan, of course...or was it? Here's an analysis from the book Behind the Hits, *by Bob Shannon and John Javna.*

This appeared in *Newsweek* on November 4, 1963. . ."There is a rumor circulating that Dylan did not write "Blowin' in the Wind," but that it was written by a Millburn, New Jersey high school student named Lorre Wyatt, who sold it to the singer. Dylan says he did write the song, and Wyatt denies authorship, but several Millburn students claim they heard the song from Wyatt before Dylan ever sang it." Who is really responsible for the song? Here is all the info we could find...what do you think?

CLUE #1

Dylan comes to New York in autumn of 1960, or February of 1961 (there are two stories), to visit Woody Guthrie at Greystone Hospital. He continues to visit through 1963.

• "In the autumn of 1960, Dylan quit the University of Minnesota and decided to visit Guthrie at Greystone Hospital, in New Jersey."—Nat Hentoff, in the *New Yorker*, 1964.

• "In February 1961, Dylan came East, primarily to visit Woody Guthrie at Greystone Hospital in New Jersey. The visits have continued..."—liner notes to "The Freewheelin' Bob Dylan," in 1963.

CLUE #2

Lorre Wyatt is doing volunteer work at Greystone at the same time Dylan is visiting it, from Autumn 1960, to Spring 1963.

• Among activities listed for Wyatt in his 1963 high school yearbook: "Folksinging at Hospitals, 1, 2, 3."

• "Lorre's sense of humor, musical ability, and strong desire to help people have made him a welcome sight to the ill and mentally retarded children at Kessler Institute and Greystone Hospital."—liner notes from "A Time To Sing," an album released in 1963 by a Millburn High School folksinging group called the Millburnaires.

Average number of earthquakes in the world every year: 50,000.

CLUE #3

Both Dylan (according to many sources), and Lorre Wyatt (according to Millburn High graduates whom we interviewed) are hanging out in Greenwich Village in 1961 and 1962. So the two might have met in either Greystone or the Village. Or both.

CLUE #4

Although "The Freewheelin' Bob Dylan," the LP on which "Blowin' In the Wind" first appears, will not be released until May 1963, Dylan actually records the song on July 9, 1962 (according to Columbia Records). This would seem to indicate that the song is legitimately his—but there is one irregularity.

CLUE #5

The song is not published and copyrighted in Dylan's name until July 30, 1962—three weeks after Dylan records it. This is highly unusual; the normal procedure is for a songwriter to write a song, get it published, and then record it. Hypothetical situation: Dylan learns the song from Wyatt, takes it into a recording session, and gets such a favorable reaction that he takes credit for it. After learning from Wyatt that he hasn't published it, Dylan has his own publisher, M. Witmark and Sons, do it in his name. Alternative hypothesis: Dylan just never bothers with the legal details until a few weeks after recording it. Would he take his own songs that lightly?

CLUE #6

A December 1962 issue of *The Miller*, the Millburn High School newspaper, mentions that Wyatt had written the song in the summer.

- "Last summer Lorre, an amateur folk singer and guitarist, put together a melody that had come to him in snatches."
- The article then adds: "He began writing lyrics to it in early autumn, inspired by Student President Steve Oxman's welcoming speech [in September of 1962]." This, of course, is at odds with the fact that Dylan recorded the song in July. However, we contacted Oxman, and he explained that the article had things reversed—his speech was inspired by the already existing song.

Queen bees don't use their stingers—except to kill other queen bees.

CLUE #7

According to *The Miller*, Wyatt sells the song to Dylan for $1000. He donates the money to CARE in memory of his deceased mother. "Blowin' in the Wind," says the paper, "a song written by senior Lorre Wyatt, and expressing the singer's own philosophy concerning the world's problems, is now the property of a well-known folksinger. Recently, the singer heard 'Blowin' In the Wind' while in New York and bought the song and the rights to it for one thousand dollars. Shortly after this, Lorre donated the money to CARE. When asked why, he replied, 'Just listen to the words in the song, and I think you'll understand.' "

CLUE #8

The Chad Mitchell Trio records "Blowin' in the Wind" for Kapp Records in early 1963.

• *The Miller* says this in its February 2, 1963 issue: "The Chad Mitchell Trio has added 'Blowin' In the Wind,' a song written by MHS senior Lorre Wyatt, to its latest album, 'Chad Mitchell in Action.'. . .The publicity department at Kapp Studios said, 'Lorre has created a beautiful ballad. A song of this nature takes longer to write and to become well-known, but it has a greater meaning and a richer melody than most of today's popular rock and roll tunes.'"

• However, when the record comes out, the song is credited to Dylan on the label.

CLUE #9

The Millburnaires, of which Wyatt is a member, record an album in April of 1963. It is called "A Time to Sing." "Blowin' in the Wind" is on the album, and is credited to Wyatt. The Millburnaires make a deal with Riverside Records to release the LP nationally.

CLUE #10

"The Freewheelin' Bob Dylan" is released on Columbia Records on May 27, 1963.

CLUE #11

Here is what Lorre says in the liner notes on the back of the Millburnaires' album: "Did you ever stop to ask yourself why the hate, the greed, the hunger—the fear?...No, they're not 'pretty' questions, but they're ones that must be asked. But we must do more than just ask: we must do something about them. It is our duty to God, ourselves, and to our fellow man. 'None is so blind as he who will not see.' The biggest criminals are people like you and I, who see things that are wrong, and know that they're wrong, and yet do nothing about them. How many times can a man turn his head and pretend that he just doesn't see?"

CLUE #12

From the liner notes of "Freewheelin':" "The first of Dylan's songs in this set is 'Blowin' in the Wind.' In 1962, Dylan said of the song's background: "I still say that some of the biggest criminals are those that turn their heads away when they see wrong and they know it's wrong."

CLUE #13

The Millburnaires' album is re-released nationally in the fall of 1963 as "Teenage Hootenanny" but gives no credits for authorship of "Blowin' in the Wind." It does have Wyatt's liner notes about "criminals," though.

CLUE #14

Dylan in his "Biograph" LP: "It was just another song that I wrote and got thrown into all the songs I was doing at the time. I wrote it in a cafe across the street from the Gaslight. Although I thought it was special, I didn't know to what degree. I wrote it for the moment."

CLUE #15

Interviews with Millburn students and teachers reveal that many recall the song being sung by the Millburnaires in a school performance in either the fall of 1962 or the spring of 1963. It was definitely introduced as Wyatt's song, and it was before the Dylan album was released. Sample interview (with Bill McCormick, M.H.S. history teacher): "[What people understood], was that one of the contingencies of the buyout was that, whatever monetary arrangements were made, it was to the effect that [Wyatt] had sold all rights and was not to ever claim that it was his. I shouldn't say it was common knowledge, but that was the hot rumor back 10, 12, 15 years ago, whatever." Ray Fowler, engineer on the

Millburnaires' LP: "Everyone I talked to at the time, said that Wyatt wrote the song."

CLUE #16

When columnist Mike Royko contacted Lorre in 1974 and asked him if he'd written "Blowin' in the Wind," Wyatt's answer was, "I don't want to talk about it." Royko: "[I told him that] all he had to do was deny writing "Blowin' in the Wind" and the matter would be closed for good. Did Wyatt deny writing it? He said, 'No comment.'" Royko contacted Anthony Scaduto, who wrote a Dylan biography, and asked what he thought. Scaduto said he believed the Wyatt story was phony, and that Dylan wrote "Blowin' in the Wind."

Did Dylan write Blowin' in the Wind? You be the judge.

✔ ✔ ✔

WORKING GIRL

Mary Tyler Moore, head of the MTM TV production company, is one of the world's wealthiest women. Some interesting facts about her:

• At age 18, she landed her first TV role. It didn't exactly make her a star. She played "Happy Hotpoint," a tiny elf with pointy ears. She jumped out of an icetray in a Hotpoint refrigerator ad and said, "Hi, Harriet. Aren't you glad you bought a Hotpoint?"

• She finally landed a regular part in a prime time series in 1959. It was on *Richard Diamond*, and she played Sam, the sexy switchboard operator. The only catch: all they ever showed of her was her legs.

• She kept auditioning. But all she could get were bit parts. Then she got a call from her agent. "He told me, 'Get over to Carl Reiner's office. He wants to talk to you about playing Dick Van Dyke's wife. I said 'No, I may just as well stay home. I'm not going to get it.'" He finally convinced her to go, and she got the part.

• With her husband, she created MTM Enterprises, which owned TV shows like "Newhart," "WKRP in Cincinnati," and "Rhoda."

• She said: "Three things help me get through life successfully: An understanding husband, an extremely good analyst, and millions and millions of dollars."

Americans eat about 5 tons of aspirin a day.

ELVIS-O-RAMA

Here's some info from Vince Staten's irreverent guidebook, Unauthorized America.

ALL SHOOK UP

"Elvis hated Robet Goulet.

"Detested him.

"Any time he saw Goulet on TV, he became violently angry. Unfortunately, in the days when Mike Douglas and Merv Griffin ruled the airwaves, Goulet was on TV a lot. Elvis shot up the TV with Goulet on it several times, usually in his suite at the Las Vegas Hilton Hotel. The most famous time Elvis pulled a derringer out of his boot and fired it into the set, sending sparks everywhere."

"Elvis didn't limit his gunplay to shooting up TV sets. He shot up lots of small appliances and a few large ones. In February 1974, he fired at light switch in his Vegas suite. The bullet penetrated the wall and just missed his girlfriend at the time, Linda Thompson. She came running into his room trembling, but Elvis was able to soothe her by saying, 'Hey now, hon, just don't get excited.'

"From then on he confined his shooting to the TV and the chandelier, explaining to his boys, 'We're in the penthouse. Nobody's gonna get hit as long as you shoot straight up.'"

THE FIRST SWIVEL

"The question of the ages is: what did he shake, and when did he shake it? Let's face it, his swivel hips were the one thing that set him apart from the other young singers of his day. They didn't call him Elvis the Pelvis for nothing.

"So when and where did he first shake his hips while singing?

"Country music legend Webb Pierce says it happened July 30, 1954, on a country music package tour that played Overton Park in Memphis. 'Elvis told me that it was the first time he had ever sung before a big crowd and that he was real scared. He said he thought he was gonna faint out there on stage, so he started flapping his legs, just to keep from passing out. Then he noticed the crowd was reacting to it, so he just kept doing it.'"

PRIMETIME PROVERBS

Here are some more TV quotes from the book Primetime Proverbs, *by Jack Mingo and John Javna.*

ON POLITICS

"When I was in third grade, there was a kid running for office. His slogan was: 'Vote for me and I'll show you my wee-wee.' He won by a landslide."

—Dorothy,
The Golden Girls

ON "FREE LOVE"

"You American girls have such big breasts all the time...So please, give us the number of your apartment so we can go up there and have sex with you now!"

—Dan Aykroyd
(The Wild and Crazy Guy),
Saturday Night Live

ON PETS

[To his dog] "You're glad to see me every minute of your life. I come home, you jump around and wag your tail. I go to the closet, I come out, you jump around and wag your tail. I turn my face away and turn it back, you wag your tail. Either you love me very much or your short-term memory is shot."

Dr. Harry Weston,
—*Empty Nest*

"The only good cat is a stir-fried cat."

—Alf, *ALF*

COP TALK

Witness [refusing to testify because he doesn't want to "get involved"]: "Mr. Friday, if you were me, would you want to get involved?"
Sgt. Joe Friday: "Can I wait a while?"
Witness: "Huh?"
Friday: "Before I'm you."

—*Dragnet*

Killer: "You made a mistake, and I'm not going to pay for it."
Sgt. Joe Friday: "You're going to use a credit card?"

—*Dragnet*

ON LINGUISTICS

"Due to the shape of the North American elk's esophagus, even if it could speak, it could not pronounce the word *lasagna*."

—Cliff Clavin, *Cheers*

"You must always keep abreast of other tongues."

—Batman, *Batman*

OH SAY CAN YOU SEE?

A Bathroom Reader's dilemma: What would do if you heard the National Anthem right now? Stay seated? Stand? Well, no one's watching. Hum it to yourself while you read this, and do whatever you want.

THE PRISONER

During the War of 1812, British troops marched on Washington, D.C. and burned down the White House. Then, with their sights set on Baltimore, they sailed up the Chesapeake River, taking a civilian prisoner with them—a Dr. William Beanes, who'd supposedly helped arrest 3 English soldiers in Washington.

THE RESCUE.

The next day Francis Scott Key, a prominent young lawyer from Washington, met with British military commanders on the Chesapeake Bay and persuaded them to release Beanes (who'd actually *assisted* wounded British soldiers). But the Brits wouldn't let Key go until the planned bombardment of Baltimore's Fort McHenry was over. So he was detained on the British boat overnight.

THE DEFENSE

During the night, Key got a first-hand look at the raging battle. He assumed that the British would take Baltimore, as they had Washington. But in the morning, he awoke to find that the American flag was still flying over Fort McHenry. Inspired by the American defense, he jotted down an emotional poem.

THE SONG

On his way back to shore, Key wrote the words down on an envelope. The next day, he showed the poem to his wife's sister. She found it so inspiring that she took it to a printer, made handbills, and circulated the poem around Baltimore. The next week, the *Baltimore American* newspaper became the first to publish it.

Surprise: the words were set to the melody of a *British* song called "Anacreon in Heaven." Another surprise: It didn't become the National Anthem until 1931—after being voted down in 1929 because it's a British tune, and a poor marching song.

90% of American business are family-owned.

CUSTOM-MADE

You know these customs. Now, here's where they came from.

CLINKING GLASSES AFTER A TOAST
Nobles and knights were sometimes assassinated by enemies who'd poisoned their wine. So when they got together socially, each poured a little of his own wine into everyone else's goblet, as a precaution. That way, if one man poisoned another, he poisoned everyone—including himself...Over the years, the tradition of exchanging wine has been simplied into this gesture of friendship.

SPLITTING THE WISHBONE
In ancient Rome, soothsayers used the bones and entrails of birds to predict the future. In fact, one Latin term for "soothsayer," *auspex*, means "one who looks at birds." The soothsayer would " throw the bones" (a precursor of throwing dice) or dissect the bird to receive insight. Nowadays, we just break the wishbone, hoping to get the larger—and luckier—piece.

BUTTONS ON COAT SLEEVES
Researchers credit this to Napoleon Bonaparte. Apparently, while inspecting some of his troops, he spotted a soldier wiping his nose on his jacket sleeve. Disgusted, Napoleon ordered all new shirts and jackets for his army—this time with buttons on the sleeves.

WEARING BLACK FOR MOURNING
Until King Charles VIII died in the late fifteenth century, Europeans in mourning wore white (for hope or renewal). But when Anne Brittany, Charles' widow, went into mourning, she donned black. The result: a funeral fashion that continues today.

THROWING RICE & EATING CAKE AT WEDDINGS
For the Romans, wheat was a symbol of fertility. In fact, the Latin term for wedding, *conferreatio*, means "eating wheat together." Weddings began with the bride holding wheat sheaves and ended with the married couple eating wheat cakes. Over the years, wheat sheaves and wheat loaves have been replaced by throwing rice and serving multi-tiered cakes.

A teaspoon holds 120 drops of water.

RADIO STUNTS

Radio stations will do practically anything for a little publicity. Three cases in point...

In 1990, WKRL in St. Petersburg, Florida introduced an all-Led Zeppelin format by playing the song "Stairway to Heaven" for 24 hours straight. According to *Pulse* magazine: "Two hours into the marathon the police showed up...Evidently a lot of listeners had called them thinking the DJ had a heart attack or was being held up at gunpoint." After 12 days of playing nothing but Led Zeppelin songs, the station decided to add another group to their format: Pink Floyd.

In 1988, the Baltimore Orioles opened their season by losing 21 straight games—a major league record. Ten games into the losing streak, Bob Rivers, a disc jockey at WIYY in Baltimore, vowed to stay on the air until the Orioles won their first game. At first it seemed like a fun idea...but then the Orioles kept losing.

Rivers kept his word—he stayed on the air 24 hours a day, sleeping only between songs. His plight made international headlines. But 258 hours later, the ordeal was finally over: the Orioles defeated the Chicago White Sox, 9-0. After playing the Who song "I'm Free," Rivers went home for some well-deserved rest.

In 1982, WSAN in Allentown, Pennsylvania announced a contest—three randomly drawn contestants would climb on top of a WSAN billboard...and live there. The one who stayed there the longest would win a mobile home. Sleeping bags and portable toilets were provided by WSAN; the rest was up to the contestants.

On September 20, 1982 the marathon began. Three men perched on a billboard off Interstate 22 in Allentown. Even through freezing winter temperatures, none would give up. Newspapers worldwide picked up the story. In March, 1983, one of the contestants was busted for selling marijuana. The two remaining billboard-sitters stayed until May 4, 1983, seven months after the contest began. Finally, WSAN declared both men winners. Each received a mobile home, a car, clothes and a free vacation. The third guy was awarded free rent for a year, a color TV and a three month supply of Big Macs.

That's a mouthful: Over 200 different languages are spoken in the African country of Zaire.

THE HAYS OFFICE

From 1922-1945, Will H. Hays—the acknowledged "czar" of Hollywood—wielded an iron hand over the Motion Pictures Producers and Directors Association (MPAA). As the moral guardian of American moviegoers, he alone decided what did and didn't make it to the screen.

BACKGROUND

Films have been censored from the beginning. In 1894, just two weeks after Edison introduced the Kinescope in Atlantic City, New Jersey, residents complained about the primitive scenes in *Dulorita in the Passion Dance*. In 1897 a New York judge closed a film that depicted a bride preparing for her wedding night, calling it "an outrage upon public decency."

By the time America entered the "Roaring Twenties," however, religious groups had upped the ante, calling for a boycott if certain moral standards were not upheld. In 1921, when popular comic Fatty Arbuckle was accused of raping and killing an actress named Virginia Rappe, America was scandalized. Arbuckle was later acquitted of the charges (although his career was ruined), but the damage was already done.

THE CZAR

To forestall public criticism, Hollywood named Will Hays as "chief censor." He was the perfect man for the job. One contemporary commentaror called him "as indigenous as sassafras root. He is one of us. He is folks."

Hays had been a rising star in the Republican Party, serving as the party's chairman in 1918. He was even briefly nominated for president in the 1920 Republican Convention and later served as Postmaster General under President Warren G. Harding.

By 1924, Hays had issued a Code of Standards which stipulated what kind of films could and could not be made. It prevented 67 books and plays from becoming films that year.

THE FORBIDDEN

In 1927, Hays issued a pamphlet called "Don'ts and Be Carefuls," which included 11 subjects "to be avoided" and 26 to "handle with care." Among the "avoided" were:

Mark Twain, Charles Dickens, and Thomas Edison never graduated from high school.

• "Scenes of actual childbirth—in fact or in silhouette."

• "Branding of people or animals."

• "Excessive or lustful kissing, particularly when one character is a 'heavy.' "

• Also banned: revealing dresses, lingerie and shots which showed a woman's inner thigh.

Several years later, the Hays Office issued amended codes including 43 words that were banned, including "broad," "cripes," "fairy," "hot" (as applied to a woman) and the phrase "in your hat."

THE PRODUCTION CODE

Despite pressure from the Hays Office, motion pictures became increasingly racy in the early 1930's due to diminishing Depression-era receipts. One Catholic group threatened a nationwide boycott, saying, "The pesthole that infects the entire country with its obscene and lascivious moving pictures must be cleansed and disinfected."

Enter Joseph Breen, appointed by Hays to enforce a strict 1934 Production Code. Among the rules of the code were: no machine guns, no gambling, no graphic killings, no dying policeman, no exposed bosoms, no excessive drinking, no lace lingerie and no drugs.

Without the Production Code Seal, a film was virtually dead in the water. Anyone distributing or exhibiting a film without the seal could be severely fined.

CHANGES

Rather than risk not getting the Production Seal refused, most movie companies made whatever changes the "Hays Office" recommended. Among the decisions were:

• Forbidding Walt Disney to show a cow's udder in a cartoon.

• Altering a Joan Crawford film title from *Infidelity* to *Fidelity*.

• Removing all references to the city of Chicago in *Scarface* and forcing producer Howard Hughes to add "Shame of the Nation" to the title.

• Ruling that adultery could not be directly mentioned in the 1935 screen adaptation of *Anna Karenina*, starring Greta Garbo—despite the fact that adultery was the subject of the book it was based on.

Bats always turn left when exiting a cave.

BODY PARTS

A few fascinating facts about your body to entertain you while you pass the…uh…time.

Your brain weighs around three pounds. All but ten ounces is water.

☛

It takes 200,000 frowns to make a permanent wrinkle.

☛

While you're resting, the air you breathe passes through your nose at about four miles per hour. At this rate, you breathe over 400 gallons of air every hour.

☛

If you stub your toe, your brain will register pain in 1/50 of a second.

☛

It takes about 150 days for your fingernails to grow from your cuticles to your fingertips.

☛

The cartilage in your nose doesn't stop growing. Expect it to grow 1/2 inch longer and wider as you age.

☛

New freckles generally stop appearing after age 19 or 20.

Bone is about four times stronger than steel. It can endure 24,000 pounds of pressure per square inch.

☛

The average adult has about 18 square feet of skin.

☛

To say one word, you use over 70 muscles.

☛

Your brain uses less power than a 100-watt bulb.

☛

Women have a more developed sense of smell than men do.

☛

The average man shrinks a little more than one inch between the ages of 30 and 70. In the same period of time, the average woman shrinks two inches.

☛

There are over 200 taste buds on each of the small bumps on your tongue.

In 1989, Americans bought over 7,000 Harlequin romance books…every hour.

LUCY THE RED

Everyone loved Lucy. When she died in 1989, newspaper obituaries mourned the passing of the brilliant red-headed comedienne. But few mentioned her brief affiliation with the Communist party in 1936...and the way it almost destroyed her career.

BACKGROUND

In the early 1950s, during the height of Senator Joe McCarthy's "red menace" witch-hunts, an appearance before McCarthy and the House Un-American Activities Committee (HUAC) could ruin anybody—especially a Hollywood celebrity. At the time, "I Love Lucy" was the number one television show in the country. But that didn't make Lucy exempt from scrutiny. In 1953, Lucille Ball's political beliefs became a nationwide controversy.

REVELATION

In 1953, in his popular newsparer gossip column, Walter Winchell reported this shocking news: Lucille Ball, "America's sitcom sweetheart," had been a "commie!" Lucy denied it, of course; and Desi emotionally proclaimed, "The only thing red about Lucy is her hair. And that's not even real!"

THE INVESTIGATION

On September 4, 1953, Ball was asked to explain to the House Un-American Activities Committee (HUAC) why she had registered as a Communist on March 19, 1936.

William A. Wheeler, an investigator for HUAC, flew to Hollywood for Lucy's testimony. In the transcripts later released, Ball explained that she had registered as a Communist "to appease an old man," namely, her grandfather Fred C. Hunt, an ardent socialist.

"How we got to signing a few things," she told Wheeler, "or going among some people that thought differently, that has happened to to all of us out here in the last ten or twelve years, and it is unfortunate, but I certainly will do anything in the world to prove that we made a bad mistake."

But why had Ball voted for the Communist candidate in a primary election? While not really denying she had, Ball claimed she "had really racked my brain...and all I remember was something like a garage and a flag, like a voting day."

As for her political leanings, Ball was more conclusive. "I am not a Communist now," she testified. "I never have been. I never want to be. Nothing in the world could ever change my mind."

THE AFTERMATH

Both the Congress and the country forgave Lucy's "mistake." After her testimony, Representative Donald J. Jackson of California revealed that the committee had known of her Communist party registration for over a year and only divulged it to quell growing rumours that Lucy was a red.

Letters of sympathy poured in from all over the nation. But a few people, including J. Edgar Hoover, apparently had their doubts.

THE FBI

According to Jack Anderson's 12/7/89 column in the *Washington Post*, Hoover kept an open file on Lucy and her husband Desi Arnaz. Among the contents:

• Lucy went to great lengths to "make her grandfather happy." Besides registering as a Communist Party member, she signed a nominating petition of the Communist candidate for the California State Assembly in 1936. She was also named as a member of the Communist party's State Central Committee in California, although Lucy later denied any knowledge of her membership.

• In testimony before the State Legistative Committee on Un-American Activities in 1943, a Hollywood writer claimed to have attended Communist Party meetings at 1344 North Ogden Drive in Hollywood—Lucy's address at the time. According to Anderson, "The writer said Ball was not there but approved of the meeting."

• In 1951, the Communist newspaper, the *Daily Worker*, alleged that Lucy had once been more outspoken in her opposition to McCarthy but had been warned to keep quiet.

• While many movie people were pilloried for less, Lucy escaped unscathed. "My conscience has always been clean," she told a press conference after her testimony in 1953. "And I have great faith in the American people. They have been very good to me in the past and I'm sure they will be now."

Two out of three Soviet doctors are women.

PIGS IN SPACE

We honor astronauts like Neil Armstrong and John Glenn for their pioneering feats in space. But animals have been the real "guinea pigs" of flight since the first balloon took off in the 1700s.

UP, UP, AND AWAY

One month before the first manned balloon flight, a sheep, duck and a chicken were loaded onto a ballon and launched in Versailles, France on September 19, 1783. They survived the eight minute, two mile flight, achieving a peak altitude of 1,700 feet. The event was witnessed by King Louis XVI and Marie Antoinette.

FLYING PIGS

• On October 30, 1909, the first pig flew on an airplane. The stunt was inspired by the expression "pigs might fly," a phrase commonly used to express skepicism about flying. Lord Barbazon of England, wanting to put the expression to rest, kept a pig in a basket during an airplane flight.

• On February 18, 1930 the first cow flew from St. Louis. In a publicity stunt, the cow was milked during the flight. The milk was parachuted to the ground in sealed paper cartons.

A DOG'S LIFE

• The first living creature to orbit the Earth was a Russian dog named Laika, who was launched in a Russian satellite on November 3, 1957. The satellite orbited the Earth 2,370 times before burning up—with Laika aboard—during re-entry.

• The first animals to orbit Earth and survive were two dogs named Belka and Strelka on Sputnik 5, which was launched August 19, 1960.

MONKEY BUSINESS

• The U.S. also sent up animals before sending a human into space. On May 28, 1959, two monkeys named Able and Baker were launched 300 miles into space from Cape Canaveral, Florida. They were recovered alive the next day in the Caribbean.

ROCK NAMES

Where do rock groups get their outrageous names? From movies, books, and medieval torture devices. Some examples:

ABBA: An acronymn of the first letters of the band's four members, Agnetha Ulugeus, Bjorn Ulugeus, Benny Anderson and Annifred Anderson.

The Bay City Rollers: Came up with their name by sticking a pin in a map of the world. It landed on Bay City, Michigan.

The Beatles: A tribute to Buddy Holly's Crickets. The "a" was added by John Lennon, who later explained that it came to him in a dream.

Buffalo Springfield: Members of the legendary L.A.-based group were stumped for a name. A member of the band was looking out their manager's window at a construction site in Hollywood, when he spotted a steamroller with the brand name "Buffalo Springfield."

The Doors: Jim Morrison got the band's name from Aldous Huxley's book *The Doors Of Perception*, which dealt with Huxley's experimentation with psychedelic drugs.

Duran Duran: Named after a character in the film *Barbarella*, starring Jane Fonda.

The Grateful Dead: The name of an Egyptian prayer which band member Jerry Garcia spotted in a dictionary.

Iron Maiden: A medieval torture device.

Jefferson Airplane: Slang for a roach clip.

Jethro Tull: Named after the 18th century British inventor of the seed drill.

A housefly can carry germs as far as 15 miles from the original source.

Led Zeppelin: Based on a comment by the late Who drummer Keith Moon, who jokingly remarked that an early live appearance of the band "went down like a lead balloon."

Lynard Skynard: Inspired by Leonard Skinner, a teacher who once suspended the original band members from high school for having long hair.

Manhattan Transfer: After the 1920 novel by John Dos Passos.

Pink Floyd: An amalgam of two American blues artists, Pink Anderson and Floyd Council.

The Ramones: After Phil Ramone, the name Paul McCartney adopted for himself when the Beatles were the Silver Beatles.

The Rolling Stones: Taken from Muddy Waters' song, "Rolling Stone Blues."

Sha Na Na: Supposedly the doo-wop lyrics from "Get A Job," a 1957 hit by the Silhouettes.

Steely Dan: Based on the name of a dildo in William Burrough's novel, *The Naked Lunch.*

The Thompson Twins: There are no Thompsons or twins in the band, which took its name from characters in the Belgian comic book, *Tintin.*

Three Dog Night: It is a practice of Australian aborigines to sleep with three dogs on particularly cold nights.

UB40: Named after the British unemployment benefit form.

The Velvet Underground: Lou Reed lifted the name from a title of a cheap paperback novel.

The Yardbirds: A tribute to legendary be-bop saxophonist Charlie "Yardbird" Parker.

About half of American men polled say they enjoy money more than sex.

MYTH AMERICA

Here we are again: You may have believed these stories since you were a kid—after all, they were taught as sacred truths. Well, it's time to take another look...

TEA TIME

The Myth: The Boston Tea Party was held because the British imposed a tax on tea.

The Truth: The exact opposite is actually true. The British did impose the Townsend Act, which taxed a number of goods—including tea—quite heavily. However, the tax on tea didn't really affect the colonists—they drank a smuggled, less expensive Dutch tea (John Hancock was a big Dutch tea smuggler).

To undercut the American tea-smuggling operation, the British rounded up between 15 and 20 million pounds of surplus tea, passed the Tea Act which eliminated taxes on British tea, and priced their huge supply below the price of the smuggled Dutch tea.

Colonists responded to this British interference by dumping the British tea before it was unloaded. That was the event called the Boston Tea Party.

FOR WHOM THE BELL TOLLS

The Myth: Alexander Graham Bell invented the telephone.

Background: About 15 years before Bell uttered the famous words, "Mr. Watson, come here; I want you," German scientist Phillip Reis had developed a crude working telephone. And about five years before Bell's historic race to the patent office, an Italian scientist named Antonio Meucci offered the patent office a rough description of a telephone's structure and principles. But nothing ever came of it.

The Truth: Bell wasn't the first to develop the device—but he was the first to patent it...barely. Many scientists were working on a telephone at the same time; one of them—Elisha Gray—arrived at the U.S. Patent Office with a model telephone just two hours *after* Bell. In fact, some say Gray's telephone was better than Bell's and more like the one we use today. By the time Bell received his patent, so many people claimed the telephone as their own invention that Bell had to defend the patent in court. In fact, the case went all the way to the *Supreme Court*. The verdict: the high court was divided in his favor, allowing him to the rights to the phone.

FULTON'S FOLLY

The Myth: Robert Fulton invented the steamboat.

The Truth: Twenty years before Fulton built his first steamboat, *Fulton's Folly*, in 1807, James Rumsey had a steamboat chugging up the Potomac and John Fitch had one traveling the Delaware. In some states, Fitch even secured exclusive rights to run passenger and freight steamboat trips. So why does Fulton get the credit for the invention 20 years later? Rumsey and Fitch died broke, while Fulton had a knack for promotion and fund-raising. But Fulton did fail to make one key sale—to Napoleon Bonaparte, who thought the idea of steamships impractical. Some historians say the little conqueror's bad decision might have saved the English.

FORD FACTS

The Myth: Henry Ford produced the first automobile.

The Truth: Karl Benz and Gottlieb Daimler, two German engineers who went on to form Mercedes-Benz, each developed working gasoline engine automobiles in 1885. The first American car was built by Charles and J. Frank Duryea in 1893. By then, Benz already had a model, the Velo, ready for sale to the general public.

The Myth: O.K., if Ford didn't invent the car, at least he invented the auto assembly line.

The Truth: No, chalk this one up to Ransom E. Olds, creator of the Oldsmobile. Olds introduced the moving assembly line in the early 1900s and boosted car production by 500%. The previous year, the Olds Motor Vehicle Company had turned out 425 cars. The year after they made over 2,500 of them. Ford improved Olds's system by introducing the conveyor belt, which moved both the cars *and* needed parts along the production line. The belt cut Ford's production time from a day to about two hours. A significant contribution, but not the original.

WHO'S ON FIRST?

The Abbott and Costello baseball routine "Who's On First?" is considered a landmark in the history of comedy.

Abbot and Costello's recording of "Who's On First?" became the first gold record placed in the Baseball Hall of Fame in Cooperstown, New York.

• "The Baseball Scene," as it was known before it was given the title "Who's On First?" was a burlesque standard long before Abbot and Costello popularized it. In fact, Abbott and Costello each performed it with other vaudeville partners before teaming up in 1936.

• When the duo first performed the routine on radio's "The Kate Smith Hour," they were forced to change the ending from "I don't give a damn!" / "Oh, that's our shortstop" to "I don't care" / "Oh, that's our shortstop." President Roosevelt was listening; he enjoyed it so much that he called them personally to offer congratulations after the show.

HERE'S THE ROUTINE

BUD: You know, strange as it may seem, they give baseball players peculiar names nowadays. On the St. Louis team Who's on first, What's on second, I Don't Know is on third.

LOU: That's what I want to find out. I want you to tell me the names of the fellows on the St. Louis team.

BUD: I'm telling you. Who's on first, What's on second, I Don't Know is on third.

LOU: You know the fellows' names?

BUD: Yes.

LOU: Well, then, who's playin' first?

BUD: Yes.

LOU: I mean the fellow's name on first base.

BUD: Who.

BUD: The fellow's name on first base for St. Louis.

LOU: Who.

BUD: The guy on first base.

LOU: Well, what are you askin' me for?
BUD: I'm not asking you. I'm telling you. Who is on first.
LOU: I'm askin' you, who is on first?
BUD: That's the man's name.
LOU: That's whose name?
BUD: Yes.
LOU: Well, go ahead and tell me.
BUD: Who?
LOU: The guy on first.
BUD: Who.
LOU: The first baseman.
BUD: Who is on first.
LOU: (*Trying to stay calm*) Have you got a first baseman on first?
BUD: Certainly.
LOU: Well, all I'm trying to find out is what's the guy's name on first base.
BUD: Oh, no, no. What is on *second* base.
LOU: I'm not askin' you who's on second.
BUD: Who's on first.
LOU: That's what I'm tryin' to find out.
BUD: Well, don't change the players around.
LOU: (*starting to get angry*) I'm not changin' anybody.
BUD: Now take it easy.
LOU: What's the guy's name on first base?
BUD: What's the guy's name on *second* base.
LOU: I'm not askin' you who's on second.
BUD: Who's on first.
LOU: I don't know.
BUD: He's on third. We're not talking about him.
LOU: (*begging*) How could I get on third base?
BUD: You mentioned his name.
LOU: If I mentioned the third baseman's name, who did I say is playing third?
BUD: (*starting all over again*) No, Who's playing first.

Bonehead fact: You have 22 bones in your skull.

LOU: Stay offa first, will ya?
BUD: Please, now what is it you'd like to know?
LOU: What is the fellow's name on third base?
BUD: What is the fellow's name on second base.
LOU: I'm not askin' ya who's on second.
BUD: Who's on first.
LOU: I don't know.
BUD & LOU: (*together*) Third base!
LOU: (*tries again*) You got an outfield?
BUD: Certainly.
LOU: St. Louis got a good outfield?
BUD: Oh, absolutely.
LOU: The left fielder's name.
BUD: Why.
LOU: I don't know. I just thought I'd ask.
BUD: Well, I just thought I'd tell you.
LOU: Then tell me who's playing left field.
BUD: Who's paying first.
LOU: Stay outa the infield!
BUD: Don't mention any names there.
LOU: (*firmly*) I wanta know what's the fellow's name in left field.
BUD: What is on second.
LOU: I'm not askin' you who's on second.
BUD: Who is on first.
LOU: I don't know!
BUD & LOU: (*together*) Third base! (*Lou makes funny noises*)
BUD: Now take it easy, man.
LOU: And the left fielder's name?
BUD: Why?
LOU: Because.
BUD: Oh, he's center field.
LOU: Wait a minute. You got a pitcher on the team?
BUD: Wouldn't this be a fine team without a pitcher?
LOU: I dunno. Tell me the pitcher's name.

Indians in the Andes mountains have 3 quarts more blood than people living at sea level do.

BUD: Tomorrow.
LOU: You don't want to tell me today?
BUD: I'm telling you, man.
LOU: Then go ahead.
BUD: Tomorrow.
LOU: What time?
BUD: What time what?
LOU: What time tomorrow are you gonna tell me who's pitching?
BUD: Now listen, who is not pitching. Who is on—
LOU: (*excited*) I'll break your arm if you say who is on first.
BUD: Then why come up here and ask?
LOU: I want to know what's the pitcher's name!
BUD: What's on second.
LOU: (*sighs*) I don't know.
BUD & LOU: (*together*) Third base!
LOU: You gotta catcher?
BUD: Yes.
LOU: The catcher's name.
BUD: Today.
LOU: Today. And Tomorrow's pitching.
BUD: Now you've got it.
LOU: That's all. St. Louis got a couple of days on their team. That's all.
BUD: Well, I can't help that. What do you want me to do?
LOU: Gotta catcher?
BUD: Yes.
LOU: I'm a good catcher, too, you know.
BUD: I know that.
LOU: I would like to play for St. Louis.
BUD: Well, I might arrange that.
LOU: I would like to catch. Now Tomorrow's pitching on the team and I'm catching.
BUD: Yes.
LOU: Tomorrow throws the ball and the guy up bunts the ball.

The first hearing aid was too large to be worn.

BUD: Yes.

LOU: So when he bunts the ball, me, bein' a good catcher, I want to throw the guy out at first base. So I pick up the ball and I throw it to who?

BUD: Now that's the first thing you've said right!

LOU: *I don't even know what I'm talkin' about!*

BUD: Well, that's all you have to do.

LOU: I throw it to first base.

BUD: Yes.

LOU: Now who's got it?

BUD: Naturally.

LOU: Naturally.

BUD: Naturally.

LOU: I throw the ball to naturally.

BUD: You throw it to Who.

LOU: Naturally.

BUD: Naturally, well, say it that way.

LOU: That's what I'm saying!

BUD: Now don't get excited, don't get excited.

LOU: I throw the ball to first base.

BUD: Then Who gets it.

LOU: He'd better get it.

BUD: That's it. All right now, don't get excited. Take it easy.

LOU: (*beside himself*) Now I throw the ball to first base, whoever it is grabs the ball, so the guy runs to second.

BUD: Uh-huh.

LOU: Who picks up the ball and throws it to What. What throws it to I Don't Know. I Don't Know throws it back to Tomorrow. A triple play!

BUD: Yeah, could be.

LOU: Another guy goes up and it's a long fly ball to center. Why? I don't know. And I don't give a damn!

BUD: What was that?

LOU: I said, I don't give a damn!

BUD: Oh, that's our shortstop.

One out of every seven birds in the world is a finch.

STRANGE LAWSUITS

Tired of being sprayed by department store employees? Are headless cartoon characters terrorizing your children? Don't take the law into your own hands. Take 'em to court.

THE PLAINTIFF: Deborah Martorano.
THE DEFENDANT: Bloomingdale's Department Store.
THE LAWSUIT: Martorano claimed she was wrongfully sprayed with perfume by a store employee. On April 30, 1984, she was shopping for a blouse on her lunch hour when a roving perfume-demonstrator approached her and squirted her with fragrance. Martorano's lawyer claimed his client, a lifelong asthma and allergy sufferer, spent 10 days in a New York hospital recovering from "respiratory distress" resulting from the unsolicited spritz.
VERDICT: She accepted a $75,000 settlement from the store.

THE PLAINTIFF: John Moore.
THE DEFENDANT: Regents of the University of California.
THE LAWSUIT: Moore claimed one of his organs was pirated. In 1976, University of California-Los Angeles Medical Center doctors removed Moore's spleen in a successful effort to cure his cancer. Doctors later found that the spleen possessed unique cancer-fighting cells; experiments with the cells led to a new discovery worth an estimated $3 billion. Moore, who was never told that his ex-organ had commercial value, sued for part of the profits.
VERDICT: In 1990, 14 years after the operation, Moore lost the case.

THE PLAINTIFF: The estate of an unidentified 34-year-old co-pilot.
THE DEFENDANT: Gates Lear Jet Corporation.
THE LAWSUIT: The estate claimed that a jet's windshield wasn't thick enough. In 1987, an 11.5 pound loon crashed through the windshield of a state-of-the-art jet during takeoff, killing the loon and the co-pilot. The man's estate contended that the windshield should have been "birdproofed." It was, Gates Lear said, but

only for birds weighing up to four pounds.
VERDICT: A Michigan circuit court awarded the man's estate $1.5 million in compensatory damages.

THE PLAINTIFF: McDonald's.
THE DEFENDANT: McDharma's Natural Fast Foods.
THE LAWSUIT: McDonald's hadn't a clue that McDharma's, a 15-employee vegetarian restaurant where cashiers wear T-shirts, shorts, and sandals, even existed until the three-year-old Santa Cruz, California eatery sought its own national trademark. McDonald's had nothing against the top-selling "Brahma Burger," a burger made of beans, nuts, seeds, grains, and soy, but objected to the McDharma's use of the trademarked "Mc." "It's such a joke," McDharma's co-owner Bernie Shapiro said, "and they're the only ones taking it seriously."
VERDICT: McDharma's was forced to drop the "Mc," but instead of removing the two letters from their sign, McDharma's painted a red circle with a slash over them. McDonald's sued again; McDharma's eventually removed the "Mc." However, McDharma's received a handful of offers for franchises.

THE PLAINTIFF: Mr. and Mrs. Lonnie and Karen B.
THE DEFENDANT: The Walt Disney Corporation
THE LAWSUIT: The couple claimed that they were falsely arrested for shoplifting while they and their daughters, Lindsay, 6, and Melissa, 2, were visiting Disneyland. They were detained for questioning. Apparently, while they waited, Lindsay caught sight of several actors dressed as Disney characters who had taken their costume headpieces off...and she freaked out. The couple sued for damages, claiming their daughter suffered nightmares and had to undergo therapy as a result of the experience.
THE VERDICT: Pending.

MISC. DID WE MENTION THIS?
From the book *George Washington Had No Middle Name:* "A biography of George Armstrong Custer, by James Warner Bellah, reads in its entirety: 'To put it mildly, this was an oddball.' "

LATE NIGHT WITH DAVID LETTERMAN

A few words from America's favorite gap-toothed talk show host.

"This warning from the New York City Department of Health Fraud: Be suspicious of any doctor who tries to take your temperature with his finger."

"Martin Levine has passed away at age 75. Mr Levine had owned a movie theater chain here in New York. The funeral will be held on Thursday at 2:15, 4:20, 6:30, 8:40, and 10:50."

"A professor at Johns Hopkins has come forth with an intriguing thought about a perennial question: He says that if an infinite number of monkeys sat typing at an infinite number of typewriters, the smell in the room would be unbearable."

"Interesting survey in the *Journal of Abnormal Psychology*. New York City has a higher percentage of people you shouldn't make any sudden moves around than any other city in the world."

"Tip to out-of-town visitors: If you buy something here in New York and want to have it shipped home, be suspicious if the clerk tells you they don't need your name and address."

"Every year when it's Chinese New Year here in New York, there are fireworks going off at all hours. New York mothers calm their children by telling them it's just gunfire."

"New Jersey announced today that they were adopting a new license plate slogan: 'Try Our Creamy Thick Shakes.'"

"Someone did a study of the three most often heard phrases in New York City. One is, 'Hey, taxi.' Two is, 'What train do I take to get to Bloomingdales?' And three is, 'Don't worry. It's just a flesh wound.' "

"High insurance rates are what really killed the dinosaurs."

MONKEE BUSINESS

The Monkees were one of the most popular bands in the world, but weren't allowed to play on their own records—until they went on strike. Here's the inside story, from Behind the Hits, *by Bob Shannon and John Javna.*

From the outside, everything looked great for the Monkees in 1967. In one year they had leaped from semi—or total—obscurity to overnight superstardom. They had a hit TV series, two #1 singles ("Last Train to Clarksville," and "I'm A Believer"), and two #1 albums ("The Monkees," and "More of the Monkees"). The only problem was the Monkees weren't allowed to play on their own records. Why not? Because Don Kirshner, the musical supervisor of the Monkees, said so. It was...well...embarrassing. Here they were, pretending to be a real group, when in fact they had almost nothing to do with "their" music. Critics made fun of them. Even worse, teenyboppers idolized them for something they weren't doing. And to add insult to injury, Kirshner made more money from their records than they did. They each got a 1.5% royalty, but Kirshner got 15%! They had their pride, after all.

Trouble had been brewing for some time between Kirshner and the group, particularly Mike Nesmith, who wasn't even allowed to play guitar on the songs he *wrote*. That was Kirshner's studio policy; the Monkees just sang vocals while studio musicians played on the tracks. But what the hell, Kirshner reasoned, he was getting results—hits—and that was his job. So what if Nesmith had to stand by and watch Glen Campbell put the guitar licks on his own song, "Mary Mary"? This was the only way management could be sure it was right. The bottom line was what counted, after all. Nesmith, a genuinely creative individual, just stewed.

"Essentially, the big collision I had with Don Kirshner was this," said Nesmith; "he kept saying, 'You can't make the music; it would be no good, it won't be a hit.' And I was saying, 'Hey, the music isn't a hit because somebody wonderful is making it, the music is a hit because of the television show. So, at least let us put out music that is closer to our personas, closer to who we are artistically, so that we don't have to walk around and have people throwing eggs at us,' which they were."

Eventually the feud came to a showdown in early '67 at Kirshner's suite at the Beverly Hills Hotel. Kirshner had just handed the four Monkees some new demos (including "Sugar, Sugar," a bubblegum hit later for Kirshner's Archies) that they would be putting vocals on. Nesmith stepped forward and demanded that musical control be give to the Monkees. When Kirshner refused, Nesmith angrily smashed his fist through the wall, declaring, "That could have been your face!" Then the Monkees went off to record some original material *without* Kirshner's approval.

What happened next is a little unclear. While the Monkees were working out their own songs, Kirshner appears to have approached Davy Jones, one of the members of the group, and talked him into going into the studio without the rest of the Monkees. Jones put the vocals on several tunes, one of which was "A Little Bit Me, A Little Bit You." But the Monkees weren't doing the backing vocals. Who was it? Eric Lefcowitz, author of *The Monkees Tale*, speculates, "Kirshner was quoted once as saying that Neil Diamond and Carole King had sung back-up vocals on some Monkees songs, and I think that if you listen closely to 'A Little Bit Me,' you can hear them. It sounds like Neil Diamond to me." And why would Jones record without the rest of his group? "I don't know, of course," Lefcowitz says, "but Davy Jones hadn't ever had the chance to sing lead before. This was *his* session. Maybe that had something to do with it."

Whatever. The important thing is that in a power play, Kirshner recorded and released "A Little Bit Me, A Little Bit You" without even telling the Monkees he was doing it! That was the last straw. Monkees' producers Bert Schnieder and Bob Rafelson wanted hits, but they weren't going to put up with that from anyone. They fired Kirshner, and yanked the single out of American record stores. Then they re-released it with a Monkees' original—Nesmith's "The Girl I Knew Somewhere"—on the B side. Finally the Monkees could smile. They were out from under Kirshner...and a song they'd actually played on made the Top 40—"The Girl I Knew Somewhere" reached #39 on the charts.

Layne Hall of New York, age 109, has been driving 75 years—without an accident.

GIVE US A HAND

You probably can't put a finger on the origins of these common gestures, but here's some info you might find handy.

THE FINGER

It doesn't matter what you call it—"the bird," "the finger," or the "freeway salute"— the middle finger is among the most well-known symbols in America. Believe it or not, the gesture can be traced to the ancient Romans, who called it the "finger without shame" or *digitus impudicus*. Psychologists say it's a symbol of phallic aggressiveness.

THE RING FINGER

Over two-thousand years ago, Greek physicians believed that a special "vein of love" connected this finger to the heart. It logically became the finger to be "bound" by an affair of the heart.

CROSSING FINGERS

Ever cross your fingers for good luck? Historians suggest this popular gesture comes from the pre-Christian belief that a cross symbolizes perfect unity. The intersection point of the fingers was said to possess a mystical quality which would hold the wish until it was fulfilled.

THUMBS UP OR THUMBS DOWN

This symbol wasn't always used to rate new movies or hitch rides. According to popular lore, it was a matter of life or death. Roman emperors would use "thumbs up" to spare a defeated gladiator's life, and "thumbs down" to order his death.

THUMBING YOUR NOSE

You've done it before—touching your thumb to the tip of your nose and extending your fingers like a fan. It's understood as an insult all over the world, but what does it mean? Some folklorists say it's a mock military salute. Others maintain that it's a graphic suggestion that someone stinks.

It costs parents about $5,800 to care for a newborn in its first year.

THE GREAT *TITANIC*

You've probably heard of the Titantic. We had, but we didn't really know much about it. So this piece by Eric Lefcowitz was particularly interesting.

BACKGROUND

Steamships were the most viable means of trans-Atlantic travel when the White Star Company decided to build the world'd largest ship, the *Titanic* in 1912. Its proposed measurements—900 feet (3-1/2 city blocks) long and 11 stories high—were enough to make it front-page news. But size wasn't all it had to offer. The company announced a breakthrough in steamship design; with 16 watertight compartments and a double bottom, the *Titanic* would be "unsinkable." If water got through the first hull, spokesmen explained, the second one would still keep the boat afloat.

The construction of the Titanic captured the public's imagination. Newspapers billed it as a "floating Camelot." By the time it was ready to sail, the whole world was watching.

THE VOYAGE

On April 12, the *Titanic* left for its maiden voyage from Southhampton, England to New York. Accommodations varied: There were cramped, low-cost quarters in the bowels of the boat for arriving immigrants; and there were luxurious upper-deck suites for the upper class. A one-way luxury ticket cost an incredible $4,350.

Fatal mistake: The captain, intent on breaking the world's record with the fastest trans-Atlantic journey ever, ignored warnings about icebergs.

The result: On April 15, four days, 17 hours, and 35 minutes later, the "unsinkable" Titanic hit an iceberg in the North Atlantic. It was 350 miles from Newfoundland. In the darkness of night, the mighty boat plunged into water two miles deep.

It was the most dramatic ship disaster of all-time; 1,512 passengers were killed.

TITANIC FACTS

• The *Titanic*'s band played on deck as the ship was sinking. The song they played was "Autumn," a popular British waltz.

Noble ladies of Greece and Rome carried the tiny Maltese dog (3-6 lbs.) in their robe sleeves.

- There was lifeboat space for only 1,200 of the 2,227 passengers.
- Only 705 people, most of them women and children, survived the disaster. They were picked up by the Cunard liner *Carpathia*.
- Among the rich and famous who went down with the ship were John Jacob Astor and Benjamin Guggenheim.
- Unlike the 1898 disaster of the French ship, *La Bourgogne*—where women and children were trampled by hysterical passengers attempting to get on lifeboats—chivalry and honor prevailed on the *Titanic*; most of the women and children survived. However, a greater proportion of first-class passengers survived than lower-class travelers, including immigrants, who were on the lower decks.
- The *California*, a freighter only 10 miles away, saw eight distress flares fired from the *Titanic* but did not respond, figuring they had been set off in celebration.
- Several changes in sea travel regulations occurred after the disaster. Every ship was required to have enough lifeboats to accommodate every passenger. The International Ice Patrol was also organized.
- Only one ship has struck an iceberg since the *Titanic* sank—it happened during World War II.
- A song called "The Wreck of the *Titanic*" became popular shortly after the disaster. Sample lyrics: "Oh, they built the ship *Titanic* to sail the ocean blue. And they thought they had a ship that the water couldn't get through. But an iceberg on the wave, Sent it to its watery grave. It was sad when that great ship went down."

DISCOVERING THE WRECK

Still controversial: For years people searched for the most famous wreck of all-time. Finally, in 1985, the *Titanic* was discovered by a U.S./French exploratory team. To keep potential looters away, its location wasn't divulged. But in 1987, the French members returned to the site and—contrary to the wishes of the U.S. team, who thought the site should be preserved out of respect to the dead—salvaged 800 artifacts from the wreck. In response, the U.S. Senate, whose members agreed the site should be left alone, passed a resolution banning the display of the recovered *Titanic* items for profit in the United States.

A recent study suggests test-takers perform better if they have a cold.

WEIRD COINCIDENCES

A reader sent us this list of the bizarre similarities between the assassinations of Lincoln and Kennedy. It's hard to believe, but they're true. Rod Serling, where are you?

Abraham Lincoln was elected in 1860, and John Kennedy in 1960, 100 years later.

Both Lincoln and Kennedy mentioned having premonitions of death before their assassinations.

Lincoln's secretary, named Kennedy, warned him not to go to the theater that fatal night. Kennedy's secretary, named Lincoln, tried to talk him out of going to Dallas.

Both men died of bullet wounds to the head.

Both were killed as they sat beside their wives.

Both were ardent proponents of civil rights.

John Wilkes Booth, Lincoln's assassin, was born in 1839, and Lee Harvey Oswald, Kennedy's assassin, was born in 1939, exactly 100 years later.

The names John Wilkes Booth and Lee Harvey Oswald each contain 15 letters.

Booth shot Lincoln in a theater and fled to a warehouse. Oswald shot Kennedy from a warehouse and fled to a theater.

Both Presidents were succeeded by vice-presidents named Johnson. Andrew Johnson followed Lincoln, and Lyndon B. Johnson followed Kennedy.

Andrew Johnson was born in 1808, and Lyndon B. Johnson was born in 1908, 100 years later.

Both were killed on Friday.

Both Johnsons were Democrats, southern, and former senators.

The names Kennedy and Lincoln each contain seven letters.

The names Andrew Johnson and Lyndon Johnson each contain 13 letters.

Both Booth and Oswald were killed before reaching trial.

According to a recent study, about 20% of men and 6% of women sleep naked.

SATURDAY NIGHT LIVE

The original version of Saturday Night Live, which ran from 1975 to about 1980, was a milestone in modern TV. Some say its hip, bold, innovative humor hasn't been matched since then. Here's how it got on the air.

HOW IT STARTED

In early 1975, NBC executives were looking to improve Saturday night ratings in the 11:30-1:00 a.m. time slot. "Tonight Show" reruns were getting stale, and research showed that viewers were constantly changing channels, indicating that a restless audience was looking for something new. . . and not finding it. "The problem," Producer Lorne Michaels explained a few years later, "was that no one in TV was accurately expressing what was going on. Carol Burnett sketches were dealing with the problems of another generation—divorce, Valium, crab-grass, adultery. It used to drive me crazy to see Bob Hope doing a sketch about marijuana and acting drunk."

When Michaels and NBC vice president Dick Ebersol suggested a 90-minute variety show featuring "rock'n'roll, satire, changing hosts, and a cast of unknown regulars who'd done almost no TV," NBC brass shocked them by accepting. Michaels also proposed going "live," sensing that the young, hip, late-nite crowd would be drawn to the "anything goes" atmosphere of such a format. "I felt that American kids knew TV as well as French kids knew wine and that there was such a thing as good TV."

Michaels began casting. He recruited some of the best young talent available, including Dan Aykroyd, Chevy Chase, Gilda Radner, and John Belushi. On Oct. 11, 1975, unaware of the profound effect they were about to have on an entire generation of American youth, the Not Ready for Prime Time Players appeared for the first time on "Saturday Night Live."

INSIDE INFO

Peanuts. The Not Ready For Prime Time Players' starting weekly salaries in 1975 were $750 per week.

Employment Opportunity. Four of the original eleven writers on SNL had just graduated from college, and the show was their first post-college job.

THE ORIGINAL CAST

• On his 21st birthday Bill Murray was in a Chicago jail (busted with eight lbs. of marijuana on him). After his release, jobless and penniless, he decided to try comedy. He joined his brother (Brian Doyle-Murray) at the Second City comedy troupe. There he found his niche; soon afterwards, SNL called and offered him a spot.

• John Belushi was the last cast-member hired for SNL. Lorne Michaels had sincere reservations about unleashing such a volatile, "on-the-edge" talent in front of a live camera, but after seeing John's "Samurai Pool Hustler," how could he resist? "Everyone in the group wanted him," Dick Ebersol said, "but we heard horrendous tales of his being a discipline problem." Said writer Michael O'Donoghue: "He wanted to grab the world and snort it."

• An experienced writer with "The Smothers' Brothers Show," Chevy Chase was originally hired only to write for SNL. But he wanted to act. One night, after dinner with Lorne Michaels, Chase took off down the street, threw himself into the air, and landed in "the biggest puddle I'd ever seen. We figured," says Michaels, "that if he wanted it that badly, we might as well give him a shot." But he'd only signed a one-year contract, so after the first season he left.

• Dan Aykroyd was hired for the show at the last minute, and for a while had to commute between Canada and the U.S. on his motorcycle.

• Laraine Newman auditioned for SNL in a hospital room, where Dick Ebersol was recuperating from an illness.

• Jane Curtin was hired out of a Boston improv group. There were equally talented applicants for the spot, but says Dick Ebersol, "we thought we needed someone who was white bread."

• The best physical comedian in the troupe, Gilda Radner was the first person hired for SNL. She was also from Second City.

• The only cast member without formal comic training (though he had formal music training at Julliard), Garrett Morris was first hired as a writer. When Michaels saw him acting in *Cooley High*, Morris was added to the cast.

FROG FACTS

Kermit the Frog says, "It's not easy being green." Maybe this is what he means.

There are around 2,600 different species of frogs. They live in every continent except Antarctica.

Frogs don't drink water—they absorb water through their skin.

Every species of frog as its own special mating call, made only by the males. The call has two parts—"a whine," which the whole species uses, and a "chuck" which is the individual frog's calling card. Females listen to the chuck carefully—the larger, more desirable frogs make longer, deeper chucks. The drawback: bats, which eat frogs, also listen for long, deep chucks.

One expert reports "A frog from Ethiopa has teethlike protusions and eats snails—shells and all."

An Australian frog hatches its offspring in its stomach, then spits out fully developed frogs—sometimes more than 20 at once.

The skin of some poisonous frogs is so toxic that it will kill any creature that bites it. Only 1/100,000 of a gram of skin poison from one species is enough to kill a man.

Have you ever heard of flying frogs? They do exist, but they don't really fly—they can't gain height in the air. Instead, they glide. Top speed: 24 kilometers per hour, fastest of all amphibians.

According to an expert, "One frog in Colombia is so toxic that local Indians merely wipe their arrows across its skin to poison the tips."

Reputedly, there's a frog in Australia that excretes a hallucenogenic slime. Natives lick it to get high.

Film for frog-fans: *Frogs*, a ludicrous 1972 horror flick starring Ray Milland. "Thousands of frogs overrun a remote, inhabited island off the southern U.S. coast, devouring any human who gets in their way." An absolutely ribbeting film.

The hamburgers McDonald's serves in a week equal more than 16,000 head of cattle.

THE NAME IS FAMILIAR

Some people have achieved immortality because their names have become product brand names. You already know the names—now here are the people.

King C. Gillette. William Painter—the man who invented the bottle cap—suggested that Gillette, a traveling salesman, invent something that people could use a few times and throw away. In 1895, while cursing his dull razor, Gillette realized that disposable razors would be a perfect invention. Devising a thin enough blade was the problem; Gillette tinkered with 700 blades and 51 razors before getting it right in 1903. Within three years, he was selling over 500,000 blades annually.

Sir Joseph Lister. Even before the mouthwash that bears his name was invented, Lister fought germs; he campaigned against filthy hospitals and against doctors who performed surgery in their street clothes. When St. Louis chemist Joseph Lawrence invented the famous mouthwash, he named it 'Listerine' both to honor and to take advantage of Lister's well-known obsession with cleanliness .

Clarence Birdseye. Brooklyn-born "Bob" Birdseye was the first person to figure out how to freeze fresh food and still preserve its taste and nutrition. Birdseye's insight came from an Arctic expedition; he observed that Caribou meat, quickly frozen in the sub-zero temperatures, retained its flavor when cooked months later. He returned to America and worked for years to develop a quick-freezing process. When he succeeded in 1929, he sold his invention for the then-enormous sum of $22 million; Birdseye foods still bears his name.

Charles Fleischmann. An Austrian native who first visited the United States during the Civil War, he found our bread almost as appalling as our political situation. At the time bread was mostly home-baked, using yeast made from potato peelings, and its taste was unpredictable. The next time he came to America,

Fleischmann brought along samples of the yeast used to make Viennese bread. In 1868, he began to sell his yeast in compressed cakes of uniform size that removed the guesswork from baking. In 1937, yeast sales reached $20 million a year. After Prohibition ended, Fleischmann and his brother Maximillian found another use for their yeast—Fleischmann's distilled gin.

William and Andrew Smith. The makers of the Smith Brothers Cough Drops were the sons of Poughkeepsie, New York restauranteur and candymaker James Smith. In 1870, one of Smith's customers gave him a recipe for a "cough candy." Smith made a batch and quickly sold it all. People in the windswept Hudson Valley—plagued by constant colds during the long winters—clamored for more... And so the Smith family became America's cough drop kings. When copycat "Smith" cough drops appeared, the bearded brothers introduced the famous box that bears their pictures, as a means of guaranteeing authenticity.

John B. Stetson. While traveling out west in the 1850s, Stetson became adept at trapping animals and sewing the skins together, making them hats for sun protection. When he returned to Philadephia, he started a hat business for $100; his mainstay, "The Boss of the Plains" hat, became the classic symbol of the Wild West.

William Scholl. As apprentice to the local shoemaker, "Billy" Scholl's work led him to two conclusions: feet were abused, and nobody cared. So, in a burst of idealism, Scholl appointed himself the future foot doctor to the world. Strangely enough, it actually happened. By the time he became a M.D. at 22, Dr. Scholl had invented and patented his first arch support; in fact, he held over 300 patents for foot treatments and machines for making foot comfort aids. And his customers seemed to appreciate it—a widow once wrote him that she buried her husband with his "Foot-Eazers" so he would be as comfortable as he was in life. Until he died, in his eighties, Dr. Scholl devoted himself to saving the world's feet, adhering always to his credo: "Early to bed, early to rise, work like hell, and advertise."

A parking space in one New York City "condo garage" sells for $29,000.

FULLER IDEAS

Buckminster Fuller, an architect, inventor, scientist, mathematician, philosopher, and we don't know what else, was considered one of the most original thinkers of the 20th century.

"Faith is much better than belief. Belief is when someone *else* does the thinking."

"If nature had wanted you to be a specialist she'd have had you born with one eye with a microscope fastened to it."

"Either war is obsolete or men are."

"Don't oppose forces, use them."

"It struck me that nature's system must be a real beauty, because in chemistry we find that the associations are always in beautiful whole numbers—there are no fractions."

"Politics is an accessory after the fact."

"People should think things out fresh and not just accept conventional terms and the conventional way of doing things."

"God to me...is a verb, not a noun, proper or improper."

"I am a passenger on the spaceship Earth."

"The most important thing about Spaceship Earth—an instruction booklet didn't come with it."

"If we do more with less, our resources will be adequate to take care of everybody."

"The end move in politics is to pick up a gun."

"When I'm working on a problem, I never think about beauty. I think only how to solve the problem. But when I have finished, if the solution is not beautiful, I know it is wrong."

"You can't reorder the world by talking to it."

"We are not going to be able to operate our spaceship Earth successfully nor for much longer unless we see it as a whole spaceship and our fate as common. It has to be everybody or nobody."

Most tornadoes occur in May.

CLOSE CALLS

Four presidents—Abraham Lincoln (1865), James Garfield (1881), William McKinley (1901) and John F. Kennedy (1963)— have lost their lives to assassins. Others have barely escaped assassination attempts. Here are the most famous "close calls" in American history.

THE ATTEMPT: On January 30, 1835, President Andrew Jackson was in the Capitol rotunda, attending funeral services for Congressman Warren B. Davis of South Carolina. He was approached by Richard Lawrence, a 35 year-old house painter, who drew two revolvers and pointed them at the president...but both guns misfired. Jackson was so incensed that he rushed at Lawrence and started to beat him with his cane.

THE MOTIVE: Lawrence had approached Jackson a week before on the White House grounds and begged the president for money. Jackson thought he was a "harmless lunatic" and dismissed him.

THE SENTENCE: Lawrence was tried by prosecutor Francis Scott Key, author of "The Star Spangled Banner." He pled insanity, claiming he was the King of England, but the verdict was "guilty." He later died in a mental institution.

THE ATTEMPT: On October 14, 1912, former President Theodore Roosevelt was campaigning for a third term in Milwaukee, Wisconsin, running as the Progressive Party candidate. Roosevelt was approaching an automobile on his way to a speech when a New Yorker named John Schrank pulled a revolver, pointed it between two spectators, and pulled the trigger. Roosevelt staggered but didn't fall. Although there was no blood, Roosevelt's handlers begged him to go to the hospital. Roosevelt refused. "I shall deliver this speech or die," he reportedly said. And that's what he did; he delivered a fifty-minute speech to a cheering throng at the Milwaukee Auditorium. When he pulled the 100-page speech out of his vest, however, he noticed a bullet hole in it. A bullet had penetrated four inches into his body, right under his right nipple. Finally, after the speech was completed, Roosevelt consented to go to the hospital where he was treated for shock and loss of blood.

Take that, Imelda! Elizabeth I of England owned 3,000 gowns.

THE MOTIVE: Schrank claimed that William McKinley, who'd been assassinated in 1901, had revealed in a dream that Teddy Roosevelt was behind his death...and that Schrank should avenge him. Schrank had stalked Roosevelt from New Orleans to Chicago and then to Milwaukee to accomplish this.
THE SENTENCE: Schrank was later found guilty of attempted murder, and was sent to an insane asylum where he spent 32 years. He died in 1943.

THE ATTEMPT: In 1933, Guiseppe Zangara wanted to kill a president—it didn't matter which one. As it happened, Franklin D. Roosevelt had just defeated Herbert Hoover in the 1932 election and was the new president-elect. So he became Zangara's target.

Roosevelt had just finished giving a speech in Chicago when Zangara approached the podium and fired his revolver five times. One shot hit Anton Cermak, Chicago's mayor; another wounded a spectator seriously. Three others were hit—but Roosevelt was untouched. Reportedly, the mortally wounded Cermak told FDR "better me than you." He died two days after FDR's inauguration.
THE MOTIVE: Zangara was a brick-layer who had emigrated from Italy. He was a self-professed anarchist and had previously considered killing Hoover and Calvin Coolidge.
THE SENTENCE: Zangara was found guilty of murder and sentenced to the electric chair. In jail, he wrote his autobiography, which ended with "I go contented because I go for my idea. I salute all the poor of the world." On the day of his execution in Florida, Zangara became enraged when he saw that no photographers were present. He reportedly said, "No pictures? All capitalists are a lousy bunch of crooks."

THE ATTEMPT: On November 1, 1950, Harry S Truman was taking a nap at the Blair House, his temporary quarters while the White House was being restored. Outside, three policeman and a Secret Service agent were on guard when two men approached the Blair House from different directions, in an attempt to kill Truman. The first, Oscar Collazo, tried to shoot an officer, but the gun didn't fire. He eventually shot the guard in the leg and ran for the steps. Meanwhile, the other conspirator, Griselio Torresola, approached and fired at an officer, Leslie Coffert, who was hit but managed to shoot Torresola in the head. Both Coffert and Torresola died later.

THE MOTIVE: Collazo, who suffered slight injuries, later stood trial. He claimed that he and Terresola—both of whom were Puerto Rican—were fighting for Puerto Rico's independence, and hoped to get attention for their cause by assassinating Truman.

THE SENTENCE: He was found guilty and sentenced to death. In a surprise move, Truman commuted Collazo's sentence to life in prison eight days before he was scheduled to die.

THE ATTEMPT: On September 5, 1975, Lynette "Squeaky" Fromme drew a Colt .45 loaded with four bullets and aimed it at President Gerald Ford during a campaign stop in Sacramento, California. Fromme managed to squeeze the trigger but the firing chamber was empty. She was wrestled to the ground by Secret Service agents.

THE MOTIVE: Fromme, a follower of Charles Manson, had once declared, "I'll die for Charlie; I'll kill for him, I'll do whatever is necessary."

THE SENTENCE: She was tried under the post-JFK-assassination law that made any attempt on a president's life a Federal offense. She was found guilty and imprisoned. On December 24, 1987, Fromme escaped from a West Virginia prison, after hearing a rumor that Manson was dying and wanted to see her. Two days later she was apprehended on a country road.

THE ATTEMPT: On September 22, 1975, a few weeks after Fromme's attempt on Ford's life, another woman in California attempted to kill the president. The woman was Sarah Jane Moore, a 45-year old police and FBI informant, who, only the day before, had been interrogated by the police for threatening the president's life (they confiscated her .44 gun). Moore's shot at Ford was deflected by a bystander in the crowd who knocked her arm as she pulled the trigger of her .38. The shot ricocheted off a concrete wall and slightly injured a nearby cab driver.

THE MOTIVE: Moore later claimed, "it was kind of an ultimate protest against the system."

THE SENTENCE: She was convicted and jailed. Like Fromme, Moore made a jail break in 1979 but was later apprehended.

THE ATTEMPT: On March 29, 1981, John Hinckley arrived in Washington, D.C. after a three-day cross-country bus trip from Los Angeles. The next day he checked out of his hotel, went over the Washington Hilton and waited for President Reagan to come out after a speech to union representatives. When Reagan emerged from the hotel, Hinckley drew out a .22 caliber "Saturday Night Special" and fired six Devastator bullets. One shot ricocheted off a waiting limousine and struck Reagan, who later recovered.

THE MOTIVE: Apparently, it was a "gift of love" to actress Jody Foster. Hinckley left a note to Foster which said "there is a definite possibility that I will be killed in my attempt to get Reagan...I'm asking you to please look into your heart and at least give me the chance with this historical deed to gain your respect and love."

THE SENTENCE: On June 21, 1982, Hinckley was found "not guilty" of attempting to assassinate the president for reasons of insanity and was admitted to St. Elizabeth's Hospital in Washington.

P.S. There is no precedent for letting attempted assassins out of jail. None have ever been released from custody alive.

A LITTLE MORE PRESIDENTIAL TRIVIA

From Sid Frank and Arden Davis Melick's book *Presidents: Tidbits and Trivia*: "On April 10, 1865, Washington crowds, overjoyed at the news of Robert E. Lee's surrender, surged around the White House, cheering and calling for the President to make a speech.

"Abraham Lincoln appeared, quieted the throng, and promised to make a few remarks. But first, he said, turning toward the members of a band which was at the scene, he had a request. He would like the band to play 'Dixie.'

" 'Dixie?' The Confederate song? Why 'Dixie?' The crowd stirred restlessly. Was this another of Lincoln's jokes?

" ' "Dixie," ' he said, 'is one of the best tunes I have ever heard, and now we have captured it.' A mighty cheer went up from the crowd and the band played 'Dixie.' "

Check a map: Reno, Nevada is west of Los Angeles, California.

TRAVELS WITH RAY

Perplexing adventures of the brilliant egghead Ray "Weird Brain" Redel. Answers are on page 223.

One morning, "Weird Brain" Redel, the most renowned thinker of our time, called and asked if I wanted to go to the gym with him and lift weights. I have to admit that weight-lifting isn't really my bag, but the prospect of spending a few hours with a brilliant man like "Weird Brain" was too good to pass up. I agreed.

When we got there, I discovered that our trainer for the day was Charles Atlas—the guy I used to see on the back of comic books. Wow!

But even Mr. Atlas, who taught thousands of people how to keep bullies from kicking sand in their faces, couldn't resist trying push "Weird Brain" around with a little weightlifter's riddle. "Okay Brain," he said to his old buddy, "try this one: *Light as a feather, Nothing in it, But a big guy can't hold it for more than a minute.*"

"Weird Brain" rolled his eyes and said, "Charlie, you ask me that every time I come to the gym. It's the same answer as last week."

What WAS the answer?

When my friend, "Weird Brain" Redel returned from the month-long Western Hemisphere Egghead Conference in Panama, I picked him up at the airport.

"I hope you brought your 1953 Chevy panel truck," he said.

"Of course I did," I replied; "You asked me to on the phone. But I don't understand why."

"Well," "Weird Brain" explained, "As you know, I had my new pre-sotonic-zorperator along, and the only thing I could find that was big enough and padded enough to ship it in was..." I saw that horrible gleam in his eye, and I knew he was going to answer me in a riddle. "Was *what?*' I shuddered. He replied: "*The man who made it didn't want it, the man who bought it didn't use it, the man who used it didn't know it.*"

What did "Weird Brain" use for a shipping crate?

There are more teenage girl smokers than teenage boy smokers.

INVASION! PART II

Most invasions of the U.S. aren't any big deal, except as footnotes in history...and as excellent bathroom reading (although we're sure that wasn't on anyone's mind at the time). Take these invasions, for example:

THE INVADERS: Pancho Villa and his guerilla army.

THE DATE: March 9, 1916.

BACKGROUND: Many folk heroes—Emiliano Zapata and Albert Obregon, for instance—emerged during the Mexican revolution in 1910. But the most notorious was a former cattle rustler named Francisco "Pancho" Villa. To the people of Chihuahua, Mexico's largest state, he and his guerilla army of 40,000 men seemed like Robin Hood, stealing from rich landlords and giving to the poor.

At first, the U.S. government supported Villa and his outlaw army. But after the war was won, Washington was forced to ally itself with a single faction of the splintered Mexican revolutionary movement...and it chose Villa's rival, Venustian Carranza. Villa was furious. He felt betrayed, and decided to retaliate against the U.S.

THE INVASION: Villa led an army of 1500 guerrillas across the border and attacked the 13th U.S. Cavalry in Columbus, New Mexico. During the raid, Villa's men killed 18 Americans, burned down several buildings, and stole a quantity of weapons. But as they retreated across the border into Mexico, 50 of Villa's troops were killed by U.S. Army personnel.

AFTERMATH: The American public was seething. U.S. president Woodrow Wilson responded to the attack by ordering John J. "Black Jack" Pershing to cross the Mexican border and capture Villa. The so-called "Punitive Expedition" was a dismal failure; the nimble Villa eluded Pershing's troops. Months later, the American army gave up and retreated emptyhanded. Pershing later claimed the campaign had given his men field experience for future battles in World War I.

Villa was assassinated in Parral, South Chihuahua in 1923.

THE INVADERS: Eight Nazi terrorists.

THE DATES: June 13 and June 17, 1942.

BACKGROUND: In early 1942, German U-boats were a menacing presence in the waters off the East Coast. Fearing a secret Nazi invasion, the U.S. ordered the approaches to harbors in New York, Boston, and Portland, Maine to be mined.

U.S. authorities had no inkling, however, that the invasion being planned by Nazi strategists involved only eight men—specially trained terrorists with instructions to bomb selected factories and bridges and shake the confidence of the American public.

THE INVASION: On the night of June 13, four Nazi agents rowed a collapsible boat from a German U-boat to a beach in Amagansett, Long Island. Fortunately for the U.S. John C. Cullen, a 21-year-old second class seaman in the Coast Guard, stumbled onto the four Germans while patrolling the beach. The nervous Nazis claimed to be shipwrecked fisherman.

Cullen was suspicious, particularly when the group's leader, Johann Dasch, tried to bribe Cullen with $300 to shut up. Cullen took the money and rushed back to Coast Guard headquarters to tell his superiors. The FBI instantly rushed in and found a cache of weapons and explosives that the Germans had buried on the beach. An extensive search was conducted but the agents had already fled.

Four days later, another Nazi foursome landed without detection on the beach of Ponte Vedra, Florida.

AFTERMATH: Dasch, leader of the Nazi mission, was unnerved by his run-in with Cullen. The Nazi spy convinced his partner E.P Burger to abandon their intricately conceived plan. The duo traveled to Washington, D.C., and turned themselves in to the FBI.

Thanks to Dasch's information, FBI officials tracked down the other six Nazis before they could carry out their mission. Dasch and Burger were sentenced to jail (Truman later commuted their sentences and sent them back to Germany, where Dasch wrote a book about the mission). The other six were executed within a month of their capture, before the public was informed.

BEN FRANKLIN SPEAKLIN': "Our Constitution is in actual operation; everything promises that it will last; but in this world nothing is certain but death and taxes."

DISNEY STORIES: CINDERELLA

In 1949, Uncle Walt released the musical cartoon version of Cinderella, which "combined realism with caricature." The people—Cinderella, her family, and the Prince, were drawn from life; the animals were just cartoon characters. Of course, the Disney version and the original story were substantially different. Here are Jim Morton's examples of how the tale was changed:

THE DISNEY VERSION

Cinderella is horribly mistreated by her mean step-mother and step-sisters. She's stuck dreaming while she scrubs floors.

• When the Prince holds a ball for the women of the Kingdom, trying to find a wife, Cinderella isn't allowed to go—she has to finish her chores. But Cinderella's Fairy Godmother appears. With her magic wand (bibbety, bobbety, boo), the Fairy turns a pumpkin into a coach and makes a beautiful gown for the girl. She warns Cinderella to be home by midnight; that's when the spell wears off.

• When the Prince sees Cinderella he immediately falls in love, and spends the entire evening with her. Cinderella loses all track of time; before she knows it, the clock strikes twelve. She flees the palace, leaving behind only a glass slipper.

• The Prince searches his Kingdom for the woman whose foot fits the glass slipper. The step-sisters try to squeeze into it, but can't. When Cinderella tries it on, the Prince realizes she's the one he's looking for. They marry and live happily ever after.

THE ORIGINAL STORY

• Most people don't realize there are two popular versions of Cinderella (it's actually a very old folktale, and there are dozens of variations all over Europe). Disney's film is a remarkably accurate retelling of Charles Perrault's version. But what about kids who don't have the Perrault fairy tales around the house and turn, instead, to the Brothers Grimm version? Boy, are they in for a surprise!

• The differences between the Perrault and the Grimm versions are startling. The Grimm tale is so gruesome it approaches Grand Guignol, and has more in common with Alfred Hitchcock's *The Birds* than it does with the Disney film.

• There is no Fairy Godmother in the Grimm story. Cinderella is helped by two pigeons, who bring her a gown and slippers, and help with her chores. The slippers in the Grimm version are gold, not glass. (In other versions, the slippers are made of fur.)

• It's not a ball, but a three-day festival, that Cinderella attends. So the Prince has three chances to find her, and narrows the search down to one household—he doesn't have to try the shoe on every woman in the kingdom. (Cinderella doesn't lose her slipper by chance, either. On the third day of the festival, the Prince, after losing Cinderella on two previous occasions, has the palace stairway coated with pitch.)

• When the Prince tries the gold slipper on Cinderella's stepsisters, the shoe is too small. The first step-sister cuts her big toe off to get her foot into the slipper. The second step-sister cuts her heel off to fit into the slipper. Each time, the blood on the slipper (pointed out by the two pigeons) betrays the women. Finally the Prince tries the slipper on Cinderella, and of course, it fits.

• Cinderella and the Prince marry, and at Cinderella's wedding, the pigeons appear once more and peck out the eyes of the two step-sisters. Gruesome.

SAMPLE PASSAGE (FROM THE GRIMM VERSION)

The Prince brings the gold slipper to Cinderella's house, and the step-sister tries it on first.

"The oldest took the shoe into a room to try it on, and her mother stood by her side. However, the shoe was too small for her, and she could not get her big toe into it. So her mother handed her a knife and said, 'Cut your toe off. Once you become Queen, you won't have to walk anymore.'

"The maiden cut her toe off, forced her foot into the shoe, and went out to the Prince. He took her on his horse as his bride, and rode off. But they had to pass the grave where the two pigeons were sitting on the hazel tree, and they cried out: '*Looky, look, look, At the shoe that she took; There's blood all over, and her foot's too small. She's not the bride you met at the ball.*' "

FILM TERMS

Every business has its slang. Here are some of the terms movie people use, some of which you've probably seen on screen.

Annie Oakley: A free ticket to a movie screening.
Apple Box: A box that actors stand on while filming a scene.
Best Boy: Assistant to the head gaffer (see gaffer).
Clapsticks: The wood sticks that are struck together to signify the beginning of filming a scene.
Click Track: Audible click used in musical scoring.
Dolly Shot: Wheeling the camera on tracks for motion in a film shot.
Dope Sheet: Storyboards (see storyboards) used in animation films.
Final Cut: The last edited version of a film ready for release.
Gaffer: Electrician on a film set.
The Grip: Head fix-it person on the set.
Juicer: Electrician in charge of the main power source.
Lap Dissolve: Editing together two shots, one fading in, the other fading out.
Matte Shot: Film editing technique where foreground and background images are placed together to form one shot.
Oater: A Western.
Outtake: Footage not used in final cut.
P-O-V: Acronym for point-of-view. Camera is positioned to simulate a character's line of sight.
Rear Projection: Cost-cutting filming technique where actors stand in front of a projection on a translucent screen.
Rushes: Daily screenings of footage from a work-in-progress.
SFX: Acronymn for sound effects.
Sky Pan: Huge floodlights used for large areas to be lit.
Slate: Board used with clapsticks (see left column) to identify scenes during editing.
Splice: Editing two pieces of film together.
Space Opera: Slang for science fiction film.
Storyboards: Sketches drawn to depict, shot-for-shot, the action to be filmed.
Swish Pan: Rapid camera movement causing a blurring sensation.
Weenie: A plot device that is considered to be a gimmick.
Walla Walla: Background noise in a scene.

Who suffers the most on-the-job back injuries? Garbage collectors & warehouse workers.

CARTOON CORNER

Miscellaneous facts about your favorite cartoon characters.

DAFFY DUCK

Daffy first appeared in the 1937 cartoon, "Porky's Duck Hunt." According to animator / director Chuck Jones in *Chuck Amuck,* he and his co-workers were looking for a voice to complete this new character—"a duck who enjoyed being nutty." While they were brainstorming, someone did an impression of their boss, producer Leon Schlesinger, who had a heavy lisp. Pressed for time, the crew impulsively decided to use that voice.

It wasn't until later that it occured to them what they'd done. Schlesinger would have to screen the cartoon and approve the new character—lisp and all. He wasn't going to think it was funny to hear his own voice coming from the duck.

Expecting to be fired, the animators wrote out their resignations and took them to the cartoon's first screening. Schlesinger arrived, the lights were dimmed, and at the producer's cry of "Roll the garbage!" Daffy Duck lit up the screen. A few minutes later, the lights went back on and all eyes focused on Schlesinger. His reaction? Jones recalls: "He said, 'Jesus Crithe, that's a funny voithe! Where'd you get that voithe?' "...He didn't have a clue!

FELIX THE CAT

You may find it hard to believe, but Felix was the first cartoon superstar—the Mickey Mouse of the silent film years. In 1919 he appeared in a short called "Feline Follies," and was so popular that Pat Sullivan's production studio could barely keep up with the demand. They turned out 26 cartoons a year—one every two weeks. Among Felix's early achievements:

- In 1922 he appeared as the New York Yankees' lucky mascot.
- In 1923, he shared the screen with Charlie Chaplin.
- In 1927, a Felix doll was Charles Lindbergh's companion on his historic trans-Atlantic flight.
- In 1928, he became the first image ever to appear on TV. When the first experimental television broadcast occurred, the subject was a Felix doll.

So what happened? Why didn't Felix remain popular? Like a lot of movie-industry people, Felix's owner, Pat Sullivan didn't believe in "talkies." So silent star Felix the Cat was eclipsed by the new talking cartoons.

YOGI BEAR

When Hanna-Barbera produced Jellystone's smarter-than-the-average-bear, New York Yankees catcher Yogi Berra threated to sue them. The grounds: Among other things, defamation of character. Although everyone in America made the connection between Yogi and Yogi, a Hanna-Barbera executive producer swore "it was just a coincidence." He said the character was inspired by Ed Norton (Art Carney), the next-door neighbor in "The Honeymooners."

HUEY, LOUIE, & DEWEY

This is one of the greatest "naming" stories we've ever heard. It comes from a fascinating book called *Cartoon Monickers*, by Walter M. Brasch.

"One day in the late 1930s, Harry Reeves, a gagman working on the Donald Duck cartoons, burst into the work area of Jim Carmichael, a layout man, proclaiming, 'Jim, we've got three new characters. Donald's nephews. And we're gonna work them into a lot of screwy situations with the duck. But we haven't got name for 'em. Got any ideas for naming three cute li'l ducks?"

"Carmichael recalls that he 'wasn't too interested that morning in the nomenclature of three cute li'l ducks, so I glanced at the front page of the newspaper...Thomas E. Dewey was doing something political in New York, and Huey P. Long was blabbering in New Orleans. So, off-handedly, I said, 'Why don't you call them Huey and Dewey?' A friend, Louie Schmitt, was passing in the hall and gave a big hello. Inspired, I said, 'Hell, call the little clunkers Huey, Louie, and Dewey.' Harry leaped up, yelping 'That's it!' "

POPEYE

The sailor man was a popular comic strip character before he made his screen appearance—in an early '30s Betty Boop cartoon. A few years later, in 1936, he won an Oscar for *Sinbad the Sailor*. If the dialogue between Popeye and Olive Oyle often seems informal, it's because a lot of it was ad-libbed.

Spectators drink more than 1,800 gallons of mint julips at each Kentucky Derby.

THE OLD BALL GAME

Baseball's unofficial anthem, "Take Me Out To The Ballgame," is one of the best-known songs in America. But only a few trivia buffs know the story behind it. Here it is:

THE WORDS: In the summer of 1908, a vaudevillian named Jack Norworth was riding the New York City subway when he noticed an advertisement that read "Baseball Today—Polo Grounds." He'd never been to a baseball game, but he knew the sport was getting popular...and it hit him that a baseball song might fit into his act. Inspired, he jotted down some lyrics about a woman named Katie who was crazy about baseball games.

THE MUSIC: Norworth rushed to the office of a music-publisher friend named Albert von Tilzer. Von Tilzer had never seen a baseball game either, but he quickly set the words to music.

THE FLOP: Norworth was convinced he had a hit...But when he sang "Take Me Out To The Ballgame" during his vaudeville act in Brooklyn that night, the crowd seemed bored. No one complained ...but no one paid much attention to it, either.

THE HIT: So Norworth tried a different approach; he turned the song into a "Nickelodeon slide show"—a sort of turn-of-the-century MTV. Slide shows, featuring sing-along lyrics and illustrations (in this case, photos of pretty Miss Katie Casey at a Polo Grounds game), were shown at movie theaters between films. Audiences "followed the bouncing ball," and sang along. Norworth's ploy worked. "Take Me Out To The Ballgame" became a hit. Ironically, it wasn't until *after* the song was popular that Norworth finally went to an "old ballgame."

THE MISSING LINK: Everybody knows the chorus to "Take Me Out To The Ballgame." But here are the verses: *Katie Casey was baseball mad. Had the fever and had it bad. Just to root for the hometown crew, Ev'ry sou, Katie blew. On a Saturday her young beau, Called to see if she'd like to go. To see a show but Miss Kate said "No I tell you what you can do..."*

LOOSE ENDS

What would a Bathroom Reader be without flushing out some new information on toilets?

TOILET ART

Two toilets have figured prominently in the art world:

• Marcel Duchamp rocked the art world in 1917 when he made a urinal into sculpture by turning it upside down and signing it "R. Mutt." The piece, entitled "The Fountain," upset an art committee's dignified sensibilites—they refused to exhibit it. According to the *New York Times*, however, the work "is now considered a masterwork," although it exists only in a photograph taken by Alfred Stieglitz.

• Another "art toilet" surfaced in 1985 when a three-hole outhouse seat was discovered to have been "painted" by famed artist Willem de Kooning in 1954. Apparently, de Kooning splattered some paint on the seat to make it resemble a marble surface as a joke for a party he was throwing in a rented home in Bridgehampton, New York. An art dealer spotted the 22" X 99" toilet seat in an auction, and bought it for $50. Theoretically, the three-seater could be worth millions, which is how much de Kooning's regular work sells for.

LOOK OUT BELOW

Gene Gordon of Fort Worth, Texas was in his backyard in late 1987 when he heard a loud bang in his house. He checked it out, and found a large hole in his roof and chunks of blue ice melting in his attic. After an investigation, it was determined that the ice originated from an airplane toilet. Apparently, blue cleaning fluid had leaked from the airplane's toilet, frozen in mid-air, and dropped to earth.

THE BOTTOM LINE

• In 1985, Lockheed Corporation charged the U.S. government $34,560 for 54 toilet seats (or about $600 a piece) for the Navy's P-3C Orion anti-submarine planes. When government officals told

Lockheed that the same seat could be purchased by mobile-home owners for $25, the price was lowered to $100 apiece.

• The most expensive toilet ever made was the one developed for the space shuttle. The price tag for NASA's waste collector: $3,000,000.

LOO-SELY SPEAKING

The popular British slang for *toilet* is the "loo." Where did the term come from? One theory suggests its roots are in a pay toilet with an L-shaped handle followed by two O-shaped coin slots—spelling out the word "loo." A more plausible explanation: it derives from the phrase "gardyloo," which Scottish people shouted before throwing trash out of the window and onto the street. Another longshot: it's a pun on the words "water closet" and "Waterloo."

EXPENSIVE TOILET PAPER

Billy Edd Wheeler, the country songwriter who penned "Coward of the County" for Kenny Rogers, also wrote a little gem of a book called *Outhouse Humor* (published by August House).

Here's a sample joke from the volume:

"At a filling station near Bland, Virginia, before they got indoor plumbing, customers had to use the outhouse if they wanted to go to the bathroom.

Actually, they had two outhouses under one roof, with side doors, but they were separated in the middle only by a partition built about a foot off the floor, and running up to about six feet...similar to the rows of stalls in restrooms in airports.

One time two men were in this outhouse at the same time. After one man finished going he noticed there wasn't any toilet paper left on the spool, so he pecked on the wall and said, 'Hey bud, would you kindly share some of your paper with me? This one's empty over here.' The voice came back from the other side: 'Sorry, pal, but there ain't much left over here, either. I'm afraid there's just enough for me.'

A few minutes passed. There was another peck on the wall, and the first man said, 'Uh, buddy...you ain't got five ones for a five, have you? Or maybe two fives for a ten?' "

BLUE SUEDE SHOES

And now, the mystery of the most famous pair of shoes in rock 'n' roll history.

Pop culture is full of contradictions. Stories about the beginnings of fads, products, books and songs are fun to tell, but you can't be sure if they're true. To illustrate the point, here are two versions of the origin of the rock'n'roll classic, "Blue Suede Shoes," each told by believable sources. One, Carl Perkins, wrote the tune. The other, Johnny Cash, has been a friend of Perkins' since the days when "Blue Suede" was recorded. If anyone should know the story, Carl should. But Johnny Cash seems to be pretty sure about his version, too. We'll never know exactly which of these stories is true.

STORY A—*"Blue Suede Shoes," according to Carl Perkins*: On December 4, 1955, a Jackson, Tennessee musician named Carl Perkins played at a local dance tht changed his life. "[I was] playin' a club in my hometown," he remembers, "for a high school sorority dance. A beautiful girl was dancin' with a boy who had on a pair of blue suede shoes...He said, 'Uh-uh, don't step on my suedes!' "

Carl couldn't believe it—this kid was with a gorgeous girl, but all he cared about were his shoes! What a nut! When the dance ended, Perkins went home and went to sleep. And then at 3:00 A.M. he suddenly awoke with a song in his head. He jumped out of bed, grabbed the first piece of paper he could find—which happened to be a brown paper potato sack—and wrote down the lyrics to "Blue Suede Shoes."

STORY B—*"Blue Suede Shoes," according to Johnny Cash*: Carl Perkins and Johnny Cash were part of Sam Phillips' fabled Sun Records stable, which included Jerry Lee Lewis, Roy Orbison, and a certain Mr. Elvis Presley. One night, Cash, Presley and Perkins were performing in Amory, Mississippi. Cash and Perkins had already done their shows and Presley was onstage. In the wings, Cash told Perkins that he really had a "feel for the 'bop' kind of song," and asked why didn't he record one? Perkins said he'd tried, but he could never come up with the right song. So Cash gave him an idea for a tune. He told Carl a story about his Air Force days. His sergeant, Cash said, was a black man named C. V. White, who was always immaculately dressed. White would come into Cash's room and ask how he looked. After Cash replied, White would say, "Just don't step on my blue suede shoes," and leave the room. Cash would yell after him that those were Air Force regulation shoes, not blue suede, and White would say, "Tonight when I get to town they're gonna be blue suede, man!" Perkins exclaimed, "That's a great idea for a bop song!" He grabbed a pencil and before Elvis was offstage, Perkins had written it.

FOR THE RECORD

• The original intro was "One for the money, two for the show, three to get ready and go, man, go." As they were recording, Perkins said "Go, cat, go" instead. The record producer asked, "This word 'cat,' what did you mean?" Perkins: "I have no idea where it came from." "Cat" was actually a slang word for "black person."

• Released on New Year's Day, 1956, "Blue Suede" took about three months to break out of the South. By March it was headed for the top of all three music charts (Pop, Country, R&B). But as Perkins was driving to appear on "The Perry Como Show," where he was to make his first national appearance and receive his gold record for "Blue Suede," he got into a serious car accident that killed one of his brothers and put him in the hospital. His interrupted career was never the same again.

THE TOP FIVE—Week of April 21, 1956

1. **Heartbreak Hotel**
   —Elvis Presley
2. **Hot Diggity Dog/Jukebox Baby**
   —Perry Como
3. **Poor People of Paris**
   —Les Baxter
4. **Blue Suede Shoes**
   —Carl Perkins
5. **Lisbon Antiqua**
   —Nelson Riddle & His Orchestra

PRIMETIME PROVERBS

Here are some more TV quotes from the book Primetime Proverbs, *by Jack Mingo and John Javna.*

ON GOD

"God don't make no mistakes—that's how he got to be God."

—Archie Bunker,
All in the Family

"Well, I certainly don't believe God's a woman, because if He were, men would be the ones walking around wearing high heels, taking Midol, and having their upper lips waxed."

—Julia Sugarbaker,
Designing Women

Archie Bunker: "All the pictures I ever seen, God is white."
George Jefferson: "Maybe you were looking at the negatives."

—All in the Family

ON BOOZE

"Never cry over spilt milk. It could've been whiskey."

—Pappy Maverick,
Maverick

"Oh, I just adore beer. It's so... so...democratic."

—Kookie's Girlfriend,
77 Sunset Strip

ON THE ARMY

"What other job lets you die for a living?"

—Hawkeye Pierce,
M*A*S*H*

THE RICH

"He's got a purse the size of an elephant's scrotum, and it's just as hard to get your hands on."

—Edmund Blackadder,
Blackadder II

[*To Mama's rich boyfriend*]
"It's a pleasure to meet a man of your charming credit rating."

—Kingfish,
Amos'n'Andy

SKEWERED SAYINGS

"You've buttered your bread, now sleep in it."

—Gracie Allen,
The George Burns and Gracie Allen Show

"People in stucco houses should not throw quiche."

—Sonny Crockett,
Miami Vice

BEWITCHED

From 1964 to 1972, Elizabeth Montgomery starred in TV's "Bewitched" as Samantha Stevens, the perky blonde housewitch who could take care of household chores with a twitch of her nose.

HOW IT STARTED

In 1942, Veronica Lake starred in the title role of a movie comedy called *I Married a Witch*. The plot: an upright, middle-class American guy discovers his bride is literally an enchanting young woman.

In 1958, Kim Novak played a witch with her sights set on future husband James Stewart in the romantic comedy, *Bell, Book and Candle*.

In 1963, William Dozier and Harry Ackerman, two executives at Screen Gems TV, decided to make a suburban family sitcom with a "brand new" twist: The husband unwittingly marries a pretty, young witch. Well it was new for TV, anyway.

They wrote the pilot script and took it to Tammy Grimes, an English actress who'd been starring in Broadway's "The Unsinkable Molly Brown." Grimes had a TV contract with Screen Gems, didn't like the script, but she refused to say whether she'd do the show or not. "Why not rewrite it," she suggested, infuriating Dozier. But he obliged; commissioning a new script.

While he was waiting, Dozier got a call from an old friend he'd been dying to work with—Liz Montgomery. Liz, it seems, had fallen in love with a TV director named William Asher and the two of them wanted to spend all their time together—so they were interested in a TV show in which she could star, while he directed. Dozier immediately decided that Montgomery would make the perfect witch, but he couldn't offer her the part in "Bewitched" ("I couldn't even mention it,")—he was already committed to Tammy Grimes.

Fortunately, Grimes didn't like the new script either. She held out for a show in which she played the part of a befuddled English heiress. (It went on the air as "The Tammy Grimes Show," and lasted about two months.) Montgomery, meanwhile, took the part of Samantha, and "Bewitched" became the hottest new show of 1964. It was in the Top 10 for five straight years.

Most Oscars: Walt Disney won 20.

JUST KIDDING

When filming for the show began, Liz Montgomery was eight months pregnant. So Asher (by now her husband, as well as the director), had to shoot the first five shows without her, adding in her parts later. A few weeks after the baby was born, Montgomery was out on the set making up for lost time.

THE NOSE KNOWS

Some people can wiggle their ears. Elizabeth Montgomery can wiggle her nose. (It's not as easy as it looks—try it.) "Bewitched" 's producers put the trick to good use by making Sam's nose her magic wand. No one else on the show could do it, so they had to settle for hand gestures, or—in the case of Tabitha (the daughter), moving her nose with her finger.

MOON SHOT

Agnes Moorhead, who played Sam's mother, Endora, was invited to Cape Kennedy by NASA to witness the Apollo 12 moon flight in 1969. She was the honorary "technical advisor," since, as Endora, she had been on the moon herself. "I distinctly remember," she said, "being on the moon at least 7 times over the past 6 years."

WHICH WITCH?

Moorhead didn't particulary like being known as "the witch." That was understandable. She was 57 and had been performing for over 50 years when she first appeared as Endora. She had starred in almost 100 films, won an Emmy, and was nominated for 5 Oscars. She died of lung cancer in 1974, ten years later.

DARRIN'S LUCK

Viewers often ask why there were two different actors playing Darrin Stephens, Samantha's husband. Here's why: After 5 seasons as Darrin, actor Dick York had to withdraw from the series because of serious back pains. It turns out that in 1959, while working on a film with Gary Cooper, he sustained a back injury, tearing all the muscles loose from his spine. Over the years the pain got worse and by the time York got to "Bewitched," the injury had become so debilitating that he missed 14 episodes of the show.Then one day he had a seizure; he was rushed to the hospital and never returned to "Bewitched" again. He was replaced by Dick Sargent.

Racehorses don't run any faster than ostriches.

FAMOUS LAST WORDS

When you gotta go, you gotta go. Here are some final quotes from people who really knew how to make an exit.

"I'll be in hell before you've finished breakfast, boys...Let her rip!"

—"Black Jack" Ketchum, ***murderer, before being hanged***

"The Countess Rouen sends her compliments but begs to be excused. She is engaged in dying."

—The Countess Rouen, ***in a letter read by her attendant to her guests***

"Go away...I'm alright."

—H. G. Wells, ***writer***

"God bless...God damn. . ."

—James Thurber, ***writer***

"If this is dying, I don't think much of it."

—Lytton Strachey, ***writer***

"Four o'clock. How strange. So that is the time. Strange. Enough."

—Sir Henry Stanley, ***explorer***

"You sons of bitches. Give my love to mother."

—"Two Gun" Crowley, ***sitting on the electric chair***

"Now comes the mystery."

—Henry Ward Beecher, ***preacher***

"Oh God, here I go."

—Max Baer, ***boxer***

"Friends applaud, the Comedy is over."

—Ludwig van Beethoven

"All my possessions for a moment of time."

—Elizabeth I, ***Queen of England***

"And now, in keeping with Channel 40's policy of always bringing you the latest in blood and guts, in living color, you're about to see another first—an attempted suicide."

—Chris Hubbock, ***newscaster who shot herself during broadcast***

"Drink to me."

—Pablo Picasso

"Why yes— a bullet-proof vest."

—James Rodgers, ***murderer, before the firing squad, asked if he had final request***

Lip Service: Reuters News Service gave its founder a 17-word obituary.

ASTEROIDS

At the B.R.I. Science Department, we have a saying: A day without Bathroom Reading is like a pain in the asteroid. Ah, but what do we really know about asteroids? Read on...

BACKGROUND

• Asteroids are collections of rocks and dust half a mile or more in diameter. Scientists theorize they are leftover fragments from the Big Bang.

• Most asteroids orbit the sun in a large belt between Mars and Jupiter. Over a billion fragments reside in the belt, ranging from dust-sized particles to Ceres, an asteroid 637 miles in diameter.

• How do asteroids escape the asteroid belt? Through the Kirkwood Gap, named for Daniel Kirkwood, an American astronomer. He discovered that the belt was separated into two different regions by a mysterious gap. Asteroids that enter the gap shift into an orbit closer to Earth's. One out of five asteroids end up crossing Earth's orbit.

A MISS IS AS GOOD AS 500,000 MILES

On March 23, 1989, a huge asteroid passed within half a million miles (approximately twice the distance from the Earth to the Moon) of hitting the Earth. If the asteroid, which was traveling at 46,000 miles an hour, had actually crashed into Earth, it would have had a devastating impact, equivalent to exploding 20,000 one-megaton hydrogen bombs.

Scientists later calculated that the asteroid missed the Earth by six hours in its orbit. If it had hit Earth, the crater would have been 10 miles long and one mile deep.

ASTEROIDS IN THE PAST

• The first scientific finding that proved asteroids were not pieces of alien spacecraft occurred in 1803 in northern France.

• In 1908, an asteroid the size of a small building crashed near the Stony Tunguska River in Siberia. Its force was later measured to be equal to 12 megatons of TNT.

Aztec Indians used a breed of small, hairless dogs to keep their feet warm.

• In 1984, a Japan Air Lines flight saw a mushroom-like cloud 70,000 feet tall and 200 miles wide. The flight landed at a U.S. base in Anchorage, Alaska for fear it had flown through radiation, but no traces were found. Eventually, scientists concluded that the airliner may have passed through a cloud created by an exploding meteor.

• Scientists have found evidence of a huge asteroid collision around 100 miles off the coast of New Jersey from 34 million ago.

• An asteroid named Icarus came within four million miles of hitting Earth in 1968. This "near miss" prompted the notion that nuclear missiles could be deployed to deflect oncoming asteroids. In 1982, a scientific conference in Colorado concluded that a one-kilometer asteroid could be diverted by the using a nuclear device only half the power of the atomic bomb dropped on Hiroshima.

THE ODDS

• According to the *New York Times*, there are more than 80 asteroids of at least one kilometer that could threaten the Earth. Other scientists estimate there are over 1,000 asteroids with orbits that could collide with Earth's.

• Despite the danger, scientists say the chances of a giant asteroid colliding with Earth in our lifetime are relatively small—it only happens once every 100,000 years or so.

THE EFFECTS

• Scientists have argued that asteroid impacts in the past may have caused the Earth's magnetic field to reverse, triggering the ice age and ultimately continental drift, the breaking up of the continents 80 million years ago.

• The biggest recorded asteroid hit Earth 66 million years ago and spread lava over India. Some scientists have argued that its enormous impact eventually wiped out the dinosaurs by enveloping the Earth in dust and smoke, causing the Earth to cool.

• The dinosaur/asteroid theory arose after the discovery of the element iridium in the same geologic layers that existed when the dinosaurs disappeared. Iridium is abundant in asteroids.

On average, Salt Lake City citizens consume more Cracker Jacks than any other Americans.

IT'S THE LAW

Believe it or not, these laws are real.

In Logan County, Colorado, it's illegal to kiss a sleeping woman.

It's illegal to ride a camel on Nevada highways.

In North Carolina motels, it's a crime to move twin beds together or to make love on the floor.

In Miami, Florida, it's unlawful to imitate an animal.

Women in Morrisville, Pennsylvania, are required by law to purchase a permit before wearing lipstick in public.

Laws in Indianapolis, Indiana, and Eureka, Nevada, make it a crime to kiss if you wear a moustache.

New York City law entitles its horses to a 15 minute "coffee-break" after each two hours of work.

Children are prohibited from doing handstands on Denver, Colorado sidewalks—it might frighten horses.

It's a crime in Zion, Illinois to offer a cigar to a dog, cat, or any pet. No mention of cigarettes or pipes.

Laws in Boston, Massachusetts prohibit sleeping in "day clothes."

If your horse is ugly, the law prohibits you from riding it down a street in Wilbur, Washington.

In Minnesota, it's illegal for a woman to be dressed-up as Santa Claus on city streets.

Kansas law prohibits catching fish with your bare hands.

Arkansas law prohibits schoolteachers with "bob" hairdos from getting raises.

Don't even think about it—*Bull throwing* is illegal in Washington D.C.

You're breaking the law if you're wearing "form-fitting" pants in Lewes, Delaware.

A law in Hartford, Connecticut, prohibits the teaching or education of a dog.

OPEN & CLOTHED

A few interesting tidbits about clothing.

BLUE FOR BOYS, PINK FOR GIRLS

The blue comes from an ancient superstition—the pink is sort of an afterthought.

According to *How Did They Do That?*, "The choice of blue dates back to ancient times, when evil spirits purportedly plagued young children but could be warded off with certain colors: blue, emblematic of the heavens, had an immanent power to dispel satanic forces (Many Arabs in the Mideast continue to paint their doorways blue.) Since it was of paramount importance to protect little boys, they were clothed in blue, while little girls were left to fend for themselves. Only much later did parents, somewhat guilty about the girls' lack of identity, assign them precious pink."

SUPERMAN'S CLOTHING

Every time George Reeves, TV's Superman, donned his costume for a public appearance, he risked kicks in the shins, fists in his back, and other assaults by young admirers eager to prove how strong the "Man of Steel" really was.

One afternoon in Detroit in 1953, the costume almost cost Reeves his life. He was making an appearance at a department store when a young fan pulled out his father's loaded .45 Army Colt and pointed it directly at Reeves's chest. Miraculously, Reeves talked the kid into putting it down. He assured the boy that Superman could stand the force of the shot, but "when bullets bounce off my chest, they might hurt you and others around here."

CHARLIE CHAPLIN'S TRAMP OUTFIT

In 1914, director Mack Sennet told Chaplin to "get into a comedy makeup." He scouted the dressing room and came up with baggy pants and derby belonging to the enormously overweight comedian, Fatty Arbuckle, a cutaway jacket from Roscoe Conklin, and a pair of size-14 shoes from Ford Sterling. They were so big that the only way to keep them on was to wear them on the wrong feet. The cane was the only thing Chaplin actually owned.

On July 22, 1972, a lady in Rome gave birth to quindecaplets—10 girls and 5 boys.

KUNG PHOOEY

Is it serious philosophy or TV gobbledygook? You be the judge of these quotes from TV's only "Buddhist" western, "Kung Fu."

"Grasshopper, look beyond the game, as you look beneath the surface of the pool to see its depths."

—Master Po

"The caterpillar is secure in the womb of the cocoon. And yet—to achieve its destiny—it must cast off its earthbound burden...to realize the ethereal beauty of the butterfly."

—Master Po

Master Po: "What have I told you, Grasshopper?"
Caine: "That life is a corridor and death merely a door."

"The blossom below the water knows not sunlight. And men, not knowing, will find me hard to understand."

—Caine

"Will shooting guns and making bombs make you men and not dogs?"

—Caine

"Seek always peace...We are all linked by our souls, and if one is endangered so are all."

—Caine

"To seek freedom, a man must struggle. To win it, he must choose wisely where and when he struggles, or it is like spitting in the wind."

—Caine

Caine: "Master Kan, what is it to be a man?"
Master Kan: "To be a man is to be one with the Universe."
Caine: "But what is the Universe?"
Master Kan: "Rather ask: what is *not* the Universe?"

"Remember always—a wise man walks with his head bowed, humble like the dust."

—Master Po

"The power to hope cannot be taken away with guns or fences."

—Caine

"Perceive the way of nature and no force of men can harm you. Do not meet a wave head-on, avoid it. You do not have to stop force; it is easier to redirect it."

—A monk

There are twice as many heart attacks in winter as in summer.

DON'T LOOK NOW

Here's a look at a few of the movies that have been banned in the U.S. over the last 75 years.

SPIRIT OF '76 (1917). A silent propaganda film made to enlist public support for America's entry into World War I. The film reenacted Revolutionary War events, like Paul Revere's ride and the signing of the Declaration of Independence.

One scene depicted British soldiers attacking women and children. Although the scene was realistic, England was America's ally in the war effort, so it was considered treasonous. Authorities seized the movie, alleging (erroneously) that the movie had been financed by Germans. The film's producer, Robert Goldstein—who later became an executive at 20th Century Fox—was convicted of violating the Espionage Act and was sentenced to jail (his sentence was later commuted by Woodrow Wilson).

THE NAKED TRUTH (1924). A silent movie about a man who gets venereal disease and marries. His brain is affected by V.D. and he kills his wife. Nudity, not subject matter, got this film banned in Newark, New Jersey due to a brief scene in which a male and female were shown partially naked.

Note: one of the main figures in the controversy, William J. Brennan (head of Newark's Public Safety Department), was the father of future Supreme Court Justice, William J. Brennan, Jr. Brennan upheld the censorship by refusing to see it and review the case. *The Naked Truth* was also banned in New York.

THE MAN WITH THE GOLDEN ARM (1955). Banned in Maryland for depicting drug use. The film, directed by Otto Preminger, was about a card shark (played by Frank Sinatra) who becomes a drug addict. The Maryland Board of Censors suggested that United Artists cut the scene of Sinatra being injected by a drug pusher. According to the *Historical Dictionary of Censorship in the United States*, the state of Maryland "was the only locality that attempted to censor this film: It was exhibited across the United States and Western Europe without problems, and even won a scientific and cultural award in the Netherlands." United Artists sued and a judge reversed the order.

TITICUT FOLLIES (1969). A documentary on the horrible conditions in a state prison for the criminally insane in Bridgewater, Massachusetts. Scenes included a forced nose-feeding of an inmate on a hunger strike.

Producer and director Frederick Wiseman received permission to make the film as long as he protected the privacy of the film's subjects. However, when the documentary was shown commercially, the state of Massachusetts filed suit, contending the film had violated their contract and the inmates' privacy. Massachusetts won, and the Supreme Court refused to hear an appeal. The result: The documentary was put under permanent court restrictions. Selected audiences were allowed to view the film as long as profits were put into a trust fund for the inmates.

Wiseman later commented, "There was no evidence introduced at the trial that the film was not an honest portrayal of the conditions...if [then State Attorney General Elliot] Richardson and the other politicians in Massachusetts were genuinely concerned about the privacy and dignity of the inmates of Bridgewater, they would not have allowed the conditions that are shown in the film to exist. They were more concerned about the film and its effect on their reputations than they were about Bridgewater."

CINDY AND DONNA (1970). The Sheriff of Pulaski Country, Kentucky went to see this X-rated film at a drive-in. After staying for the entire motion picture, the Sheriff arrested the manager of the theatre and confiscated the film. The manager was convicted of exhibiting an obscene film. He appealed to the Supreme Court, which overturned the conviction on the grounds that no warrant had been served.

CARNAL KNOWLEDGE (1971). This film starring Jack Nicholson, Art Garfunkle, Candice Bergen, and Ann-Margaret was a critically-acclaimed drama about two college friends who take different roads in life; one straight, the other a swinger. The state of Georgia ruled that the film was obscene. In 1974, the Supreme Court found that it was not obscene. William Rehnquist delivered the opinion, stating, "the subject of the picture is, in a broad sense,

Americans eat over 7 billion quarts of popcorn a year. 10% of it is eaten at movie theaters.

sex...(but) the camera does not focus on the bodies of the actors at such times."

DEEP THROAT (1972). The most-banned film in United States history (25 states brought it to trial) starred Linda Lovelace and Harry Reems. The X-rated skin flick was first ruled obscene in Georgia. Lovelace later denounced her role in the film, which made millions at the box-office.

CALIGULA (1980). *Penthouse* publisher Bob Guccione produced this screen version of Gore Vidal's novel about the bloody reign of the Roman Empire's fourth Caesar. The film, starring Malcolm McDowell, Sir John Gielgud, and Peter O'Toole (all of whom later officially "disassociated" themselves from the final product),showed explicit sex and violence, earning an X rating. It was banned in Boston and Atlanta, but a judge in Boston refused to uphold an obsenity claim, ruling the subject was related to historical facts. The Supreme Court ruled in 1984, agreeing that the film was not obscene. "Caligula" became the largest-grossing X-rated film ever produced independently, although critics hated it, and at least one of the actresses tried to sue the producer for talking her into performing in an X-rated scene.

THE WINDY CITY

Chicago is the "Big Banned" of America when it comes to motion pictures. Among the censorship battles that have taken place there:

• Chicago censors denied licenses to show newsreels criticizing Nazi Germany before WWII. They also banned Charlie Chaplin's "The Great Dictator," a parody of Hitler, for fear of upsetting the large German population of the city.

• They banned newsreels which showed scenes of Chicago policemen shooting at union protestors.

• They refused to issue a permit for the movie *Anatomy of a Murder* because the words "rape" and "contraceptive" were used.

• They deleted scenes of a buffalo giving birth in Walt Disney's "Vanishing Prairie," the 1954 Academy Award-winning documentary.

Florida isn't the southernmost state in the United States—Hawaii is.

STENGEL-ESE

Legendary New York Yankees and Mets manager Casey Stengel offers a few confusing words of wisdom.

To a hitter with the bases loaded: "Let him hit 'ya; I'll get you a new neck."

"There are three things you can do in a baseball game. You can win, or you can lose, or it can rain."

"Now all you fellers line up alphabetically by height."

"You have to have a catcher, because if you don't, the pitch will roll all the way back to the screen."

"They say you can't do it, but sometimes it doesn't always work."

"Look at that guy. Can't run, can't hit, can't catch. Of course, that's why they gave him to us."

On two 20-year-old players: "In 10 years, Ed Kranepool has a chance to be a star. In 10 years, Greg Goosen has a chance to be 30."

"We're in such a slump that even the ones that are drinkin' aren't hittin'."

"Good pitching will always stop good hitting, and vice versa."

"I love signing autographs. I'll sign anything but veal cutlets. My ballpoint pen slips on veal cutlets."

"The secret of managing a club is to keep the five guys who hate you away from the five who are undecided."

"The Mets have come along slow, but fast!"

"Being with a woman all night never hurt no professional ballplayer. It's staying up all night looking for a woman that does him in."

"I'll never make the mistake again of being 70 years old."

"They say some of my stars drink whiskey, but I have found that the ones who drink milkshakes don't win many ball games."

"Most ball games are lost, not won."

The fourth most common language in the U.S. is sign language.

MYTH AMERICA

1992 is the 500th anniversary of Columbus's historic voyage. So it's a good time to clear up a few myths about him.

THE MYTH: Columbus proved the Earth was round.
THE TRUTH: The ancient Greeks knew the world wasn't flat two thousand years before Columbus was born. Pythagoras came up with the theory in the in sixth century B.C., and Ptolemy proved it in the second century A.D. Before Columbus even left on his first voyage to the New World, he studied globes and maps depicting a round planet. He had a hard time finding funding for his voyage, not because his contemporaries thought he would sail off the earth's edge, but because they thought the Orient was too far to reach by sailing west.

THE MYTH: He was the first European to discover North America.
THE TRUTH: Columbus never even set foot on the North American continent. The closest he ever came was the islands of the Caribbean and South America. The America whose "discovery" we celebrate is actually a tiny island near San Salvador, which was already inhabited anyway. Even Columbus wouldn't take credit for discovering a new continent—he died thinking he he had reached India. Actually, the Vikings were the first Europeans to reach North America, around 1000 A.D.

THE MYTH: Columbus was a friend to the Indians.
THE TRUTH: Sad to say, that's not even close. Take his Haitian exploits for example: According to historian Howard Zinn, Arawak Indians who didn't honor Columbus and his crew with regular contributions of gold "had their hands cut off and bled to death." After two years, half of Haiti's 250,000 inhabitants were dead "through murder, mutilation, or suicide." Many of the native Indians who survived were enslaved and brought back to Spain. "Let us in the name of the Holy Trinity, go on sending all the slaves that can be sold," Columbus wrote.

You get more Vitamin C from strawberries than from oranges.

MILITARY DOUBLE-TALK

What is the Pentagon spending our money on this year? See if you can figure it out. Try to match these official U.S.military terms with their civilian meanings.
Answers on page 223.

1. "Interlocking slide fastener."

2. "Portable hand-held communications transcriber."

3. "Weapons system."

4. "Hexiform rotatable surface compression unit."

5. "Special weapon."

6. "Habitability improvements."

7. "Vertically deployed anti-personnel device."

8. "Aerodynamic personnel decelerator."

9. "Wood interdental stimulator."

10. "Universal obscurant."

11. "Kinetic kill vehicle launcher."

12. "Missionized crew station."

13. "Radiation enhancement weapon."

14. "Interfibrous friction fastener."

A. Neutron bomb

B. Hammer

C. Parachute

D. Toothpick

E. Cockpit

F. Smoke from smoke bombs

G. Steel nut

H. Anti-satellite weapon

I. Bayonet

J. Pencil

K. Zipper

L. Atomic bomb

M. Furniture

N. Bomb

Forty percent of Americans have never visited a dentist.

YOU BE THE JUDGE

On July 20, 1969, Neil Armstrong became the first human being to set foot on the moon. But his famous comment, "That's one small step for man, one giant leap for mankind" has caused some controversy. Did he write the words himself...or did someone at NASA slip him the line? No one knows for sure, but here are some clues that may help you decide for yourself.

CLUE #1

The quote doesn't make sense. Apparently, Armstrong meant to say "one small step for a man" instead of "one small step for man." What are the odds that he would have misquoted himself? (Armstrong claims he said "one small step for a man" but the "a" dropped out during transmission).

CLUE #2

In 1983, Armstrong told *Esquire* that he made the words up after—not before—landing on the Moon. With all the pressure and details to take care of, how likely is it that he could have come up with such an eloquent phrase?

CLUE #3

The quote—with the correct "a" included—appeared on a NASA press blackboard only minutes after Armstrong uttered the words. Did NASA know in advance about the quote?...And if so, doesn't that contradict Armstrong's own testimony?

CLUE #4

Armstrong is often described as the archtypical "strong and silent type." Many thought the words didn't sound like something he'd ordinarily say. Wouldn't Armstrong have asked a writer to help coin a phrase for such a momentous event?

CLUE #5

Space flight is a highly regimented process. Would NASA allow an

Ho, Ho, Ho: Americans use as many artificial Christmas trees as real ones.

astronaut to write the history of the space agency's finest hour with just anything that came into his mind? Don't forget—billions of people were watching and listening.

CLUE #6

One writer, Oriana Fallaci, tried to prove Armstrong would not have been allowed to improvise on the spot. She bet astronaut Pete Conrad that he wouldn't be allowed to say "It may be a small step for Neil, but it's a big step for a little fellow like me" during the Apollo 12 mission. But Conrad did say the words (he claims Fallaci never paid up the $500 bet).

YOU BE THE JUDGE

No one's ever proven whether or not Armstrong authored the phrase. Buzz Aldrin, his Apollo moonwalking partner, has defended Armstrong. So has every NASA official. What do you think?

★ ★ ★

MORE JUNK ABOUT SPACE JUNK

- After only a handful of human visits, the moon is already littered. Apollo astronauts left behind a space buggy, camera equipment (worth $5,000,000) and the two golf balls that Alan Shepard hit.
- On the average, more than three man-made objects crash into Earth each week.
- In 1969, five crewmen on a Japanese freighter in the Sea of Japan were seriously injured after debris from a Soviet spacecraft crashed into their ship.
- Thus far, the most famous object to fall to earth was the 78-ton U.S. Skylab, which caused a world scare during the days leading up to its reentry. Despite an international scare, the debris from Skylab did not kill anybody; instead it exploded over the Indian Ocean and the Australian Outback. The debris from Skylab was considered public domain; i.e., finders, keepers. A 17-year truck driver named Stan Thornton won a $10,000 prize from the *San Francisco Examiner* by being the first person to turn in a piece of Skylab.

EDISON ENLIGHTENS

Thomas Edison was a genius inventor who gave us the electric light, the phonograph, and movies. He also gave most of the credit for his accomplishments to hard work, not brilliance. Some of his ideas:

"Genius is one percent inspiration and ninety-nine percent perspiration."

"The chief function of your body is to carry your brain around."

"We don't know a millionth of one percent about anything."

"Restlessness and discontent are the first necessities of progress."

"I am glad that the eight-hour day had not been invented when I was a young man. If my life had been made up of eight-hour days I do not believe I could have accomplished a great deal. This country would not amount to as much as it does...if the young men had been afraid that they might earn more than they were paid."

"I am long on ideas, but short on time. I expect to live to be only about a hundred."

"The inventor tries to meet the demands of a crazy civilization."

"I never did anything worth doing by accident, nor did any of my inventions come by accident; they came by work."

"Everything comes to him who hustles while he waits."

"To my mind the old masters are not art; their value is in their scarcity."

"Not only will atomic power be released, but someday we will harness the rise and fall of the tides and imprison the rays of the sun."

"There is no substitute for hard work."

"When down in the mouth remember Jonah—he came out all right!"

"The English are not an inventive people; they don't eat enough pie."

RECYCLING FACTS

Here are some fascinating facts from the EarthWorks Group's handy new book, "The Recycler's Handbook."

Some 94,000 cans are recycled every minute in America.

• Americans use 100 million steel and tin cans every day. We recycle about 5% of them...which means we dump more than 30 billion into landfills every year.

• Americans use enough corrugated cardboard in a year to make a bale the size of a football field and the height of the World Trade Center. About 40% of it is recycled.

• If Americans recycled half our newsprint every year, we'd need 3,200 fewer garbage trucks to collect municipal trash.

• Americans throw away enough used motor oil every year to fill 120 supertankers. It could all be recycled.

• According to the EPA, we create enough garbage every year to fill a convoy of 10-ton garbage trucks 145,000 miles long—more than halfway from here to the moon.

• About 70 million car batteries are recycled in the U.S. each year. The other 15-20%, with 165,000 tons of lead, go to landfills.

• To make plastics, the U.S. uses about a billion barrels of petroleum by-products each year. How much is that? Enough to fill over 56,000 olympic-sized swimming pools.

• According to the Glass Packaging Institute, we now use around 41 billion glass containers a year—an average of about 165 per person. How much of that is recycled? About 30%...which means nearly 30 billion glass containers go into landfills.

• Every year, Americans dispose of 1.6 billion pens, 2 billion razors and blades, and 18 billion diapers. They're all sitting in landfills somewhere.

• In 1988, about 9 million automobile bodies—more than American automobile plants produced that year—were recycled.

New York City has been host to only 27 ticker-tape parades, total.

COLLEGE NAMES

We know the names—Cornell, Harvard, Stanford...
Here's where a few of them come from.

Brown University. Nicholas Brown, a member of a wealthy Rhode Island shipping family, gave a $5,000 endowment to Rhode Island College in 1804. By that time, Brown's family had given the school more than $160,000, and officials decided a name-change was in order.

Cornell University. Samuel Morse invented the telegraph, but it was Ezra Cornell who put it to work. He devised a practical method of stringing insulated wires along telephone poles, and provided the first telegraph service to the cities of the northeast. His initial donation of land and $500,000 put the school on its feet.

Stanford University. Amasa Leland Stanford, a robber baron who got himself elected governor of California and a U.S. senator, founded the university in memory of his son, Leland Jr., who died of typhoid fever at the age of 15.

Johns Hopkins University. Humbled by his own poor education, Johns Hopkins, a wealthy Baltimore merchant and banker, willed $7,000,000 to found the now famous university and hospital.

Duke University. Once there was a school in North Carolina called Trinity College. Then, in 1925, a wealthy tobacco, textiles and utilities magnate named James B. Duke gave them $107 million. Suddenly, the name Duke had a certain ring to it.

Harvard University. In 1638 John Harvard, a wealthy Massachusetts settler, left half his estate—$1,480—to a two-year-old local bible college. It was the largest gift to the new school at that point; the school repaid the favor by calling itself Harvard College.

Brigham Young University. Named after one of the founding fathers of the Church of Jesus Christ of Latter Day Saints (the Mormons).

There are about 800 tombstones in Tombstone, Arizona.

SPACE NAZIS

Whatever happened to the scientists who supplied Hitler's war machine with its advanced weaponry? Many of them moved to the U.S. at our government's invitation, to join our space program.

Following the defeat of Germany at the end of World War II, the United States began Project Paperclip, a secret program that employed "ex"-Nazis in U.S. scientific efforts. Many of the scientists smuggled into America by our government had committed war crimes—but U.S. officials didn't care. In fact, information about their past was deliberately covered up to circumvent laws that prohibited Nazi collaborators from entering the country.

CODE NAME: OVERCAST

According to Linda Hunt's 1985 exposé in the *Bulletin of the Atomic Scientists*, the scheme "grew from the notion that German and Austrian scientists were part of the spoils of the war which had been won against Nazi Germany." Initially, the top secret program, whose code name was Overcast, called for temporary immigration of "Nazi experts in rocketry, aircraft design, aviation, medicine, and other fields," writes Hunt. "But by early 1946, the War Department found their skills too valuable to lose and pushed for a revised program that would allow them to stay in the United States."

SEAL OF APPROVAL

In early 1946, Overcast was renamed Project Paperclip and the operation was approved by President Harry S. Truman. According to official policy, "No person found...to have been a member of the Nazi Party and more than a nominal participant in its activities or an active supporter of Naziism or militarism shall be brought to the U.S."

But government agencies ignored these regulations. Records of the German scientists' Nazi backrounds were routinely altered and sometimes deleted altogether. As a result, perpetrators of some of the most heinous war crimes in World War II soon became full-fledged American citizens. From 1945 to 1952, 765 German scientists were admitted to the U.S. All of them were committed Nazis.

If a black cat crosses your path in Japan, it's considered good luck.

CASE HISTORIES

Arthur Rudolph. Designed the Saturn 5 rocket used in the Apollo moon landings. During World War II, he was the operations director of the Mittelwerk factory at the Dora-Nordhausen concentration camp in Germany, where 20,000 workers were tortured to death. At first, Rudolph denied to U.S. officials that he had witnessed any incidents of abuse at the camp, but later admitted seeing 12 prisoners hanged from a crane ("I do know that one lifted his knees after I got there," Rudolph testified).

An earlier 1945 military file had concluded that Rudolph was "100% Nazi, dangerous type, security threat!!!" This appraisal was ignored, however, and Rudolph was allowed to become a U.S. citizen. In 1984, while under investigation for his war record, Rudolph fled to West Germany.

Wernher von Braun. Instrumental in many areas of NASA's Apollo program. In 1947, von Braun was labeled an "SS officer" and "potential security threat" to the United States. But several months later, a new security evaluation, specifically rewritten to allow von Braun to emigrate, claimed "no derogatory information is available...like the majority of members, he may have been a mere opportunist." Von Braun was subsequently allowed to come to the U.S., despite the fact that his V-2 rocket had been used to bombard London during World War II. He became an American celebrity and was even showcased as a role model for American children during the 1950s and early 1960s.

Kurt Blome. A high-ranking Nazi scientist who was put on trial at Nuremberg in 1947 for conducting human experiments. Although he was acquitted there, it was generally accepted that the charges had basis in fact: During a 1945 interrogation by the U.S. military, Blome admitted that he had been ordered in 1943 to experiment with plague vaccines on concentration camp prisoners.

Two months after his Nuremberg acquittal, Blome was being interviewed in Camp David, Maryland, for information about biological warfare. He supplied technological details and names of Nazi collaborators in his experiments.

Nearly 50% of Americans read, work or watch TV while they eat dinner.

In 1951, the U.S. Army Chemical Corps chose to ignore Blome's background when it hired him to work on chemical warfare for "Project 63," the U.S.'s secret effort to hire Germans scientists before the Russians got to them. Nowhere in Blome's files did it mention his arrest or trial at Nuremberg.

Hermann Becker-Freysing and ***Siegfried Ruff.*** Both Becker-Freysing and Ruff (and 21 others) were charged at the Nuremberg War Crimes trials for participating in cruel medical experiments on Dachau concentration camp inmates. Before the trials began, however, both were contacted by the Army Air Force Aero Center in Heidelberg, Germany. According to the *Bulletin of the Atomic Scientists*, Becker-Freysing and Ruff were paid "to write reports or conduct laboratory tests for the Army Air Force's use that were based on wartime experiments which Nuremberg prosecutors later charged had been conducted on concentration camp victims." Becker-Freysing was later found guilty and sentenced to 20 years in jail for conducting seawater experiments on prisoners at Dachau. Ruff was acquitted for conducting experiments that killed over 80 Dachau inmates who had been locked in a chamber that simulated high altitude pressure.

Konrad Schaefer. Schaefer was charged in the Nuremberg trials for his role in Becker-Freysing's sea water experiments. According to the charges, Schaefer oversaw experiments on Dachau concentration camp inmates who were starved and then force-fed sea water that had been chemically altered to make it drinkable. Like Becker-Freysing and Ruff, Schaefer was paid by the Aero Center to inform the Army and Air Force about his experiments.

In 1949, Schaefer was allowed to enter the United States in spite of the fact he had admitted to having been tried at Nuremberg (he was acquitted, despite evidence that he had attended planning meetings for the experiments.) Ironically, when Schaefer was sent back to Germany in 1951, it was not because of his war crimes—the Air Force simply could not find a job for him.

OBJECTIONS

In 1947, the *Bulletin of the Atomic Scientists* ran one of the first exposes on Project Paperclip. The two authors of the piece, Hans Bethe and H.S. Sack argued against the immigration of the

The American slogan, "In God We Trust," was not adopted until 1956.

ex-Nazi scientists: "Is it wise, from a long-range point of view, or even compatible with our moral standards, to make this bargain? Would it not have been better to restrict the stay of these scientists in this country to the absolute minimum? For it must be borne in mind that many of them, probably the majority, are diehard Nazis, or at least worked wholeheartedly with the Nazis; otherwise they would not have held their high posts so vital for the Nazi war machine."

JUSTIFICATION

Addressing the moral argument about using war criminals, Bosquet Wev, the director of the Joint intelligence Objectives Agency said in a 1947 memorandum: "The best interests of the United States have been subjugated to the efforts expended in 'beating a dead Nazi horse'...the return of these scientists to Germany would present a far greater security threat to the United States than their retention."

DENUNCIATION

In December, 1946, Albert Einstein, Norman Vincent Peale and other prominent Americans issued protests to the American government concerning Project Paperclip. But the issue quickly died down, since little information was made public.

THE END OF PAPERCLIP

Project Paperclip came to an end in 1957 after 11 years. Ironically, the government of West Germany began to complain of a "brain drain" of its best scientists. Since that time, writes Linda Hunt, many of imported ex-Nazi scientists "have received the highest honors bestowed by the military on civilians and have risen to top positions at NASA and other governmental agencies and in private industry."

And Now for Something Completely Different...

"What kind of animals were the dinosaurs? Up until the last decade, many scientists would have answered with confidence: Dinosaurs were huge, slow-moving, cold-blooded reptiles of the past... Today some paleontologists offer radically different views: Dinosaurs were active, perhaps even warm-blooded animals, comparable to modern mammals and birds." —*National Geographic*, 1978

DISNEY STORIES: PINOCCHIO

The original Pinocchio was written by an Italian educator named Carlo Lorenzini (using the name Carlo Collodi) in 1883. It was adapted by Disney at a cost of $2.5 million and released in 1940. Although it contains "some of the finest art and animation sequences every produced," it wasn't a big hit. Of course, the Disney version and the original story were substantially different. Here are Jim Morton's examples of how the tale was changed.

THE DISNEY VERSION

• Geppetto, a kindly old wood carver, makes a marionette named Pinocchio. Then he wishes (on a star) that the puppet were a real boy, so he could have a son.

• A talking bug named Jiminy Cricket is appointed Pinocchio's conscience. He follows Pinocchio on a series of adventures.

• Pinocchio is accosted by a fox and a cat—two humorous con artists—is sold to Stromboli, and sent to Pleasure Island, where dumb, selfish boys are turned into beasts. Pinocchio narrowly escapes being turned into a donkey.

• He's eventually reunited with Geppetto in the belly of a whale; Geppetto was swallowed while he was out looking for Pinocchio.

• Pinocchio helps the wood carver escape, and for his unselfishness, he's turned into a real boy. Jiminy Crickett beams and sings.

THE ORIGINAL VERSION

• Disney follows the main themes of the book, but skips over the grim moments from the original story.

• For example: When Pinocchio hides his gold coins in his mouth, the cat attempts to force Pinocchio's mouth open with a knife. Pinocchio bites the cat's paw off and spits it out. While he's running away, Pinocchio meets a zombie girl. Then the fox and cat hang him by the neck, trying to make him spit out the gold.

• The biggest difference between the Disney Version and the book is Jiminy Cricket. In the book, the cricket has no name. It appears early in the story and is promptly smashed with a hammer by Pinocchio. Later in the tale, the cricket's ghost pops up as a sort of insect Obi Wan Kenobi, offering Pinocchio guidance (rarely heeded) as he goes on his journeys.

• Also in the original, on Pleasure Island (called Playland in the book), Pinocchio does turn into a donkey and is sold at the market. He's forced to perform in a circus before going lame. Then he's sold to a man who plans to use Pinocchio's skin to make a drum. The man tries to drown Pinocchio, but fish eat the donkey skin off him, revealing the puppet inside.

• Pinocchio does rescue Geppetto, but from the belly of a shark, not a whale. This deed alone isn't enough to turn Pinocchio into a boy. The puppet works from sunrise to sundown every day for five months before his wish is finally granted.

SAMPLE PASSAGES (FROM THE ORIGINAL)

"'Why are you sorry for me?' Pinocchio asked the cricket.

"'Because you are a puppet, and—what is worse—you have a wooden head,' the cricket replied.

"At these last words, Pinocchio lost his temper and, seizing a mallet from the bench, threw it at the cricket.

"Perhaps he did not mean to hit him, but unfortunately the mallet struck the cricket right to the head. The poor insect had scarcely time to cry 'Cri-cri-cri,' and there he was, stretched out stiff, flattened against the wall."

• • •

The fox and cat are trying to rob Pinnochio.

"'Ah-ha, you rascal! So you hid your money under your tongue! Spit it out at once!'

"Pinocchio did not obey.

"'Oh, so you can't hear? Then we'll make you spit it out.'

"And one of them seized the puppet by the end of his nose, and the other by his chin, and they pulled without mercy, one up, the other down, to make him open his mouth; but it was no use.

"Then the smaller assassin drew a horrid knife and tried to force it between his lips, like a chisel, but Pinocchio, quick as lightning, bit off his hand and spat it out. Imagine his astonishment when he saw that it was a cat's paw."

The heads of a two-headed snake will fight over food—even though they share one stomach.

THE ARCHIES

When you were a kid, were Archie *comics part of your bathroom reading? Here's a new Archie story from* Behind the Hits, *by Bob Shannon and John Javna.*

If you grew up in post-World War II America, the chances are you've read at least one *Archie* comic book in your life. As Maurice Horn says in *The World Encyclopedia of Comics*, "Archie, like Batman, Superman, and a small handful of others, has transcended comic books into pure Americana. There will, it often seems, always be an Archie. It is inevitable as death and taxes."

THE '40s & '50s: ARCHIE'S EARLY DAYS

Archie Andrews, a red-headed, freckle-faced creation of cartoonist Bob Montana, first appeared in *Pep* comic books in 1941. He was portrayed as the "typical" American teenager of the '40s, and he was so popular that within a year he had his own comic book. His audience increased. He starred in a radio show. By the '50s, a whole cast of characters—and more comic book titles—had evolved.

Now Archie and his pals from Riverdale High were the "typical" American teenagers of the '50s. Maybe you remember that Archie had a red jalopy and a big crush on rich and snooty Veronica Lodge; Jughead Jones wore a strange-looking beanie and loved hamburgers; Betty, Veronica's best friend and rival, was hopelessly in love with Archie; Moose was a super-strong but super-dumb athlete; and so on. They all hung out at Pop's Malt Shoppe when they weren't in school under Mr. Weatherbee's watchful eye.

ARCHIE IN THE '60s

But as popular as the Archie clan was in the '40s and '50s, the '60s was their golden decade. With the help of the cartoon show that premiered on CBS in 1968, sales of everything connected to Archie characters, from lunch boxes to comic books, skyrocketed. For example, best-selling comics normally sold about 300,000 copies a month in the '60s; in 1969, at the height of the cartoon show's popularity, *Archie* comics sold over a million a month!

ARCHIE ANDREWS, ROCK STAR

Included in this fantastic marketing windfall was a scheme to

The cold season: Divorce rates rise in the winter.

merchandise the Archie characters as a Monkees-style rock 'n' roll group. The Monkees had already proven TV's effectiveness in selling records to American kids. Now the people behind the Archie TV show wanted to cash in on the same appeal. They hired the man behind the Monkees' hits, Don Kirshner, as "music supervisor," and he began putting together a session group to make records as the Archies. Since the stars of this TV series were animated, Kirshner didn't have to put up with what he must have regarded as prima donna actors again (his association with the Monkees ended on unfriendly terms). For this job, he could just hire anonymous studio singers.

DANTE'S INFERNO

Enter Ron Dante, an out-of-work jingle and demo singer whose only previous hit ("The Leader of the Laundramat") had been credited to the Detergents. Says Dante, "[Kirshner] was casting for the Archies, and he was listening to a lot of singers. I heard that a musician friend of mine was playing on the session, and I just happened to fall by and say, 'Why don't you try me?' I auditioned for it because I had just written a Broadway show that bombed, and my career in Broadway had gone down the drain. So I said, 'I think I'd better jump back into records and take anything I can get my hands on,' and that was the beginning of it. I went and auditioned; I sang for about a half-hour.

"The next day, they called me and said, 'All right, you're gonna do the season's music.' We must have done a hundred tunes that first season. Over the years, I must have done about three or four hundred songs for the Archies. I auditioned with songs like 'Bang Shang-A-Lang' and 'Truck driver,' and I said, 'Here I go again.'"

HOW SWEET IT IS

The Archies released an album in 1968, and had a moderate hit with "Bang Shang-A-Lang" that year. But their second single—"Sugar Sugar"—was a smash. It became the biggest-selling record of 1969, with total sales of over four million. It was even covered by Wilson Pickett, who turned it into a Top 25 hit as a soul song. The Archies had two more Top 40 singles in the next year. But a proposed Archies tour was not to be. "They wanted me to dye my hair and put freckles on and go out as Archie," Dante says, "and I said, 'Oh boy, is this a career move, or what?' "

In anonymous surveys, 40% of Americans confessed cheating on their taxes.

GROUCHO GOSSIP

How did the Groucho Marx and his brothers get into show business? And where did they get those funny names? Now it can be told. From Cult TV by John Javna.

Julius Henry Marx (Groucho's real name) wasn't happy when his mother pushed him into becoming a vaudevillian. His dream was to become a doctor. But soon he, two brothers and a friend were touring backwater theaters as the Four Nightingales.

WISECRACKS

They were less than successful. During a performance in Texas, the entire audience left the theater to catch an escaped mule. When they returned, the angry brothers dropped their regular act and ad-libbed a routine mocking the patrons instead. They expected boos, but they got laughter. It changed the Marx brothers' act forever: they learned they could make fun of people and get away with it.

NAME GAME

Years later, another piece fell into place. Julius and his brothers were playing poker with a friend who was making fun of a popular comic character named "Knocko the Monk." The friend made up a similar name for each of them. Leo became Chicko because he chased women constantly. Adolph became Harpo (he played the harp). Milton became Gummo (because he liked to chew gum?). And Julius, who groused constantly, became Groucho.

LUCKY BREAK

The Marx Brothers might never have become stars if it hadn't been for a lucky accident. One night in 1924, a major play-opening was cancelled in New York. Reviewers, left with nothing else to see that night, showed up at the opening of a new Marx brothers' vaudeville act instead. They expected to find a typically boring variety act—but the surprised reviewers loved the Marx Brothers. Their rave reviews made Groucho and his family instant celebrities and Broadway stars...which led to Hollywood.

The most profitable supermarket aisles: 1. Meat 2. Fresh produce 3. Pet food.

BANNED BOOKS

It can't happen here? Guess again. Each year, the American Booksellers Association holds a "Banned Books Week" to call attention to the issues surrounding censorship. Here are some books that were banned, or nearly banned, during the 1980s.

The Diary of Anne Frank, by Anne Frank. In 1983 members of the Alabama State Textbook Committee wanted the book rejected because it was "a real downer."

Lord of the Flies, by William Golding. In 1981 the book was challenged by a high school in Owen, North Carolina because it was "demoralizing inasmuch as it implies that man is little more than an animal."

Biology, by Karen Arms and Pamela S. Camp. In 1985 the Garland, Texas textbook selection committee complained of "overly explicit diagrams of sexual organs."

The American Pageant: A History of the Republic, by Thomas A. Bailey and David M. Kennedy. In 1984 officials in the Racine, Wisconsin School District complained the book contained "a lot of funny pictures of Republicans and nicer pictures of Democrats."

Zen Buddhism: Selected Writings, by D.T. Suzuki. In 1987 the school system of Canton, Michigan was informed that "this book details the teaching of the religion of Buddhism in such a way that the reader could very likely embrace its teachings and choose this as his religion."

1984, by George Orwell. In 1981 the book was challenged in Jackson Country, Florida because it was "pro-communist and contained explicit sexual matter."

Slugs, by David Greenburg. In 1985 an elementary school in Escondido, California banned the book for describing "slugs being dissected with scissors."

One third of all the fresh water on Earth is in Canada.

A Light In the Attic, by Shel Silverstein. In 1986 the popular children's book was challenged at an elementary school in Mukwonago, Wisconsin because it "gloried Satan, suicide and cannibalism, and also encouraged children to be disobedient."

The Crucible, by Arthur Miller. In 1982 citizens of Harrisburg, Pennsylvania complained about staging a play with "sick words from the mouths of demon-possessed people. It should be wiped out of the schools or the school board should use them to fuel the fire of hell."

Slaughterhouse Five, by Kurt Vonnegut. In 1985 complaints were made in an Owensboro, Kentucky high school library because the book had "foul language, a section depicting a picture of an act of bestiality, a reference to 'Magic Fingers' attached to the protagonist's bed to help him sleep, and the sentence: 'The gun made a ripping sound like the opening of the fly of God Almighty.' "

Meet the Werewolf, by Georgess McHargue. In 1983 the school district of Vancouver, Oregon claimed the book was "full of comments about becoming a werewolf, use of opium, and pacts with the devil."

Album Cover Album, by Roger Dean. (A book of album covers). In 1987 the Vancouver, Washington school district objected to a photo of the "Statue of Liberty with bare breasts as exemplary of several photos that were pretty raw toward women."

The Amazing Bone, by William Steig. In 1986 a parent in Lambertville, New Jersey complained to the local school library about "the use of tobacco by the animals" in this fantasy.

The Haunting Of America, by Jean Anderson. In 1985 an elementary school in Lakeland, Florida claimed it "would lead children to believe in demons without realizing it."

SIDENOTE: Lewis Caroll's **Alice's Adventures In Wonderland** was banned in China in 1931. Authorities objected that "animals should not use human language, and that it was disastrous to put animals and human beings on the same level."

An automatic spaghetti-spinning fork was patented in 1950.

DON'T QUOTE ME ON THAT

You'd be surprised how many famous quotes were never actually said by the people they're attributed to. Here are some classic examples.

The Quote: "Play it again, Sam." —*Humphrey Bogart*
The Truth: The real line from *Casablanca* is "You played it for her, you can play it for me. If she can stand it, I can—Play it." Dooley Wilson (Sam) didn't really play it. In real life, Wilson couldn't play the piano; the accompaniment was dubbed in afterwards.

The Quote: "Elementary, my dear Watson." —*Sherlock Holmes*
The Truth: Arthur Conan Doyle wrote four novels and 56 short stories that feature his detective; Holmes doesn't say it in any of them. Basil Rathbone, an actor who portrayed the sleuth in films of the 1930s and 1940s, was the one who made the line famous.

The Quote: "I cannot tell a lie." —*George Washington*
The Truth: Washington's biographer, Mason Weems, fabricated the whole cherry tree incident six years after Washington's death.

The Quote: "Hold on, Mr. President!" —*Sam Donaldson*
The Truth: The aggressive White House television reporter claims he never said it at any of the presidential press conferences he covered, although it is the title of a recent book he wrote.

The Quote: "Win one for the Gipper." —*George Gipp*
The Truth: Knute Rockne, the Notre Dame football coach to whom dying player George Gipp allegedly spoke his final words, was known for embellishing the truth to inspire his players. Experts believe that Rockne—who first told the story a long eight years after Gipp's death—made it up.

In the United States, there are four times more astrologers than astronomers.

The Quote: "You dirty rat!" —*James Cagney*
The Truth: Cagney denied ever saying this in any of his movies.

The Quote: "Go west, young man." —*Horace Greeley*
The Truth: A man named John Babsone Soule first wrote it in an article for Indiana's *Terre Haute Express* in 1851. Greeley reprinted the article in his *New York Tribune*, but gave full credit to Soule.

The Quote: "On the whole, I'd rather be in Philadelphia."
—*W.C. Fields*
The Truth: Fields' alleged epitaph first appeared as a joke in a *Vanity Fair* magazine around 1950, after his death.

The Quote: "The government is best which governs least."
—*Thomas Jefferson*
The Truth: Historians can't find evidence that the founding father ever said it.

The Quote: "There are three kinds of lies: lies, damn lies, and statistics." — *Mark Twain*
The Truth: In his autobiography, Twain credited this saying to Benjamin Disraeli.

The Quote: "Judy, Judy, Judy." —*Cary Grant*
The Truth: The line comes from a popular impersonation of Grant by comedian Larry Storch.

The Quote: "War is hell." —*William T. Sherman*
The Truth: The Union general really said, "There is many a boy here today who looks on war as all glory, but, boys, it is all hell."

The Quote: "He who hesitates is lost." —*Joseph Addison*
The Truth: The original line from his play *Cato*, is, "The woman that deliberates is lost."

Every single day, L.A. residents drive 142 million miles—the distance from Earth to Mars.

AIN'T THAT A SHAME

Here's an interesting commentary on old-time rock, from Behind The Hits, *by Bob Shannon and John Javna.*

One of the more sordid aspects of rock'n'roll's early history was "cover artists," the white guys who imitated black artists who created the songs, the arrangements, and the harmonies. But the worst part wasn't that the cover artists were imitators—the worst part was that they copied the black artists' records while the original version was still new. So the cover versions competed with—and usually did better than—the originals. The difference between them was often minor; one rendition sounded like it was done by white singers, the other sounded like it was done by black singers. So lily-white radio stations pushed the songs done by by "acceptable" (white) artists. And these artists became stars.

MR. RIPOFF

A good example is Pat Boone. Pat, a pious fellow, got onto the charts doing cover versions of the El Dorados' "At My Front Door" (Pat: #7; the El Dorados: #17), the Charms' "Two Hearts (Pat: #16), Little Richard's "Tutti Frutti" (Pat: #12, Richard: #17), and a bunch more. Little Richard was so incensed by Boone's cover version of "Tutti Frutti" that he purposely made the follow-up, "Long Tall Sally," too fast for Boone to sing. Nonetheless, Boone figured out how to adapt "Long Tall Sally" to his style, and gave Richard a run for his money. Little Richard's version did beat Boone's, but only by one place on the charts (Richard: #7, Pat: #8).

WHITE BUCKS

There was also a huge difference in the attitudes of the artists toward their songs. To the originators, the songs were a part of life. To the rip-off artists, it was just business. Take, for example, one of Pat Boone's biggest hits, "Ain't That a Shame"—which actually belonged to Fats Domino. Fats, who was an established artist, wrote this song from a personal experience.

"I usually record my songs like things that people say everyday," Fats says. "Like 'Ain't That A Shame.' I was passin', walkin' down the street and I saw a little lady beatin' a little baby, you know,

Highest altitude for a bird—a Ruppell's Vulture hit a plane over Africa at 37,000 feet.

spankin' a baby. And I heard somebody say, 'Ain't that a shame.' "

In 1956, Fats released the song and it went to #10. Not bad, except that Pat Boone covered it right away, and his version went to #1, obviously taking some sales from Fats.

Pat, however, didn't really identify with the tune. In fact, he objected to it because the grammar was bad.

PROPER ENGLISH

" 'With 'Ain't That A Shame,' I balked," Boone says. "I said, 'Look, I just transferred to Columbia University, I'm an English major. I don't want to record a song called 'Ain't That A Shame.' I mean, 'ain't' wasn't an accepted word. It is now in the dictionary, but I was majoring in English and I felt that this was going to be a terrible thing if it was a hit. I tried to record it, 'Isn't That A Shame,' and it just didn't work."

Boone continues: "And I must say that I was complimented...I would go to radio studios, walk in, and the deejays were astonished to see that I was white."

Maybe they'd been listening to Fats' record.

THE STONES

The Rolling Stones have written some great original music, but they've also liberally "used" other people's music from the very beginning of their recording careers. "Stoned," the flip side of their first British hit ("I Wanna Be Your Man"), for example, was a copy of a 1964 hit called "Green Onions." An album cut called "Prodigal Son," which is credited to Jagger/Richards, is virtually a note-for-note copy of an old blues tune by Furry Lewis. Even the guitar licks are the same.

The Stones' first American Top 10 record, "Time Is On My Side," is another imitation, a note-for-note copy of the original version by New Orleans singer Irma Thomas. Even Mick Jagger's "rap" in the middle of the song is lifted from Irma's rendition. "Time On My Side" should have been the successful follow-up to her Top 20 tune, "I Wish Someone Would Care," but before Irma's record had a chance, the Stones' version was already rocketing up the charts. "I really liked the song, and I put my heart and soul into it," Irma says. "Then along comes this English group that half-sings it and gets a million-seller. And after that I stopped doing it."

America has more senior citizens than teenagers.

BODY LANGUAGE

Here are some fascinating facts about the human body.

IT'S A GAS

• An average person releases nearly a pint of intestinal gas by flatulence every day. Most is due to swallowed air. The rest is from fermentation of undigested food.

• Burping while lying on your back is a lot harder than burping while you're sitting or standing.

• The two things that make farts smell, *skatole* and *indole*, are commonly used in making perfumes.

• Your stomach produces a new lining every three days. Reason: It keeps stomach acids from digesting your stomach.

TAKE A BREATHER

• The average person breathes 70 to 80 million gallons of air in a lifetime.

• A newborn's first breath requires 50 times the suction of an ordinary breath.

• You inhale over 3,000 gallons of air every day.

• An infant breathes about three times faster than a 20-year-old.

• On the average, a person who smokes a pack of cigarettes a day will die at 67, seven years earlier than the average nonsmoker.

THE EYES HAVE IT

• Most men's pupils get 1/3 bigger when looking at pictures of sharks, but shrink in reaction to pictures of babies.

• 33% of the population has 20/20 vision.

• The muscles in the average eye move up to 100,000 times in a day.

• Every time you blink, you wash irritating contaminants out of your eyes.

• 1 out of every 500 people have one blue eye and one brown eye.

• You can't keep your eyes open when you sneeze.

DON'T SWEAT IT

• One square inch of your skin has over 600 sweat glands and 90 oil glands.

• In a hot climate, a person can perspire up to 3 gallons of sweat a day.

In a UCLA study, 87% of the people researchers smiled at smiled back.

SHARK !!!

Some fascinating factoids about the ocean's most feared predator.

Sharks lived more than 400 million years ago—200 million years before dinosaurs existed.

Shark skin is covered with small teeth-like denticles which can tear human skin on contact. It was once used as sandpaper by coastal woodworkers.

In a single year, a shark goes through more than 20,000 knife-like teeth.

Unlike other fish, sharks lack air bladders and consequently have to keep moving to avoid sinking and drowning.

To a shark, a swimmer in a black wetsuit looks a lot like a seal or sea lion.

Sand Tiger shark embryos fight to the death inside the mother's womb until only one shark is alive at birth.

In May 1945, fishermen off Cuba caught the largest Great White shark on record—measuring over 21 feet and weighing 7,302 pounds.

The Great White shark has no natural enemies and it never gets sick.

Sharks have no bones in their body—only cartilage.

Three times as many people are killed by lightning as are killed by sharks.

A plankton-eating Whale shark caught off Pakistan measured over 41 feet and weighed over 33,000 pounds.

Sharks have three eyelids on each eye to protect against the thrashing of its prey.

Don't swim or dive with cuts—some types of shark can smell one part of blood in 100 million parts of water.

An attacking shark can sometimes be confused and diverted by a hard blow to the nose, or a poke in the eye or nostrils.

Sharks live only in salt water, except for the mysterious Bull sharks, sometimes found swimming miles up rivers.

Napoleon Bonaparte was afraid of cats.

SITUATION TRAGEDY

Ever wish your family could be more like the Partridge Family or the Nelsons? It turns out, there were no families like that.

Back in the "golden age" of TV, situation comedies presented audiences with the image of an ideal Middle Class America. Parents were patient, neighbors were nice, and kids were neat (even their bedrooms were spotless). In reality, however, many of the child actors in these "perfect" TV families had less-than-perfect lives offscreen.

FATHER KNOWS BEST

From 1954-63, the "white-bread" Anderson family of Springfield, U.S.A., could do wrong. But two of the main actors ran into trouble after the show went off the air.

• Billy Gray (who played the son, Bud) spent 45 days in jail on marijuana charges and later dropped out from society. He told *TV Guide*, "I look back at the show and see it as a lie, a lie that was sold to the American people."

• Like Gray, Lauren Chapin (who played the youngest daughter, Kathy) also had drug troubles. She became addicted to heroin and speed, and did jail time for forging a check.

THE PATTY DUKE SHOW

Many people were shocked when Patty Duke revealed in her autobiography, *Call Me Anna: The Autobiography of Patty Duke*, that she had suffered from severe manic-depression during her TV sitcom days. She wrote, "I hated being less intelligent than I was, I hated pretending that I was younger than I was."

• From 1963-66, Duke starred in the popular series, but gradually the stress of playing two roles—herself and her look-alike cousin—caught up with her; she became depressed, anorexic and eventually an alcoholic and drug addict.

The screen on the first home television set was only 3 X 4 inches.

• To make matters worse, her managers, John and Ethel Ross, were not only physically and emotionally abusive (they wouldn't allow Duke to watch her own show) but, according to Duke, embezzled her savings as well.

THE PARTRIDGE FAMILY

• The happy-go-lucky Partridge Family was a favorite of pre-teens in the early 1970s.

• After the show ended, Danny Bonaduce, the cherubic bass player, developed drug problems. By age 21, he had squandered $350,000 in savings on his cocaine habit. In 1985 he was arrested for possession of cocaine, but the charges were dismissed after drug counseling. In 1989, Bonaduce resurfaced as a DJ in Philadelphia, claiming "My only reponsibility is not to promote drugs." Within a year, Bonaduce was busted again, this time for purchasing crack.

• Susan Dey, who was 16 when the show began, later claimed to have suffered from severe anxiety which resulted in anorexia and bulimia.

THE ADVENTURES OF OZZIE AND HARRIET

• For 14 years, 1952-66, Americans tuned in to "The Adventures of Ozzie and Harriet." The Nelsons were a real-life family, which certainly added to their appeal, but it didn't exclude them from real-life problems.

• Fans of Ricky Nelson were shocked when his autopsy revealed that he had been freebasing cocaine just prior to the plane crash that killed him on December 31, 1984 in DeKalb, Texas.

FAMILY AFFAIR

In 1976, Annissa Jones, who played "Buffy" on the series "Family Affair" was found dead of an overdose after a party in Oceanside, California. The coroner reported that Jones had "the largest combination of drugs in any cases I've ever encountered." Toxological tests showed massive amoungs of cocaine, Quaaludes and barbituates. Jones was 18.

The diameter of the wheel on TV's "Wheel of Fortune" is 8' 6".

NAME & PLACE

Planning to move? Why not make your home in Sodom... or Elephant's Playground? Or any of these other strangely-named places:

Sodom, Vermont: Its name was changed to Adamant, VT in 1905, by people who shuddered at the thought of having their incoming mail addressed to Sodom.

Mount Derby, Colorado: It's hat-shaped.

Coffee-Los Lake, Maine: Locals, who like to call nearby Telos Lake "tea-less lake," thought they should have a "coffee-less lake" too.

Einanuhto Hills, Alaska: From the Aleut word meaning "three breasts."

Phoenix, Arizona: Traces of an Indian or pre-Indian village were found at the site. Town founders, taking the name from the mythological bird who rises form the ashes, hoped their new town would rise from the village's ruins.

Bosom, Wyoming: A town with two peaks.

Mistake Peak, Arizona and Mistaken Creek, Kentucky: Wrong peak, wrong creek.

Elephant's Playground, California: Home of large boulders in a meadow.

"Gotham City": In England, during the reign of King John, Gotham villagers all feigned lunacy to discourage the king from establishing a hunting lodge nearby that would lead to an increase in taxes. The name now means a city overrun by madness. Washington Irving coined the phrase in a description of New York in 1807.

Bimble, Kentucky: From the names of Will and Rebecca Payne's prize oxen—Bim and Bill.

Portland, Oregon: The two men who named the city couldn't decide—Portland (like the Maine city)...or Boston? A coin flip settled the debate in favor of Portland.

The most popular American dog names are Rover, Spot, and Max—in that order.

COMMON PHRASES

In the first two Uncle John's Bathroom Readers, *we gave you the origins of some familiar phrases. Here are a few more.*

SECOND STRING
Meaning: Replacement or backup.
Background: You might have caught William Tell without an apple, but not without a second string. In medieval times, an archer always carried a second string in case the one on his bow broke.

IN THE LIMELIGHT
Meaning: The center of attention.
Background: In 1826, Thomas Drummond invented the limelight, an amazingly bright white light, by running an intense oxygen/hydrogen flame through a lime cylinder. At first, the intense light was used in lighthouses to direct ships. Later, theatres began using the limelight like a spotlight—to direct the audience's attention to a certain actor. If an actor was to be the focal point of a particular scene, he was thrust into the limelight.

MAKE THE GRADE
Meaning: To fulfill expectations, or succeed.
Background: In railroad jargon, the term "grade" refers to the slope of the hill. When a train reaches a plateau or mountaintop, it has "made the grade."

FLASH IN THE PAN
Meaning: Short-lived success.
Background: In the 1700s, the pan of a flintlock musket was the part which held the gunpowder. If all went well, sparks from the flint would ignite the charge, which would then propel the bullet out the barrel. However, sometimes the gun powder would burn without igniting a main charge. The flash would burn brightly but only briefly, with no lasting effect.

ELVIS: STILL DEAD?

Here's a piece about the Phantom of the Rock World, Elvis. It's taken from Vince Staten's irreverent guidebook, Unauthorized America.

"In 1988, for some reason, people all across America got the idea that Elvis wasn't really dead, that he had faked his death to get a little peace and quiet, and that he had actually spent the previous eleven years enjoying himself, wandering the country, seducing fat waitresses who knew who he was but decided not to tell until the *Weekly World News* called.

"He was spotted in Georgia and in Germany; in Texas and in Tennessee. But the majority of the sightings centered in the Kalamazoo, Michigan area."

INSIDE SOURCES

"The Elvis Is Alive mania began the last week in May, 1988 when the *Weekly World News* broke the story: After faking his tragic death [in 1977], exhausted idol Elvis Presley was secretly flown to Hawaii, where he began his new life under the name John Burrows.

"The newspaper quoted from a new book, *Is Elvis Alive? The Most Incredible Elvis Presley Story Ever Told*, by author Gail Brewer-Giorgio, who—just coincidentally—also wrote the novel *Orion*, about a rock star who faked his own death. The Elvis book came complete with an audiocassette tape of conversations with Elvis *after* his death."

ELVIS SPEAKS

"'Everything worked just like it was meant to be,' E said on the secret tape. 'There was an island I had learned about a long time ago. I must have spent a year there. I really needed the rest.'

"Voice analyst Len Williams of Houston verified that the voice on the tape was Elvis's, and that the tape had been edited. Brewer-Giorgio shrugged that one off, saying it was edited to take out the voice of the person talking with Elvis."

Every year, Americans send three billion Christmas cards.

PROGRESS REPORT

"So how has Elvis been since his death? 'It's been enjoyable, but it's been a constant battle, growing a beard and this and that, to keep from being recognized…I'm hoping that a lot of people out there are not disappointed with me. I mean, I didn't mean to put anybody through any pain. It's taken a lot to have to do what I had to do. But in the long run it's going to pay off.'"

MORE ON TAPE

"The tape was supposedly made in 1981. Elvis said he hadn't had a sleeping pill in three years and didn't like the films about him. He said he plans to come out when 'the time is right.'"

HE'S BACK

"Soon America's tabloids were swamped with tales from chubby waitresses who had lived with Elvis and pimply-face teenagers who saw someone who looked like him at the local hamburger heaven.

"In the June 28, 1988, issue of the supermarket tabloid *Weekly World News*, amid such headlines as 'Space Aliens Graveyard Found!' and 'Man Keeps Wife's Body in Freezer for 23 Years!' and 'Cheeseburger Kills Space Alien!' was this shocker:

I'VE SEEN ELVIS AND HE'S ALIVE AND WELL!
Woman spots Presley at a Kalamazoo Burger King"

EYEWITNESS ACCOUNT

"The diligence of *Weekly World's* reporters had turned up an eyewitness, Louise Welling, fifty-one, a Kalamazoo, Michigan housewife, who said she saw Elvis twice; in September she had gone to Felpausch's grocery in suburban Vicksburg, Michigan, after church, and spotted him in the next checkout lane. He was buying a fuse. 'He was dressed in an all-white jumpsuit and holding a motorcycle helmet,' she said. 'He'd lost weight, and he didn't have sideburns.'

"She spotted him a second time two months later at the J. C. Penney entrance of the Crossroads Mall. And in May her children saw Elvis in a red Ferrari at a Burger King drive-through window."

43% of Americans surveyed say they'll never eat snails.

TOUGH QUESTIONS

"Was Elvis Alive?

"And if so, why hadn't he had a hit lately?

"I conducted my own investigation.

"The first thing I had to answer was: why Kalamazoo?

"Why did Elvis Presley, Tupelo, Mississippi native and longtime Memphis, Tennessee resident pick Kalamazoo for his hideaway?

"I had no clue. I didn't even know where Kalamazoo was."

THE INVESTIGATION

"To help unravel the mystery, I sent for the Kalamazoo Chamber of Commerce's newcomer guide. I assume Elvis must have done this in those hectic last days before his death...What was it about Kalamazoo, I kept asking myself?...the annual Michigan Wine & Harbor Festival in September?...the Kellogg Bird sanctuary? The NASA/Michigan space center?

"Terrific stuff, sure, but nothing Elvis would have cared about.

"I couldn't find any plausible explanation until I spotted a short paragraph on the back of the Kalamazoo County 'come and see our corner of Michigan' brochure. It leaped out at me: 'Kalamazoo County...is the world headquarters of the Upjohn Company, and you can take a fascinating tour of their pharmaceutical production facility.'

"Bingo."

DRUG STORE COWBOY

In the last 7 months of his life, Elvis had 5,300 uppers, downers, and painkillers prescribed for him.

ELVIS LIVES AGAIN

"Just when you thought it was safe to read a supermarket tabloid again, the *National Examiner* was back on the Elvis Lives story. E had been spotted living on a farm near Cleveland, Alabama. He'd been glimpsed at the local pharmacy and at the Dogwood Inn in Oneonta, Alabama. He was using the name Johnny Buford during his Alabama sojourn."

The average American kid will watch 30-40,000 TV commercials this year.

GOLDWYNISMS

Samuel Goldwyn was one of Hollywood's great movie producers. He was also famous for murdering the English language—sort of the Yogi Berra of the film world. In Hollywood, his sayings were called Goldwynisms. Here are some classic examples:

"All this criticism—it's like ducks off my back."

"Too caustic? To hell with the cost—we'll make the movie anyway."

"We've all passed a lot of water since then."

Asked about the message of one of his films: "I'm not interested in messages. Messages are for Western Union."

"I'm willing to admit that I may not always be right...But I'm never wrong."

"Tell me, how did you love the picture?"

"I want a movie that starts with an earthquake and works up to a climax."

"I'll believe in color television when I see it in black and white."

"Don't let your opinions sway your judgment."

"Let's have some new clichés."

"These days, every director bites the hand that laid the golden egg."

"In two words: im possible."

"This music won't do. There's not enough sarcasm in it."

"Let's bring it up to date with some snappy 19th century dialogue."

"If you can't give me your word of honor, will you give me your promise?"

"A verbal contract isn't worth the paper it's written on."

"Anyone who goes to see a psychiatrist ought to have his head examined."

"The most important thing in acting is honesty. Once you've learned to fake that, you're in."

"If I could drop dead right now, I'd be the happiest man alive."

The island of Cyprus has one movie theater for every eight of its inhabitants.

TISSUE TALK

According to Harry L. Rinker, "all toilet paper is not created equal." Rinker should know—believe it or not, he collects the stuff. Here's "Rinker on Collectibles," a column excerpted from Antiques and Collecting *magazine.*

If you have traveled abroad or used an outhouse, you are aware of one basic truth—all toilet paper is not created equal. What a perfect excuse to collect it.

BEGINNER'S NOTE

On the surface, collecting toilet paper need not be an expensive hobby. Select pilfering from public restrooms and friends' bathrooms will provide enough examples to begin a collection. Of course, if you travel abroad to obtain examples, the costs increase considerably. However, I discovered that once my friends found out that I have a toilet paper collection...their personal contributions rolled in.

GETTING STARTED

I became aware of the collectible potential of toilet paper in the late 1970s when I learned about a woman who was appearing on the Women's Club lecture circuit talking about the wide assortment of toilet paper that she encountered during her travels. She charged a fee for her presentation and did not seem to lack bookings. She obviously was cleaning up.

After resisting the urge to follow suit for almost a decade, I simply gave up and began my own toilet paper collection. My initial beginnings were modest. I wrote to several German friends and asked them to send me some examples of German toilet paper. Udo, my friend in Hamburg, outdid himself. Among the examples he sent was toilet paper from the German railroad.

A close examination of the light gray textured paper revealed that each sheet was stamped "Deutsche Bundesbahn." This says something about a nation's character. The German railroad administration is so concerned about a roll of toilet paper that they find it necessary to stamp their name on every sheet. The ridiculousness of the German railroad administration is surpassed by the English government. When you use the public restrooms at government museums throughout England, you quickly notice that each sheet of toilet paper is marked "Official Government Property." What a subtle way to recognize that your tax dollars are at work.

GI T.P.

The U.S. military now issues its field troops camouflage toilet paper. It seems the Viet Cong used mounds of used white stuff to track our troop movements during the Vietnam War. What happened to the good old, collapsible GI shovel?

THE RULES

Since toilet paper collecting is in its infancy, now is an excellent time to create rules concerning how to validly accumulate this important new collectible. For example, how many sheets are necessary to have a valid example? Ideally, I suggest four to six; but, a minimum of two, one to keep in mint condition and the other to record the time and place of acquisition, will do in a pinch.

Do you collect single sheets or the entire roll? This is a tough one. I started out by collecting sheets. Then I began thinking about the potential value of wrappers and added them to my collection. Since I had gone that far, I figured why not save the entire roll. When I realized that same rolls were packaged in units of four to six, I was forced to save the entire package. My collection, which originally was meant to be confined to a shirt box, now occupies several large boxes.

TALKIN' TOILETS

Toilet paper collecting provides an engaging topic for cocktail parties and other social gatherings. Everyone has a toilet paper story to tell. I remember the time I had to use the facilities in the basement of the Moravian Archives in Herrnhut, East Germany. The nature of the call required my immediately locating a toilet with no regard to the toilet paper status. Later examination revealed no toilet paper, but rather an old railroad time schedule booklet with some of the pages torn out. As I tore a sheet loose, the ink on the paper came off in my fingers. You can imagine the rest. I should have saved an example, but I wasn't thinking of toilet paper collecting at the time.

The number one use of gold in the United States: Class rings.

BE A T.P. CONNOISSEUR

I think everyone should be required to use a farm or camp outhouse at some point in his or her life. The stories of corn cobs and Sears catalogs are true. I know. I remember the concern espressed by my rural relatives when Sears switched to glossy paper stock. I have a number of old catalogs in my collection.

As my toilet paper collection grew, I became fascinated with the composition and variety of designs and patterns of toilet paper. When I first visited Germany in the late 1960s, their extremely coarse gray toilet paper had the quality of sandpaper. It was rough, but you had confidence the job was getting done. In 1987 I found that German toilet paper tastes now matched the Americans' desire for soft, almost tissue-like paper. The significance of this shift and what is says about the development of the German character should not be overlooked.

FAVORITE THINGS

As with all my collections, I have some favorite examples, among which are a half roll of toilet paper that a friend brought me from England that has a surface texture equivalent to wax paper and a German aluminum foil package that contains toilet paper moistened and perfumed to act and smell like a wash and dry. I have a special box in which I put translucent examples, those you can see through when held up to the light. Their use gives real meaning to the phrase "doubling up."

HELLO OUT THERE

Thus far, I have been unsuccessful in locating other serious toilet paper collectors. They exist; there are collectors for everything. If I can locate them, I would be glad to discuss swapping duplicates.

Meanwhile, you can help. The next time your travels in the U.S.A. or abroad bring you into contact with the unusual during a period of daily meditation, save a few examples and send them to me (care of *Antiques and Collecting* magazine, 1006 S. Michigan Avenue, Chicago, Illinois 60605). Is there the making of a future museum collection here? Time will tell.

SAY GOODNIGHT, GRACIE

George Burns and Gracie Allen were two of the only performers to successfully jump from vaudeville to radio to TV. Their sitcom, "The George Burns and Gracie Allen Show," aired from 1951 to 1958. It's been seen continuously in reruns for the last three decades.

HOW IT STARTED

George was a small-time vaudevillian and Gracie was jobless and broke when they met in 1924. Gracie went to a New Jersey club to watch a friend of hers perform. Also on the bill: a duo called "Burns and Lorraine." Gracie thought the dancer (Burns) would make a good partner and approached him about working together. George figured he had nothing to lose. At age 27, he had been a flop at everything he'd tried.

In their original act, Gracie was the "straight man," and George got the funny lines. But even as a "straight man," Allen got more laughs than Burns. So he rewrote the act, creating the daffy character that made Gracie famous. It was a selfless, professional gesture for which she always admired him. It was also a canny one—the new act was a hit. By the end of the '20s, the pair were vaudeville headliners. By 1932 they had their own radio show, which grew in popularity until they had a weekly audience of 45 million people.

Then, in the late '40s, George decided radio was on its way out (though not everyone realized it), and he decided to jump to television. Gracie, on the other hand, steadfastly refused to be a part of a TV show. George figured she was just afraid to see how she looked on the small screen—which he considered ridiculous. Some radio stars disappointed their fans with they way they looked, but Burns and Allen didn't have to worry. "Gracie," said George, "looked even better" than she sounded. So he offered her a deal. If she did a test shot on-camera and didn't like the way she looked, he'd forget all about television. She agreed, and he got his way.

Next question: what was the show going to be about? There were hours of meetings with CBS, and according to Burns, he finally asked why they couldn't do their radio program on TV. "Why give us a new look," he asked, "when nobody's seen the old one yet?"

Tallest man on record: Robert Wadlow— 8 feet 11 inches. He died at age 22, still growing.

It made sense. The radio series had featured Burns and Allen as themselves, and Blanche and Harry Morton as their next door neighbors. So did the TV series.

NAME & RANK

• George Burns's real name is Nat Birnbaum. He was born in New York City to a poor, Orthodox Jewish family. Trying to make it in show business before he met Gracie, he'd been "a singer, a dancer, a yodeling juggler, did a roller skating act, an act with a seal, worked with a dog...You name it, I did it."

• As a youth in San Francisco, Gracie hung around theaters, dreaming of becoming an actress. When she graduated from high school, she joined an Irish act as a "colleen," and headed for Broadway. It didn't work—the act fell apart when they got to New York. When she met George she was taking odd jobs just to keep eating, and was seriously considering giving up and going back home.

LOST TREASURE

The first 50 TV shows B&A did were live. It wasn't until their third season that the program was saved on film, so the reruns we watch today actually begin in 1953, not 1951. What did we miss? George says he appeared in an entire episode with his fly open.

HEADACHES

It's not easy being a scatterbrain. Despite her three decades in show business, Gracie suffered from severe stage fright...not to mention camera fright. And her concentration on her work was so intense that she frequently suffered from debilitating migraine headaches. She seldom had time to rest in bed, so she had their home decorated in subdued shades of green, pink, and brown to soothe herself.

SAY GOODNIGHT, GRACIE

• In 1958, Gracie retired. She died in 1964 of heart problems.

• George tried going solo, teamed up with comedienne Carol Channing, and even did a sitcom called "Wendy and Me," with Connie Stevens as a daffy blonde (a bomb). Nothing worked until 1975, when he won an Oscar for *The Sunshine Boys*. After that he became one of America's most venerated—and visible—actors.

ALLENISMS

Gracie Allen was one of America's funniest comediennes for 40 years. Here are some of her classic TV lines.

"This recipe is certainly silly. It says to separate two eggs, but it doesn't say how far to separate them."

Harry von Zell: "You're sending your mother an empty envelope?'
Gracie: "I wanted to cheer her up. No news is good news."

"I read a book twice as fast as anybody else. First I read the beginning, and then I read the ending, and then I start in the middle and read toward whichever end I like best."

"There's so much good in the worst of us, and so many of the worst of us get the best of us, that the rest of us aren't even worth talking about."

Gracie: "Every time I bake a cake, I leave it in five minutes too long and it burns."
Harry von Zell: "So?"
Gracie: "So today I put in one cake, and I put in another five minutes later. When the first one starts to burn, I'll know the second one's finished."

Gracie: "You can't give up, Blanche. Women don't do that. Look at Betsy Ross, Martha Washington—they didn't give up. Look at Nina Jones."
Blanche Morton: "Nina Jones?"
Gracie: "I never heard of her either, because she gave up."

Harry von Zell: "Gracie, isn't that boiling water you're putting in the refrigerator?"
Gracie: "Yes, I'm freezing it."
Harry: "You're freezing it?"
Gracie: "Um-hmmm, and then whenever I want boiling water, all I have to do is defrost it."

Gracie: "Something smells good."
Peter: "It's Mr. Morton's ribs."
Gracie: "Really? George only puts cologne on his face."

George: "What's that?"
Gracie: "Electric cords. I had them shortened. This one's for the iron, this one's for the floor lamp."
George: "Why did you shorten the cords?"
Gracie: "To save electricity."

Switzerland's roads are mined in 2,000 strategic places; they can be blown up in 10 minutes.

ALL-AMERICAN SPORTS

Football and basketball are American creations, right? Well, sort of. Here's where "our" sports really come from.

FOOTBALL

Historical Origin: Football is a hybrid of soccer and rugby, two sports imported by British colonists. Rugby, which allows players to pick up the ball and run with it, was adapted by the British from a 2nd century Roman game called "harpastum." Soccer originated in Florence, Italy, in the mid-1500s.

American Origin: Harvard University is credited with establishing American football, which was introduced on the campus in 1869 as "The Boston Game." In 1875, Harvard beat Yale in the first U.S. intercollegiate game; there were 15 players on each team. The 11-man team with a quarterback was added five years later.

• Football got so violent that, in 1905, 18 men died from injuries sustained on the field. There was a public outcry to ban it, but a football enthusiast named President Theodore Roosevelt stepped in. He called an emergency meeting of college football officials and instituted safety measures that enabled football to survive.

BASKETBALL

Historical Origin: 16th century Aztecs played "ollamalitzli," a basketball-like game: Players tried to "shoot" a rubber ball through a stone ring on a stadium wall and the team that scored first won. Ollamalitzli "professionals" didn't play for huge contracts and shoe endorsements. The player who scored the goal won all of the audience's clothes. And the losing team's captain was...beheaded.

American Origin: In 1891 James Naismith, a gym teacher at the Young Men's Christian Association Training School in Springfield, Massachusetts created a game for his bored students. He hung two peach baskets on opposite ends of the gym, chose two 9-man teams, and told each team to try to score without running, or kicking the ball. Kids spread the new game to other schools.

• Two initial differences: An unlimited number of players could play at the same time (even 100), and baskets still had bottoms in them. Every time someone scored, they had to stop and get the ball out. It took two decades to come up with an open-bottom net.

In 1989, Graceland received nearly 100 valentines addressed to Elvis Presley.

PUBLIC ENEMY #1

In the '20s and '30s, gangsters like Machine Gun Kelly, Pretty-Boy Floyd, and Baby-Face Nelson literally shot their way into the headlines. All of them became legendary figures, but one captured the public's imagination more than any other—John Dillinger. Here is his story.

BACKGROUND

During the Depression, the American public developed an insatiable appetite for crime-buster stories. John Dillinger seemed to be the perfect romantic criminal—handsome, dapper, arrogant and audacious.

In reality, Dillinger's life was less romantic than his image. Born in Indianapolis in 1902, he was a chronic drifter. He enlisted in the U.S. Navy in 1923 after being dropped by his girlfriend, and five months later, deserted to take up armed robbery. His first prison sentence soon followed—ten years at the Indiana State Reformatory for a grocery store stick-up in Mooresville, Indiana. Twice Dillinger tried to escape. He failed both times.

Then, in 1933, he was released on parole. Three weeks later he robbed a factory manager in Illinois. One week after that, he pulled off his first bank robbery—$3,000 from a Daleville, Indiana bank. Seeing that crime could (at least temporarily) pay, Dillinger formed a gang. Within three weeks they robbed $10,000 from a Montpelier, Indiana bank and $28,000 in Indianapolis.

Dillinger was captured in Dayton, Ohio but his gang stormed the jail, killed the sheriff and freed their boss. Two days later they stole an arsenal of machine guns and bullet-proof vests from an Auburn, Indiana police station. Now Dillinger was officially Public Enemy Number One, according to the FBI.

THE HUNT

A nationwide manhunt ensued. By this time, Dillinger's antics were a nationwide obsession. *Time* magazine ran an article called "Dillinger Land," which included a board game listing all of his crimes.

Dillinger's gang moved onto Wisconsin, where they heisted $28,000 from a bank in Racine. In early 1934, they robbed an East

Chicago, Indiana bank, killing a bank guard in the process. Once again, Dillinger was captured—this time in Tuscon, Arizona. Dillinger was flown to Indiana to be tried for the bank guard murder.

A month later, in perhaps his most outrageous exploit, he broke out of jail again—by carving a look-alike pistol out of a washboard, which he used to threaten the sheriff, Mrs. Lillian Holley. To add insult to injury, he used the sheriff's car to escape.

Over 600 FBI agents were now assigned to capture Dillinger. But backed by a gang of bandits that included Baby Face Nelson, Dillinger eluded FBI agents. In St. Paul, Minnesota, the FBI cornered the gang but allowed Dillinger to escape through the back door. On May 15, Congress asked for the public's help—offering a $25,000 reward for his capture.

THE CAPTURE

Finally, on July 22, 1934, the FBI got their man. Thanks to a tip from Anna Sage, the so-called "Woman In Red," the FBI learned that Dillinger planned to attend a movie in Chicago that night with Sage (who ran a local brothel) and his new girlfriend, a waitress named Polly Hamilton. The trio went to see *Manhattan Melodrama* (starring Clark Gable and William Powell) at the Biograph Theater.

Sage wore a red dress for identification. When Dillinger emerged from the theater, Melvin Purvis, the head of the FBI's manhunt, lit a cigar as a signal to waiting agents. The two women disappeared. Sensing something suspicious was going on, Dillinger reached into his pocket for his pistol. Before he could fire, the FBI killed him in a volley of gunfire.

DILLINGER FACTS

• Reportedly, several people dipped their handkerchiefs in his blood outside the Biograph Theatre for a future souvenir.

• After Dillinger's death, the Chicago morgue opened its doors, so the public could view the corpse of "public enemy number one."

.• FBI Chief J. Edgar Hoover kept a plaster facsimile of Dillinger's death mask at the FBI in one of his offices. Alongside it was Dillinger's straw hat and the unsmoked cigar he was carrying on the night of his death.

DISNEY STORIES: THE LITTLE MERMAID

Disney Studios' 1989 cartoon, The Little Mermaid, was adapted from a story by the Brothers Grimm. Of course, the Disney version and the original story were substantially different. Here are Jim Morton's examples of how the tale was changed.

THE DISNEY VERSION

A young mermaid, infatuated with humans, saves a Prince from drowning and immediately falls in love with him. But she realizes that there's no way he'll ever love her unless she can walk on land, so she goes to the evil Sea Witch and asks for help.

• The Witch agrees to help...but with certain conditions: The mermaid must give up her voice; and the Prince must fall in love with her within a week. The mermaid agrees without hesitation.

• When it looks like the Little Mermaid may actually win the prince's love in time, the Sea Witch uses the mermaid's voice to trick him. He falls in love with the witch instead, and—still under her spell—agrees to marry her.

• The Little Mermaid and her animal friends stop the wedding in the nick of time. Enraged by the interruption, the Witch tries to drown the Prince, but he kills her first.

• The Little Mermaid gets her wish to walk on land, and she joins the Prince she loves. They live happily ever after.

THE ORIGINAL VERSION

• The Little Mermaid does save the prince from drowning, and does go to the Sea Witch for help. But the similarities end there.

• The Sea Witch doesn't magically steal the mermaid's voice—she cuts her tongue out.

• When the Little Mermaid shows up at the prince's door, he says she reminds him of the girl who saved him from drowning. It sounds promising, but apparently the prince isn't too good with faces—while he's visiting a neighboring kingdom, he meets a princess and decides she's the one who saved him. So he decides to marry her, ruining the mermaid's chance for true love and eternal life. (In this version mermaids don't have souls, so they can't go to heaven when they die. Only humans can).

• The Little Mermaid gets one last chance to save herself. Her sisters go to the Sea Witch and trade their hair for a magic dagger. If the mermaid kills the prince with the dagger before sunrise, she can be a mermaid again.

• She goes to kill the prince while he's sleeping, but she can't do it. Instead, she jumps into the ocean, and she dissolves into sea foam.

SAMPLE PASSAGES (FROM THE ORIGINAL)

"'You must pay me,' said the Witch; 'and it is not a trifle that I ask. You have the finest voice of all here at the bottom of the water; you think you can use it to enchant the Prince, but you have to give it to me.'

"'But if you take away my voice,' said the Little Mermaid. 'What will remain to me?'

"'Your body,' replied the Witch; 'your graceful walk, and your eyes should be enough to capture a human heart. Well, have you lost your nerve? Put out your little tongue, and I'll cut it off.'

"...And she cut off the little mermaid's tongue. Now the Princess was dumb; she could neither sing nor speak."

• • •

The Little Mermaid's sisters show up carrying a knife.

"'The witch has given us a knife; here it is...Before the sun rises you must thrust it into Prince's heart, and when the warm blood falls on your feet, they will grow together again into a fish-tail...Hurry up! Either he or you must die before the sun rises! ...Kill the Prince and come back! Hurry up!'

"And they vanished beneath the waves. The Little Mermaid drew back the curtain and saw the beautiful bride lying with her head on the Prince's breast. She bent down and kissed his brow...Then she looked at the sharp knife in her hands, and again looked at the Prince, who in his sleep murmured his bride's name ...The knife trembled in the mermaid's hand. But then she threw it far away into the waves—they turned red where it fell, and it seemed as though drops of blood spurted up out of the water. Once more she looked at the Prince; then she threw herself into the sea, and felt her frame dissolving into foam."

ALFRED HITCHCOCK PRESENTS

Alfred Hitchcock was one of the first Hollywood greats to lend his name to a TV show. His acclaimed anthology series ran from 1955 to 1965.

HOW IT STARTED

How did Alfred Hitchcock, one of the best-known film directors in the world, wind up on TV at a time when most Hollywood greats were avoiding it? Good advice, that's how. His friend and former agent, Lew Wasserman, was the head of MCA, a burgeoning "entertainment conglomerate" that was itching to get into TV. Wasserman thought Hitch was the perfect vehicle. First, he was a "name." Second, he traditionally made a cameo appearance in each of his enormously successful firms, so people knew what he looked like. And third, a major magazine publisher had just contracted with Hitchcock to produce *The Alfred Hitchcock Mystery Magazine*, reinforcing his public image as master of suspense/mystery. Wasserman's immortal comment, uttered at a meeting in early 1955: "We ought to put Hitch on the air."

Wasserman then had to convince Alfred, who was unsure about getting involved. He feared it would hurt his image as a filmmaker, since the movie world looked down on the small screen. But he also trusted Wasserman, who offered him full creative control and advised that he get involved while the medium was young. Hitchcock agreed, and the show was bought by CBS. His appeal was so great that neither the network or sponsor needed a pilot—it simply went on the air. The success secured his place as the personification of "mystery and suspense" in American culture.

INSIDE FACTS

Good E-E-Evening

Hitchcock's lead-ins and closing comments often had nothing to do with the episode being aired. They were actually shot 24 at a time, 4 times a year, and spliced into completed episodes.

Cher, Tom Cruise, Richard Chamberlain, and Greg Louganis are dyslexic.

Crime Does Pay

The ownership of each episode of "Alfred Hitchcock Presents," after showing on TV once, reverted to Alfred Hitchcock. In 1964, he traded the rights to the series (along with ownership of *Psycho*) to MCA for 150,000 shares of the company's stock. This made him MCA's 4th largest shareholder, and an extremely wealthy man.

Unlikely Source

The Hitchcock theme song was actually a classical piece chosen by Alfred himself. It is Gounod's "Funeral March of a Marionette."

Just Kidding

Sponsors weren't happy with Alfred's constant put-downs of their commercials, until they discovered that the audience liked the companies better for having a sense of humor (which they didn't really have). Then they stopped hassling him about it.

Un-Sawn Episode

The only episode of *Hitchcock Presents* which was never shown was called "The Sorcerer's Apprentice." It was a story about a retarded boy who watched a magician saw a man in half and then killed someone trying to duplicate the trick. CBS refused to allow it on TV, saying it was too morbid.

Guest Star

In 10 years, Alfred Hitchcock actually directed only 20 out of the 362 episodes of the show.

Doodling

Hitchcock, who was once a commercial artist, drew the famous sketch of his profile that appeared on the show.

Buried Treasure

Most of the story ideas for the program came from short stories and novels. Hitchcock believed that if an author had a really good idea, he wouldn't use it in a TV script—he'd save it and use it in his own work. One year, his staff read more than 400 novels before they found 32 stories they could use.

Two cultures in the world don't use fire—Andaman islanders and Pygmies.

GOOD E-E-EVENING

Before each episode of "Alfred Hitchcock Presents," the "Master of Suspense" offered a few pearls of wisdom, like these.

"There is nothing quite so good as a burial at sea. It is simple, tidy, and not very incriminating."

"We seem to have a compulsion these days to bury time capsules in order to give those people living in the next century or so some idea of what we are like. I have prepared one of my own. I have placed some rather large samples of dynamite, gunpowder, and nitroglycerin. My time capsule is set to go off in the year 3000. It will show them what we are really like."

"The paperback is very interesting, but I find it will never replace a hardcover book—it makes a very poor doorstop."

"These are bagpipes. I understand the inventor of the bagpipes was inspired when he saw a man carrying an indignant, asthmatic pig under his arm. Unfortunately, the man-made sound never equalled the purity of the sound achieved by the pig."

"When I was a young man, I had an uncle who frequently took me out to dinner. He always accompanied these dinners with minutely detailed stories about himself. But I listened—because he was paying for the dinner. I don't know why I am reminded of this, but we are about to have one of our commercials."

"The length of a film should be directly related to the endurance of the human bladder."

"In each of our stories, we try to teach a little lesson or paint a little moral—things like Mother taught: 'Walk softly and carry a big stick'; 'Strike first, ask questions after'—that sort of thing."

"I seem to have lost some weight and I don't wish to mar my image. I cannot reveal exactly how much weight. I can only say that had I lost ten more pounds, I would have had to file a missing persons report."

The Roman emperor Nero married his male slave Scotus in a public ceremony.

INVASION! PART III

This wasn't exactly an invasion—but in 1942, the Japanese did attack California...sort of. Actually, the reaction was more memorable than the invasion itself.

THE INVADERS: A Japanese submarine.

THE DATE: February 23, 1942.

BACKGROUND: On December 7, 1941, Japan attacked Pearl Harbor. The U.S. responded by declaring war on Japan. Did Japan plan to attack the West Coast next? Californians watched the skies warily.

THE INVASION: About three months after America entered World War II, a Japanese submarine surfaced near the town of Goleta, California, eight miles north of Santa Barbara. It hurled 15 shells at refineries owned by the Bankline Oil Company, and disappeared. It escaped, despite an all-out search launched by the Navy and Air Force.

The shelling was the first attack on the U.S. mainland since 1918 when a German U-boat fired shells at Cape Cod. There was minimal damage—estimated at $500—and there were no injuries. However, reports that an airplane hangar was spotted on the submarine's rear deck caused jitters in Southern California. People began preparing for an imminent air attack.

AFTERMATH: Two days later, on February 25, shaky nerves gave way to general hysteria in Los Angeles. Early that morning, authorities believed they spotted an enemy plane. Assuming L.A. was under attack, they dispatched Army planes to defend them. The city was blacked out and air-raid alarms went off while local Army officials tried to locate equipment they'd lent to Paramount Pictures for a war movie.

According to the *San Francisco Chronicle*, authorities tried to blow the "enemy plane" out of the sky. They reported: "Anti-aircraft guns pumped thousands of rounds of ammunition toward an objective presumed fixed in the piercing beams of uncounted searchlights."

Then red-faced officials realized it was a false alarm; the object in question turned out to be the planet Venus.

At last count, there were only ten Rolls Royces in the Soviet Union.

THE BASEBALL MYTH

According to traditional baseball lore, our national pastime was invented by Abner Doubleday, in Cooperstown, New York. Was it? Not even close. Here's the truth.

THE MISSION

At the turn of the century, baseball was becoming a popular pastime...and a booming business. Albert G. Spalding, a wealthy sporting goods dealer, realized that the American public would be more loyal to a sport that had its origins in the U.S. than one with roots in Europe. So it became his mission to sell baseball to America as an entirely American game.

THE COMMISION

In 1905, Spalding created a commission to establish the origin of baseball "in some comprehensive and authoritative way, *for all time*." It was a tall order for any historian, but Spalding was no historian—and neither were the friends he appointed to his blue-ribbon commission.

Spalding gave six men honorary positions: Alfred J. Reach, head of another sporting goods company (known by many as the "Business Genius of Base-Ball"), A.G. Mills, the third president of the National League; Morgan G. Bulkeley, first president of the National League; George Wright, a businessman; and Arthur P. Gorman, a senator who died before the study was completed. James Sullivan, president of an amateur athletic union, functioned as secretary for the commission.

THE SUBMISSIONS

In 1907, the Special Baseball Commission issued the Official Baseball Guide of 1906-7, a report which A.G. Mills said "should forever set at rest the question as to the origin of baseball." What research had the group compiled in almost three years? Their files contained just three letters—one from Henry Chadwick, an Englishman who had helped popularize baseball; one from Spalding himself; and one from James Ward, a friend and supporter of Spalding.

In his letter, Chadwick pointed out the obvious similarities

Bela Lagosi was buried wearing his vampire outfit.

between baseball and a game called "rounders," a popular sport in England as well as Colonial America. Rounders was played on a diamond with a base on each corner. A "striker" with a bat would stand beside the fourth base and try to hit balls thrown by a "pecker." If he hit the ball fair, the striker could earn a run by "rounding" the bases. If the striker missed the ball three times, or if his hit was caught before touching the ground, he was "out." After a certain number of outs, the offensive and defensive teams switched. Ring a bell? It didn't with Spalding and his men. The commission, which selected Chadwick's letter to represent the "rounder's contingent," quickly dismissed it because Chadwick was born in England.

In deference to Spalding, James Ward supported the theory of American origin, though his letter stated that "all exact information upon the origin of Base-Ball must, in the very nature of things, be unobtainable." His testimony amounted to no more than a friendly opinion.

Spalding's letter vehemently argued "that the game of Base-Ball is entirely of American origin, and has no relation to, or connection with, any game of any other country." On what evidence did he base this argument, as well as the Doubleday/Cooperstown theory? On the letter of a mystery man named Abner Graves, a mining engineer from Denver, who claimed to recall Doubleday inventing the game of baseball *sixty-eight* years earlier (Graves was over eighty years old when he gave his account).

THE OMISSION

In his report, Spalding stated that Graves "was present when Doubleday first outlined with a stick in the dirt the present diamond-shaped field Base-Ball field, including the location of the players on the field, and afterward saw him make a diagram of the field, with a crude pencil on paper, memorandum of the rules of his new game, which he named 'Base Ball.'" However, none of this romantic imagery was actually in the Graves letter—no stick and no "crude pencil diagram of the rules"—Spalding made the whole thing up. Nor was Graves present at the first game, as Spalding claimed. Graves stated in his letter, "I do not know, nor is it possible to know, on what spot the first game was played according to Doubleday's plan." Graves' letter simply recounted the rules of the game, and how he thought Doubleday "improved" an *already existing game* called Town Ball. Spalding cleverly embellished and promoted the old miner's tale to make it the stuff of legends.

Spalding was also clever enough to know that Doubleday, a famous Civil War general, was "legend material" and would be an effective marketing tool in selling the Doubleday/Cooperstown myth. "It certainly appeals to an American's pride to have had the great national game of Base Ball created and named by a Major General in the United States Army," wrote Spalding.

DOUBLEDAY AND BASEBALL

- No record associated Doubleday and baseball before 1905.
- Doubleday entered West Point September 1, 1838, and was never in Cooperstown in 1839.
- Doubleday's obituary in the New York Times on January 28, 1893, didn't mention a thing about baseball.
- Doubleday, himself a writer, never wrote about the sport he supposedly invented. In a letter about his sporting life, Doubleday reminisced, "In my outdoor sports, I was addicted to topographical work, and even as a boy amused myself by making maps of the country." No mention of baseball.

BASEBALL IN EARLY WRITTEN RECORDS

The game of "baseball" was well documented long before its purported invention in 1839.

- In 1700, Revered Thomas Wilson, a Puritan from Maidstone, England, wrote disapprovingly about some of the events taking place on Sunday. "I have seen Morris-dancing, cudgel-playing, baseball and cricketts, and many other sports on the Lord's Day."
- In 1774, John Newberry of London published a children's book named *A Little Pretty Pocket-Book.* The 30-page book presents a number of games, each one with a rhyme and woodcut illustration. One of the games in the book is "BASE-BALL," which is described in the following rhyme:

BASE-BALL
The Ball once struck off,
Away flies the Boy
To the next destin'd Post
And then Home with Joy.

The accompanying illustrations depicts some young boys playing what is clearly a hit-the-ball-and-run kind of game. Posts mark separate bases at the corners (posts were used as bases in American baseball well into the 1860s). One boy is tossing the ball; another is waiting to strike the ball, while waiting beside a base; at a different base, another boy is poised to make a dash for "home."

Other early written references to baseball include the following:

- A 1744 book describes a rounders-like game as "base-ball."
- So does an 1829 London book called *The Boy's Own Book.*
- The acclaimed author Jane Austin refers to "baseball" in her 1798 novel, *Northanger Abbey.*
- C.A. Peverlly, in *The Book of American Pastimes*, published in 1866, clearly affirms that baseball came from the English game of rounders.

AT THE TIME

- Francis C. Richter said Spalding "...was the greatest propagandist and missionary the game ever knew and spent more time, labor, and money in spreading the gospel of Base Ball than any other man of record."
- The *New York Times* said: "The canny sports writer now refers to Abner with his tongue in cheek." *The Sun* of New York called it "a popular and harmless legend."

NUTS TO YOU

The average American eats about nine pounds of peanuts per year.

- Americans eat about 800 million pounds of peanut butter each year, enough to spread across the Grand Canyon's floor.
- The peanut wasn't popular in America until the late 1800s, when the Barnum Circus began selling them under the Big Top.
- Arachibutyophobia is the fear that peanut butter will stick to the roof of your mouth.
- One of Elvis Presley's favorite foods was a fried peanut butter and banana sandwich; Chef Julia Child loves peanut butter on corn chips.

LANDSLIDE LYNDON

In 1964, Republicans claimed that Democratic Presidential nominee Lyndon B. Johnson had a sordid past that included stealing his senate seat in 1948. It turns out they were right. This wonderful piece was contributed by B.R.I. member Michael Dorman.

THE RACE BEGINS

In 1948, while serving as a relatively obscure member of the House of Representatives, Lyndon Johnson entered the race for a vacant Texas seat in the Senate. Four other candidates were campaigning for the position in the Democratic primary. The most prominent among them was Coke Stevenson, who had served two terms as governor of Texas.

Since the Republican party fielded only token candidates in those days in Texas, victory in the Democratic primaries was equivalent to election. In the first primary for the Senate seat, Stevenson led the balloting with 477,077 votes—71,460 more than Johnson, who finished second. But because the remaining votes were divided among the other three candidates, Stevenson failed to win a majority of all ballots cast. Under Texas law, a second (or runoff) primary between Stevenson and Johnson was required to choose the winner of the Senate seat.

MR. BIG

During the period between the first and second primaries, Johnson forged a political alliance with a notoriously corrupt southern Texas political boss named George P. Parr. For almost four decades, Parr and his father before him had ruled as virtual feudal barons over a five-county area of oil-rich, sagebrush country just north of the Mexican border. Their subjects—thousands of Mexican-Americans—lived in terror of the Parr political machine.

Year after year, the frightened citizens trudged to the polls and voted the straight Parr ticket. This solid bloc of votes, guaranteed to any politician who won Parr's favor, could tip the balance in a close statewide race.

In the runoff, the initial returns from the five counties controlled by Parr gave Johnson 10,547 votes and Stevenson only 368. But Stevenson had run strongly in other parts of the state. When the statewide returns were tabulated, they showed Stevenson defeating Johnson by the razor-thin margin of 112 votes out of a total of almost 1 million cast.

HEADS I WIN, TAILS YOU LOSE

It was then that George Parr reached into his bag of political tricks and produced for Lyndon Johnson what came to be known as "the miracle of Box 13." After all the statewide returns were in and Johnson appeared to be the loser, Parr's election officials in Precinct (Box) 13 in the town of Alice suddenly claimed they had discovered some additional votes that had not previously been counted. Johnson's campaign manager, John Connally (who would later serve as Governor of Texas and U.S. Secretary of the Navy and Secretary of the Treasury), rushed to Alice to confer with the officials who would count the ballots that had supposedly been found. Former Governor Stevenson—fearing that Parr was in the process of trying to steal the election for Johnson—also hurried to the scene to protect his interests. He took with him two aides, James Gardner and Kellis Dibrell, who had formerly been FBI agents.

The ballot box from Precinct 13 was put away, purportedly for safekeeping, in a bank vault. The hitch was that the bank, along with almost everything else in the area, was controlled by George Parr.

It was not until six days after the election that Parr's officials submitted their revised tally of the votes from Box 13. They claimed they had found 203 ballots that had not previously been tabulated. Of those, they maintained, 201 had been cast for Johnson and only 2 for Stevenson. Thus, if these supposed ballots were allowed to stand, Johnson would win the primary by 87 votes.

By the time the additional votes were tabulated, a subcommittee of the Texas Democratic Executive Committee—assigned to count and certify the statewide ballots—had already issued a report declaring Stevenson the winner. But within hours after the subcommittee's declaration of what were assumed to be the final results, Johnson's aides announced that they expected the tabulation of the additional votes from Box 13 to change the outcome.

With the claim that the 201 newly discovered votes for Johnson would give him the victory, the situation in Parr's territory grew tense. Former Governor Stevenson and his aides demanded to see the list of registered voters in Precinct 13 so that they could check whether fraudulent ballots had been cast. Like the supposed ballots, the list of voters had also been locked in the bank vault. Bank officers, some of whom served as election officials for Parr, initially refused to allow Stevenson's men to see the list. Stevenson's aides had intended to examine it, note the names of the supposed voters, and then check whether such persons actually existed and had voted. Rumors swept Parr's territory that he and his henchmen were prepared to resort to gunplay, if necessary, to prevent inspection of the voting list. Standing by was his force of heavily armed *pistolero* sheriff's deputies. Stevenson appealed for help from the state capital in Austin, asking that a force of Texas Rangers be dispatched to the scene to prevent violence and ensure an honest count of the ballots. State officials responded by sending one of the most famous Texas Rangers of all time, Captain Frank Hamer, the man who had tracked down the notorious Bonnie Parker and Clyde Barrow and led the posse that killed them in a blazing Louisiana gun battle.

BULLETS AND BALLOTS

On the morning after Hamer's arrival, a showdown loomed in Wild West fashion on the street outside the bank. Five of Parr's henchmen, with loaded rifles at the ready, stood ominously across the street from the bank. A dozen others, with *pistolas* conspicuously displayed, formed a semicircle directly in front of the bank. Former Governor Stevenson, fearing Parr's men might try to shoot him and his aides and then claim self-defense, ordered his assistants to take off their coats before approaching the bank—to make clear they were carrying no concealed weapons.

Then, minutes before the bank was scheduled to open, Captain Hamer led Stevenson and his aides toward the bank. He halted a few feet from the semicircle of Parr men, stepped out in front of Stevenson's group, and stood there for a few moments to make sure everyone present recognized him.

In a scene that could have come right out of *High Noon*, Hamer crossed the street and set himself squarely in front of the five riflemen. He pointed his finger to the far end of the street and ordered, "Git!"

The men grumbled and swore for a few seconds, but then obeyed. Hamer next crossed back to the semicircle of men in front of the bank, surveyed the group silently at first, then barked, "Fall back!" The men cleared a path for Hamer, Stevenson and his aides to enter the bank.

LOOK, BUT DON'T TOUCH

Tom Donald, a Parr aide who ran the bank and also handled political chores for the local organization, opened the door. Stevenson and his assistants entered, but Hamer would not let the *pistoleros* inside. A short time later, Democratic party officials with responsibility for counting the votes and certifying the election results arrived. One of them, H. L. Adams, demanded that Donald open the bank vault and hand over the election records, since the Democratic party was entitled to serve as custodian of its own primary race documents. But Donald, acting on George Parr's orders, refused to comply.

"I will permit you to see the voting list, but not to handle it," he said. All he would agree to do was remove the voting list from the vault, hold it up, and allow the Stevenson men and party officials to view it from across a wide table. Stevenson and his aides began taking down names and immediately spotted several oddities. The persons whose ballots had been belatedly "found" had all signed their names in what seemed to be the identical handwriting.

Furthermore, their names appeared in ink that differed in color from all other names on the rolls. As if those facts were not suspicious enough, the "late" voters had somehow managed to cast their ballots in alphabetical order. Since voters usually show up at the polls in haphazard fashion, there seemed no reasonable explanation of why all these citizens would have appeared alphabetically.

After Stevenson and his men had recorded the names of only 17 voters, however, a telephone rang and was answered by Parr aide Donald. He listened for a minute, then folded the voting list and put it back in the bank vault. "That's all," he said.

Frustrated but determined to plod ahead, Stevenson's men began trying to locate the 17 persons whose names they had noted.

They quickly discovered that four of them could not have voted: the foursome had long been buried in a local cemetery. Another man whose name appeared on the list was found alive, in a distant Texas city. He denied even being in Parr's county on election day, much less voting there. A local housewife whose name appeared on the list said she had not voted and was not even qualified to vote. After a dogged investigation, Stevenson's aides were unable to find a single person from among the 17 who had actually voted.

AND THE WINNER IS...

Stevenson and Democratic party officials went into court, charging that Parr had tried to steal the election for Johnson. They asked the courts to take speedy action to prevent such a theft from receiving official sanction. But Johnson and his forces took court action of their own, seeking to certify Johnson as the winner of the election. They accused Texas Ranger Captain Hamer of entering into a conspiracy with Stevenson, various Democratic party officials, and others to have the belatedly "found" votes set aside as fraudulent. And they asked the court to bar any further recount of the votes. While the rival court actions were pending, the Texas Democratic Executive Committee met in Fort Worth to consider which candidate to certify as the winner. On the first ballot there was a 28-28 deadlock between Stevenson and Johnson. A second ballot produced identical results. Then Johnson, his campaign manager, John Connally, and his lawyer, John Cofer, left the room where the meeting was taking place, after being promised no additional votes would be taken until they returned. They made arrangements to have a member of the executive committee who had not been present for the prior votes flown to Fort Worth from Amarillo, almost 350 miles away. They did not return to the executive committee meeting until the previously absent member, C. C. Gibson, arrived.

On the next ballot, Gibson voted to certify Johnson as the winner—making the tally 29 to 28. The committee then adjourned its meeting.

Although winning the Democratic primary run off guaranteed election in Texas, there was still the formality of a general election. The slate certified by the Texas Democratic Executive Committee was ordinarily listed on the ballot for the general election alongside token slates of candidates fielded by the Republicans and minority parties. In many races, the Republicans did not even bother to nominate candidates. But in any event, it would be necessary for the winners of the Democratic nominations to go through the motions of running in general election campaigns.

Responsibility for printing the official general election ballots rested with Paul Brown, the Texas secretary of state. At the time of the tight, controversial Democratic Executive Committee meeting, Brown was already facing the deadline for ordering the printing of the ballots. But he could not do so until he knew the outcome of the Johnson-Stevenson contest. Once the committee voted to certify Johnson, Brown ordered the ballots printed with Johnson's name as the official Democratic candidate for the Senate.

Former Governor Stevenson then went into the United States district court in Dallas and filed a new lawsuit seeking to overturn the certification of Johnson as winner by both the Democratic Executive Committee and Secretary of State Brown. Federal Judge T. Whitfield Davidson, in whose court the case was filed, had left Dallas for a weekend of relaxation at a farm he owned near Marshall, Texas. Stevenson drove all night to reach Davidson's farm and asked him to sign a court order preventing, at least temporarily, what the former governor contended was the "theft" of the election.

A BLANK SLATE

Judge Davidson, after reading the legal petition presented by Stevenson, agreed to sign the order. It instructed that all election returns and ballots from George Parr's territory be seized, pending court examination. It also barred Secretary of State Brown from printing the general election ballots until the court examination was completed. A hearing on Stevenson's suit was set for September 21.

Immediately after learning of the court order, Secretary of State Brown rushed to the print shop where the ballots were to be produced. He discovered the ballots were about to begin rolling off the presses. At the last moment, he ordered Johnson's name stricken and the ballots printed without a Democratic senatorial candidate listed.

No Sugar Added: People in western China, Tibet, and Mongolia put salt in their tea.

Johnson and his forces soon counterattacked. They tried to persuade a federal appeals court to overturn Davidson's order, but the best they could do was get the appeals court to set a hearing on the matter for October 2—eleven days after Davidson's own hearing. Meanwhile, Davidson appointed a San Antonio attorney, William R. Smith, to conduct an investigation of the purported vote theft for the court. Smith was empowered to go to Parr's territory, take possession of the election records, subpoena witnesses, and gather evidence on all facts related to the run off election.

Smith lost no time in hurrying to the scene, taking with him federal marshals to help in the investigation. But when they arrived, they discovered that the election records were missing and that the Parr lieutenants whose testimony was wanted had mysteriously gone to Mexico—beyond the reach of the court—on what they claimed was urgent business. The ballot boxes were ultimately found, but all they contained were old newspapers and other trash.

JUSTICE TO THE RESCUE

Thus, when the hearing opened on September 21 in Judge Davidson's court, the most critical evidence was absent. The voting list, the ballots, and other election materials were gone. Johnson's team of attorneys, including both John Cofer and a friend of Johnson's named Leon Jaworski (later Watergate special prosecutor), seized the opportunity to claim that Stevenson had no case.

"This plaintiff [Stevenson] lost his race for United States senatorial nominee in a Democratic primary, over which only the regular Democratic officials have jurisdiction," Cofer told Judge Davidson. "This court has no jurisdiction. He [Stevenson] has no civil rights [that are being violated], as pleaded in his petition. He is merely a poor loser."

The judge, however, had little patience for such an argument. Banging his gavel to silence Cofer, Davidson denied his request to throw the case out of court. "This plaintiff, Mr. Stevenson, has alleged he has been robbed by fraud of a seat in the United States Senate," the judge said. "Not a shred of evidence has been submitted to disprove his claim. He...is entitled to a hearing in open court. And that hearing he shall have. This court will decide on the merits of his petition."

There are over 200 people on the waiting list to witness an execution in Florida.

Davidson was wrong. He would not have a chance to conclude his hearing or decide the case on its merits. Lyndon Johnson had retained a noted Washington lawyer, Abe Fortas, to file a petition with U.S. Supreme Court Justice Hugo Black asking him to order Davidson's hearing halted. (Fortas himself would later serve a controversial term on the Supreme Court, on appointment from his former client, then-President Lyndon Johnson.) Fortas's petition to Justice Black did not deal with the merits of the election fraud charges, but merely contended that the issues in the case should be resolved by the Democratic party and not by the federal courts. Justice Black signed an order forbidding Judge Davidson to proceed further with the hearing or otherwise consider Stevenson's case.

ORDER IN THE COURT

Justice Black was empowered to issue such an order on his own because the full Supreme Court was not in session at the time. Theoretically, the full court ultimately could have reversed his ruling. But the effect of the order was to halt Judge Davidson's consideration of the case indefinitely. Since the general election was quickly approaching, there would be little time for the full court to hear arguments and reverse Black's decision in time to allow Stevenson to get his name on the general election ballot.

Black's court order was flown from Washington to Texas and presented to Judge Davidson by a federal marshal. Davidson reluctantly halted his hearing. "This court has no choice but to submit to the mandate from the Supreme Court, although, in my opinion, Mr. Justice Black has acted hastily and probably illegally," Davidson said.

For all intents, Justice Black's order put an official seal on what many considered Johnson's theft of the Senate seat—with a major assist from George Parr. Time ran out on Stevenson's further efforts to win court consideration of the vote-fraud charges. Secretary of State Brown ordered Johnson's name listed on the ballot as the official Democratic Senate nominee. Johnson then easily swept to victory in the general election.

SENATOR JOHNSON

When he returned to Washington as senator, he had a new

Only 1 of 6 able-bodied men in the American colonies fought in the Revolutionary War.

nickname—“Landslide Lyndon”—derived from his 87-vote “victory” in the race against Stevenson. Within a few years, he would become the Senate majority leader and be considered the second most powerful man in Washington. Some said he was the most powerful, because President Dwight D. Eisenhower was in the White House at the time and was considered by many a weak chief executive. In 1960 Johnson would be elected vice president on John F. Kennedy’s ticket; he would become president upon Kennedy’s assassination in 1963 and win his own presidential election a year later.

THE COURSE OF HISTORY

Thus there is strong reason to speculate that the entire history of the United States might have been radically different if George Parr and his cohorts had not “stolen” the 1948 election for Johnson. If Stevenson had been declared the winner of the senatorial primary, Johnson would have remained in the House for at least several more years. He could not have become Senate majority leader when he did and thus probably would not have been the vice presidential candidate in 1960. As a result, he would not have become president. He himself observed many times that only a fluke could have put him or anyone else from the South or Southwest in the White House under the political conditions prevailing in the United States in the 1950s and 1960s. Actually, in his case, it took two flukes: the first was the purported “theft” of the Senate election, the second was President Kennedy’s assassination.

Meanwhile, George Parr continued delivering one-sided majorities at the polls for his pet candidates. Johnson was a major beneficiary of such election manipulation. Another beneficiary was John Connally, who was elected governor of Texas with help from Parr.

NO JOY IN PARRVILLE

During the early 1970s Parr was indicted on charges of failing to list on his tax returns income of more than $287,000. In March 1974 he was found guilty and sentenced to 10 years in prison. By the time his final appeal was turned down, Parr was 74 years old. He had been convicted of other crimes in the past but had served only one prison term.

Giraffes can go longer without water than camels can.

He was due to appear in court for a hearing. When he did not show up, he was listed as a fugitive. Federal marshals were sent to hunt for him, and they found him slumped over the steering wheel of his car in a pasture near his palatial home. He was dead, with a bullet wound in his head. A .45-caliber pistol and an M-14 military rifle lay on the car seat. A local justice of the peace ruled the death a suicide, apparently prompted by Parr's reluctance to serve any prison time at his advanced age.

By the time of Parr's death, Lyndon Johnson lay in his own grave. There were those who felt the story of the theft of the 1948 Senate election should be buried along with them.

✓ ✓ ✓

TV TIME: ALL IN THE FAMILY

• "All in the Family"'s twelve-and-a-half season run was second only to "Ozzie and Harriet" (which ran fourteen) among TV sitcoms.

• The original title of the show was "Those Were the Days"—hence the name of the theme song.

• The theme was performed with only a piano and two voices (Archie's and Edith's) because Norman Lear had only $800 in his budget to record it and that was the cheapest way to go.

• When Gloria gave birth to "Joey" in 1975, the event inspired another first—the "Joey" doll, billed as the first "anatomically correct male doll."

• Rob Reiner wore a toupee for his role as the long-haired Mike Stivic—he's actually as bald as his father, Carl Reiner. Even without hair, however, fans recognized him on the street wherever he went and yelled "Meathead" after him. He hated it.

• In 1974, Carroll O'Connor went on strike for more money. At first it seemed that his demands couldn't be met—so, according to *TV Guide*, the show's writers came up with an emergency plan to have Archie attend a convention, where he would be mugged and murdered. That way the show could continue with the rest of the cast. O'Connor settled for $2 million per year.

• Edith Bunker was so important to Americans that when she "died" of a stroke in 1980, *Newsweek* ran a half-page obituary, as they would have for a real world leader.

TRAVELS WITH RAY

Perplexing adventures of the brilliant egghead Ray "Weird Brain" Redel. Answers are on page 223.

On occasion, "Weird Brain" Redel, the celebrated thinker, would host a party at his plush home in the Hollywood hills. Of course, everyone who "mattered" in Tinseltown wanted an invitation. But "Weird Brain" had his own agenda... and his own friends. Some were well-known socialites, like Grace Kelly and Prince Ahmed Faroul; some were big brains like Einstein, and others were just...well, people like me.

One starry evening "Weird Brain," Al Schweitzer and Al Einstein were deeply engrossed in a discussion about biology with Jayne Mansfield. Jayne had them enthralled. "Well," she said, "you big, silly brains talk all the time about evolution and that sort of thing. That's so cute." She gave Einstein a peck on the forehead, leaving a big lipstick smear. "OOO, why, I'll bet you don't even know what a duckling becomes when it first takes to water."

"Of course we do, Miss Mansfield," Al Schweitzer interjected, "—a semi-mature aquatic web-toed aviant."

"No, honey," Jayne cooed. "That's not it." And when she explained it to them, the smartest guys in the world had to admit Jayne was right.

What DID she say?

Later that evening, "Weird Brain" and a few physicist buddies were discussing their newest discoveries. One little bearded guy with a German accent, dressed in a white smock that made him look as if he had just left Dr. Frankenstein's laboratory, volunteered some startling data. "I have stumbled upon something," he intoned, "that comes once in a minute, twice in a moment, but not once in a thousand years."

The eggheads gasped. How was this possible? "Weird Brain" reached over and gave the guy's beard a tug. It came off...revealing Peter Lorre. "Okay, Pete, enough jokes. Tell them what you mean."

What did Lorre have in mind?

FAMOUS CHEATERS

In the last Bathroom Reader, we introduced a feature called "Famous Cheaters." Here's another installment.

BACKGROUND: In the mid-50s, quiz shows, like "Tic Tac Dough," "21," and "The $64,000 Question," were the hottest thing on TV. The public couldn't get enough of them. ("The $64,000 Question" was the only show to beat "I Love Lucy" in the annual ratings, ranking as the #1 program of 1955.) Network executives loved them, too, because they were cheap to produce, and extremely profitable. By 1958, over 24 game shows were on the air. The competition grew increasingly fierce.

QUIZ CROOKS: Unknown to the public, a number of shows, including "The $64,000 Question," had begun rigging the competition to increase their entertainment value and improve their ratings.

It turned out that answers were often provided to preferred contestants—such as Charles Van Doren, an assistant English professor at Columbia University, who'd been making $5,500 a year. In 1956, the 29-year-old Van Doren became an overnight celebrity thanks to his appearances on the show "21." After knocking off the champion Herb Stempel, Van Doren went on to win $129,000. The media dubbed him "the quiz whiz." Soon after he appeared on the cover of *Time* magazine and was hired by NBC's "Today" show for $50,000.

THE ACCUSATION: Stempel was bitter at being defeated by Van Doren. He complained to several New York newspapers that "21" was fixed. There were no immediate reactions to Stempel's revelations, but in 1958 a contestant on CBS's game show "Dotto"—where contestants connected dots to reveal celebrity faces—claimed to have found an opponent's notebook with answers in it.

THE INVESTIGATION: In response to growing speculation, the House Committee on Legislative Oversight investigated allegations that quiz shows were fixed. Among the first witnesses to come forward was actress Patty Duke, who had won $64,000 on "The

A hole-in-one in golf is more common than a triple-play in baseball.

$64,000 Question." Duke claimed that the show's associate producer, Shirley Bernstein (the sister of conductor Leonard) had secretly given her the correct answers before the show.

But the most damaging revelations were made by Van Doren. In a dramatic confession on November 2, 1959, before the U.S. Senate, he admitted that all his "21" victories had been fixed. Van Doren claimed that producer Albert Freedman "told me that Herbert Stempel, the current champion, was an unbeatable contestant because he knew too much. He said that Stempel was unpopular, and was defeating opponents right and left to the detriment of the program. He asked me if, as a favor to him, I would agree to an arrangment whereby I would tie Stempel and thus increase the entertainment value of the program."

Van Doren appeared remorseful. "I would give almost anything I have to reverse the course of my life in the last three years...I was involved, deeply involved, in a deception." He immediately resigned from his teaching post at Columbia and was fired at NBC's "Today Show" as well.

THE RESULT: The nation was shocked by Van Doren's testimony: *Life* magazine wrote that it had "exposed a nation's sagging moral standards." Then-president Eisenhower was quoted as saying "it was a terrible thing to do to the American people." The *Washington Post* ran an editorial saying "it will render very little service to the public to make Charles Van Doren a scapegoat. It is an industry, not an individual, that stands in need of redemption." Almost immediately all game shows—even honest ones—were removed from the air. Congress passed legislation making quiz show fraud punishable by law.

MISCELLANEOUS

• Charles Van Doren later became an executive with *Encyclopedia Brittanica.* He refused to discuss the scandal after his congressional testimony.

• Dr. Joyce Brothers won $64,000 fielding questions on boxing; Barbara ("Get Smart") Feldon won $64,000 answering questions on Shakespeare. Consolation Prize: Anyone who made it to the big $64,000 question and blew it, still got to drive home in a new Cadillac.

Each year, Americans trash enough disposable diapers to stretch to the moon and back 7 times.

REAL PEOPLE

Some rock songs are about real people, though most of us never know it. Here are three examples:

BAD, BAD LEROY BROWN, by Jim Croce
Jim Croce met the man who inspired "Leroy Brown" while he was in the Army, stationed at Fort Dix, New Jersey. He and Croce were both going to school to learn how to become telephone linemen. Croce recalls: "He stayed there about a week and one evening he turned around and said he was really fed up and tired. He went AWOL, and then came back at the end of the month to get his paycheck. They put handcuffs on him and took him away. Just to listen to him talk and see how 'bad' he was, I knew someday I was gonna write a song about him."

THE SULTANS OF SWING, by Dire Straits
The Sultans of Swing was a jazz band that Mark Knopfler, leader of Dire Straits, happened to see at a pub one night.

Knopfler: "My brother Dave was living somewhere in Greenwich and we went out to the pub—I think it was called the Swan...and we had a game of pool and a couple of pints. There was a jazz band playing and there was nobody in there except us and a couple of kids in the corner. They did a couple of requests. I asked them for 'Creole Love Call,' and it was great. There are loads of bands like that. They're postmen, accountants, milkmen, draftsmen, teachers. They just get together Sunday lunchtimes, nighttimes, and they play traditional jazz. It's funny, because they play this New Orleans music note-for-note...in Greenwich, England."

PEGGY SUE, by Buddy Holly
This was Buddy Holly's first solo record, and one of the most famous "girl-name" records in rock history. But although Buddy made Peggy Sue famous, she wasn't in love with him—she was Cricket drummer Jerry Allison's girlfriend. Later Jerry and Peggy Sue tied the knot, and Buddy celebrated with a tune called "Peggy Sue Got Married." By the time they got divorced, Buddy was dead.

MAGAZINE ORIGINS

They're American institutions now, but once they were just someone's ideas. Here's a quick look at the origins of a few U.S. mags.

Reader's Digest. A young Minnesotan named DeWitt Wallace realized that modern Americans didn't have time to get all the latest information. They needed quick, easy access to it, and he could provide it in a magazine. Why didn't people just tune in to radio or TV? It was 1920.

On October 15, 1921 DeWitt Wallace and Lila Acheson were married. They also sent out several thousand mimeographed fliers asking people to subscribe to their new digest. When they returned from their honeymoon, more than 1,000 subscriptions were waiting. *Reader's Digest* was born.

Time. In 1923, two Yale friends—Britt Hadden and Henry Luce—also created a sort of "digest." They scoured dozens of newspapers for important news and synopsized it in "approximately 100 short articles, none of which are over 400 words." The first issue (March, 1923), financed by wealthy Yale acquaintances, was a bomb. So they changed directions, hiring a news staff and developing the pointed, pun-filled, opinionated writing style that's now the standard in American magazines. That worked; *Time* flew.

Fortune. Started in February 1930 as a way to use the excess material being produced by *Time*'s business department.

Newsweek. It looks and sounds like *Time* magazine? That's because it was started by a man who'd worked at *Time*, and whose fondest wish was to drive *Time* "out of business." Thomas Martyn started it on February 17, 1933. Today it's owned by the *Washington Post*.

TV Guide. TV was becoming an American institution in 1952 when Philadelphia publisher Walter Annenberg spotted an ad for a magazine called *TV Digest*. Was there really a market for it? His staff said yes...so he decided to start a national TV magazine with regional listings. He bought up the half-dozen regional TV magazines that had already sprung up and consolidated them into a single new publication. The Apr. '53 debut issue featured Lucy's baby.

SOLUTION PAGE

TRAVELS WITH RAY, PAGE 18

• Ray tossed Bogart a pack of matches. The answer to Bogart's riddle was "Fire." And since he was pointing to a cigarette, "Weird Brain" figured he wanted a light. Bogie, furious, jumped up and challenged "Weird Brain" to a drinking match. They tied three times, then both passed out.

• Casey was talking about a river, of course. I assume it was the Nile, though Casey kept calling it the "Vile."

TRAVELS WITH RAY, PAGE 66

• A map. We bought another one, but got lost anyway, and stumbled into the valley full of prehistoric creatures...but that's another story.

• The wind. Never leaves a shadow, as far as I know.

TRAVELS WITH RAY, PAGE 131

• "Your breath," Charlie guffawed.

• "Weird Brain" shipped his scientific equipment in a coffin. "I hope that doesn't mean my idea is dead, nyuk-nyuk-nyuk," he said. I told him he'd been hanging around the 3 Stooges too long.

MILITARY DOUBLE-TALK, PAGE 158

1-K, 2-J, 3-N, 4-G, 5-I, 6-M, 7-A, 8-C, 9-D, 10-F, 11-H, 12-E, 13-L, 14-B

TRAVELS WITH RAY, PAGE 218

• "You big brains are so-o-o-o goofy," Jayne giggled. "The first thing a duckling becomes when it takes to water is...wet." Not even Einstein could argue with that.

• Lorre was talking about the letter M, a letter he was quite fond of. "M" was the title of the film that made him a star.

Most likely, your left foot is bigger than your right.

THE LAST PAGE

FELLOW BATHROOM READERS:
The fight for good bathroom reading should never be taken loosely—we must sit firmly for what we believe in, even while the rest of the world is taking pot shots at us.

Once we prove we're not simply a flush-in-the-pan, writers and publishers will find their resistance unrolling.

So we invite you to take the plunge—"Sit down and Be Counted"—by joining The Bathroom Readers' Institute. Send a self-addressed, stamped envelope to: B.R.I., 1400 Shattuck Avenue, #25, Berkeley, CA 94709. You'll receive your free membership card and earn a permanent spot on the B.R.I. honor roll.

UNCLE JOHN'S *FOURTH* BATHROOM READER IS IN THE WORKS
Don't fret—there's more good reading on its way. In fact, there are a few ways you can contribute to the next volume:

1) Is there a subject you'd like to see us cover? Write and let us know. We aim to please.

2) Got a neat idea for a couple of pages in the new Reader? If you're the first to suggest it, and we use it, we'll send you a free copy of the book.

3) Have you seen or read an article you'd recommend as quintessential bathroom reading? Or is there a passage in a book that you want to share with other B.R.I. members? Tell us where to find it, or send a copy. If you're the first to suggest it and we publish it in the next volume, there's a free book in it for you.

Well, we're out of space, and when you've gotta go, you've gotta go. Hope to hear from you soon. Meanwhile, remember:

Go With the Flow.